Praise for *One Bird, One Stone*

"Sean Murphy's eloquent book is thought-provoking and lovely. This collection of 108 new teaching stories in the American Zen Buddhist tradition is a poetic account of the transplanting of Zen Buddhism to this new Western soil and some of the various ways it has taken root here in the lives of a wide spectrum of teachers and practitioners."

—Sharon Salzberg, Author and Co-Founder of The Insight Meditation Center

"Anyone looking for insightful quotes, humor, Zen wisdom, or even just a good story will find something in these bite-sized anecdotes."

—*Tricycle Magazine*

"The book gives you a profound glimpse into the well of the Zen mind."

—*Santa Fe New Mexican*

"Intelligent, funny, wise and, best of all, speaks to the heart."

—Rafe Martin, *Zen Bow*

"A genuine Zen classic."

—Brian Bruya, *Amazon Reviews*

"Highly recommended."

—Peter Haskel, *Zen Notes*

LOOK JUST LOOK
AT THE CROWS
LAUGHING DANCE
& TELL ME THERE
AREN'T MYSTERIES
RIDING ON EACH
BREATH WE TAKE
FOR GRANTED
A SMILE A LOVING
TOUCH LAUGHTER
NIGHT MOVING ASIDE
FOR A NEW DAY

Art by Diana Stetson
Poetry by Streams Kakudo Peterka

one bird one stone

108 CONTEMPORARY ZEN STORIES

sean murphy

HAMPTON ROADS

Cover design by Jim Warner
Interior designed by Frame25 Productions
All illustrations © Keith Abbott unless otherwise noted.

Hampton Roads Publishing Company, Inc.
Charlottesville, VA 22906
Distributed by Red Wheel/Weiser, LLC
www.redwheelweiser.com

Sign up for our newsletter and special offers by going to
www.redwheelweiser.com/newsletter.

Library of Congress Cataloging-in-Publication Data
Murphy, Sean.
  One bird, one stone : 108 American Zen stories / Sean Murphy. -- [Second edition].
     pages cm
  Summary: "Drawn from the archives of major Zen centers in America and interviews with some of the most seminal figures of American Zen, including Philip Kapleau, Bernie Glassman, Robert Aitken, Gary Snyder, Alan Watts, and Walter Nowick, Murphy presents moments of insight and wisdom, quotable quotes, and the humor of Zen as it has flowered in America over the last hundred years"-- Provided by publisher.
  ISBN 978-1-57174-697-9 (pbk.)
  1. Zen Buddhism--United States. 2. Zen Buddhists--United States--Anecdotes. 3. Zen Buddhists--United States--Quotations. I. Title.
  BQ9262.9.U6M87 2013
  294.3'4432--dc23
                         2013000287

Nyogen Senzaki poem "Parting," reprinted from *Like a Dream, Like a Fantasy: The Zen Writings of Nyogen Senzaki*, edited and with an introduction by Eido Shimano Roshi. Japan Publications, Inc., 1978. Reprinted with permission from Eido Roshi.

Material from First Zen Institute archives and Zen Notes reprinted with permission, copyright © First Zen Institute of America.

Jack Kerouac letter excerpts reprinted by permission of SLL/Sterling Lord Literistic, Inc. Copyright by John Sampas, Literary Representative of the Estate of Jack Kerouac.

Allen Ginsberg letter excerpt reprinted with permission from Allen Ginsberg Trust.

Printed on acid-free paper in the United States of America

TS

10 9 8 7 6 5 4 3 2 1

Dedicated to the many teachers who have carried the Zen teachings to the West; to Daido Roshi; and to all sentient beings.

Shunryu Suzuki Roshi once told a group of American Zen students: "You have a saying, 'to kill two birds with one stone.' But our way is to kill just one bird with one stone."

CONTENTS

ACKNOWLEDGMENTS

This book has been very much a collaborative effort. I would like to extend my particular thanks to the nearly one hundred interviewees and contributors to the collection, most of whom the reader may find acknowledged individually in the text and in the Endnotes. Their patience and generosity in meeting and sharing so openly with me was truly extraordinary. Of these, I would especially like to thank Roshi Philip Kapleau, Walter Nowick, Robert Aitken Roshi, Kobun Chino Roshi, Bernie Glassman, Mel Weitsman, Blanche Hartman, Gerry Shishin Wick, Steve Allen, Michael Wenger, Jitsudo Ancheta, Mitra Bishop, Anne Waldman and Andrew Schelling of Naropa University, and Michael Hotz and Peter Haskel of The First Zen Institute of America. Great gratitude goes also to Maezumi Roshi for being my first teacher, and providing me with such an impeccable introduction to the dharma.

The present form of this book owes much to the influence of John Daido Loori Roshi, and in particular, to my editor at Renaissance Books, Joe McNeely, both of whom pushed me (sometimes against my considerable resistance!) to add extensive background information and personal accounts into what I'd originally conceived of as a simple assembly of Zen anecdotes. The book is much the better for their efforts. I would also like to thank my agent,

Peter Rubie, for seeing the potential of the project and for placing the book so skillfully, and my editor at St. Martin's Press, Marie Estrada, for her clear vision and for picking up the project with such enthusiasm.

In addition I would like to express my deepest appreciation to my wife, Tania, whose editorial assistance in multiple close readings of the text was invaluable and whose patience throughout the duration of this project was inexhaustible, and to my parents, Harold and Ruth Garner, whose unflinching faith and support through my years of spiritual exploration has gone far beyond the call of duty. And, of course, to Natalie Goldberg, for her unrelenting encouragement, and for sharing so deeply of herself, her experiences, and her many friends and contacts in the dharma.

I would also like to extend my sincere gratitude and acknowledgments to the many people at Zen Mountain Monastery who helped in the process of writing this book: to Geoffrey Shugen Arnold, and the ZMM and Dharma Communications staff and residents, for facilitating my multiple visits and allowing me to pursue my writing and research as an aspect of my practice, as well as for giving me free access to the library, media archives, and themselves. To Konrad Ryushin Marchaj, Ron Hogen Green, and Joy Jimon Hintz, who read and commented on the project at various stages of its development and provided valuable guidance and clarification; to Hogen (again) and Cindy Eiho Green, as well as to Rafe Martin, for their great generosity in arranging my meeting with Roshi Kapleau, and to Stephen Leff for contributing greatly of his time and energy in helping to arrange my meeting with Walter Nowick. To Bonnie Myotai Treace, Jody Hojin Kimmel, Yukon Grody, Pat Jikyo George, Lisa Kyojo Smith, Diane Kosei Hartel, Sybil Seisui Rosen, Chris Trevelyan, Kay Senyu Larson, and anyone else I've inadvertently overlooked, for their support, information, and encouragement, and for pointing me in various right and helpful directions.

To Miss Christy Bright, Setman Walker, Cliff Clusin, and Madeleine, Moira, Mark, and Kristen Murphy, and Mirabai and

Jenny Starr for providing essential assistance with shelter and accommodations; to George Cane, Clark Strand, Peter Matthiessen, Jean Smith, Sandy Boucher, and David Chadwick, for various aspects of writerly advice; to Arthur Morey, for formatting the final manuscript; to Diana Stetson, Keith Abbott, and Lisa Levine, for providing artwork; to Lynn Beheler, for assisting with transcriptions and proofreading; to Michael Sierchio, for permitting use of his Den Chun stories despite my clumsiness in asking; to Marcia Rose, Steven Smith, Colin Egan, Paul Sowanick, Angelique Farrow, Kensho Miyamae, Diane Chase, Michele Huff, Jean Leyshon, Lou Hawthorne, Anne Cushman, Peter Gregory, Joe Kinczel, Steve Kishin Shupe, Katharine Kaufman, and Paul Gyodo Agostinelli for numerous valuable forms of assistance.

And to additional participants Bodhin Kjolhede Sensei, Ilia Shinko Perez, Syd Musei Walter, Taiyo Lispcomb, Guoyan Fashi, Ji Hyang Su Nim, Nancy Maxo, Shinpo Matt Seltzer, Molly Gordon, Stephen Rose, Barbara Zaring, Alvaro Cardona-Hines, Barbara McCauley, David and Rebecca Slaymaker, and Lucy Brennan, for their time and efforts.

I'd like also to extend my gratitude to all the staff, residents, and practitioners at the many dharma centers to which I traveled, who were universally welcoming, enthusiastic, and helpful to the project.

Although I have tried to be as comprehensive as possible, within the limits of such a broad-ranging project it has simply not been possible to give all lineages and teachers of Zen in America the equal representation they deserve. I therefore offer my sincere apology to any individuals or sanghas who have been overlooked in this collection.

Finally, a big thank you goes to my current editors, Greg Brandenburgh and Vanessa Ta and their staff at Hampton Roads Publishing, for their great patience and care in seeing the possibilities for this new edition and guiding it into print.

In closing I feel compelled to note, and pay respect to, a number of teachers who participated in this book, but who have passed on since the first edition appeared in 2002. These include my own beloved primary Zen teacher, John Daido Loori, as well as Philip Kapleau, Robert Aitken, Seung Sahn, Kobun Chino, and Philip Whalen. Time moves on and the dharma wheel turns, but my heart swells with gratitude and sorrow as I type their names here. All of them are sorely missed..

FOREWORD

The lore of Zen is filled with stories.

Here is a simple and famous one. Twelve hundred years old, it has touched and transformed the lives of countless Zen practitioners across every continent of this planet.

In the late 800s, as Zen was establishing itself as a new and vital school of Buddhism in China, Master Chao-chou, a prominent sage living in the northern region of the country, had an apparently insignificant encounter with a visiting monk. The monk posed to Chao-chou a question: "Does a dog have buddha nature or not?" Chao-chou, without a moment's hesitation, answered, "Mu." (Translated as "No.") On the surface, Chao-chou's response seems to contradict one of the basic tenets of Zen, which emphatically states that all beings are intrinsically perfect and complete, lacking nothing. All beings are buddha nature itself. The visiting monk was aware of this scriptural teaching, yet he still asked the question. Chao-chou lived his life out of the realization of that inherent perfection, yet he apparently denied it.

Chao-chou must have conversed with monks regularly. His monastery was famous across the countryside and many adepts flocked to the region to hear him teach, sharpen their understanding, or test their insight. This was just another encounter. Yet someone felt that it was important enough to record. Maybe the monk who asked the question, unsettled by the unexpected, sensed the transformative potential of Chao-chou's answer.

Maybe an alert witness was stirred to spiritual doubt by the exchange. Or perhaps, everything that Chao-chou said in his later years was carefully documented. One way or another, the dialogue made its way into a collection of sayings attributed to Chao-chou, probably gathered by one of his immediate disciples. By the year 1000, the text was in circulation throughout China.

Two centuries later, the story of Chao-chou, the monk, the dog, and buddha nature was encountered by Master Wu-men. When he came across it, Wu-men was already practicing Zen, and was thoroughly familiar with Buddhist doctrine and zazen meditation. When he read the exchange, it shattered his religious complacency. For the next six years, he secluded himself in a cave, trying to penetrate Chao-chou's meaning. His efforts eventually resulted in an experience of enlightenment. Years later, when Wu-men began to teach, he used this dialogue as a koan—a unique tool of spiritual exploration—to help his students gain understanding. He also used other stories. Recognizing the importance of these ancient encounters and conversations, Wu-men compiled them and wrote commentaries for each. His *Gateless Gate,* with Chao-chou's Mu as its first chapter, is an excellent example of this form of spiritual literature. Wu-men knew through his experience that a simple story about awakening is a seed of awakening. When a practitioner fully engages one of these stories within a supportive matrix, it can become a powerful aid for realizing the nature of the self and the universe.

At the turn of the millennium, thousands of years and miles away from Chao-chou's mountain, his Mu lives on. Invariably, today's Zen students engaging in koan study come across it at some point in their training. Inevitably, they are driven deep into the territory of their minds, where they have a chance to meet Chao-chou and intimately experience his clarity. When they do, this simple story transforms into a spark of spontaneity and an expression of boundless freedom.

Chao-chou's Mu is one of countless stories in Zen. Some 1,700 of these, recognized as having the unique potential to facilitate awakening, have been gathered into various koan collections, and they continue to inspire, frustrate, mystify, amuse, and enlighten modern-day readers and practitioners. Thousands of others have been swept up by the wind of time, disappearing forever.

In creating this volume, Sean Murphy continues an ancient tradition by collecting modern stories from teachers and practitioners of different lineages of 20th- and 21st-century Zen in America. Recognizing the timelessness and immense potential of these stories, he gathers them with care and delight, offering them with the conviction and enthusiasm of someone who has had direct experience with their workings through his own practice. His cataloguing and interviewing efforts should be especially applauded since these exchanges also provide a glimpse of the early evolution of Zen in the West, with the appearance of new masters, new students, and new language.

At this time, who knows the significance of these encounters for the generations to come? While it is too early to tell which of today's stories may go on to function as koans and be used as tools in the formal training of Zen students, hopefully some of these words will fall on a mind ripe to recognize their generosity and aliveness. And maybe they will touch future lives in the same way that Chao-chou's sparkling words continue to nourish and guide us on our journey to awakening.

John Daido Loori, Roshi
Zen Mountain Monastery
October 5, 2001

INTRODUCTION

It was one of those hard weeks. I was in Italy with forty American students from the East Coast who were poorly prepped to study with me. They wanted their Italian holiday, which included drinking. You don't drink at my retreats. They couldn't shut up during the silent periods. And there were five women in particular I called the bad girls. Skin-tight jeans, thick Jersey accents, they hunched in the back of the room together, giving the high five when one of them read aloud, and poured into the local bar each evening in the small town adjacent to this eighty-acre organic farm. One even brought a local boy home for loud sex through the night. I had definitely become a public high school teacher again, telling her that this was not allowed.

On top of this, the last day I caught a cold virus going around and had to lecture on creative writing in Rome to a room full of university students majoring in engineering. ("Who thought up this trip?" I asked myself.) It turned out the engineering students had gravitas, an ability to concentrate, to listen and be curious. Ah, I thought, the Italians. Serious young men and women, Europeans with history behind them.

Though I was sick, we—Wendy Johnson, my co-teacher and I—managed to be guided around Rome for two days by Paulo, an Italian student, and his ardent American friend Paul. Time stopped in front of Keats' grave at the non-Catholic cemetery for foreigners at Via Caio Cestio; Keats was only twenty-six when he died. I remembered my heavy navy cloth *Norton Anthology of English*

Literature, the thin pages, and the "Ode on a Grecian Urn" I'd read over and over.

Further down the line of stones and Italian cypress was Shelley's grave and right close in front, Gregory Corso's. Corso didn't die in Rome. His daughter brought his ashes from St. Paul, Minnesota. At seventeen Gregory was the youngest prisoner ever to be in maximum security in Clinton, New York on three counts: stealing a suit to go to a wedding, sleeping in his teacher's room, and the final straw, stealing a toaster. The last inhabitant in the cell was Lucky Luciano, a Mafioso, who also showed the Allies the way into Italy through Sicily. He'd left all his books behind and it was there that Corso discovered Shelley. His life was saved, turning in the direction of poetry, and he always wished to be buried near the great master romantic poet. On Corso's stone was writ:

Spirit
is life
it flows thru
the death of me
endlessly
like a river
unafraid
of becoming
the sea

That last night I took Wendy out for a fancy dinner for her sixty-fifth birthday at a café on a broad avenue across from the nunnery where we were staying. Coughing, nose running, having just got word a friend canceled the next leg of my trip, I decided to fly home with Wendy as far as Atlanta, then on to our separate destinations. This change in plans cost the price of the original round trip, but sometimes money shouldn't matter. You take a step outside logic—or into a bigger logic.

The nine hours crunched in a small seat with Wendy, who was ensconced in *The Leopard* half a plane away, was no fun. Bleary-eyed and jetlagged, I waited at Customs. A guard dog had sniffed three Italian lemons in Wendy's duffle. She wanted to bring them to Peter, her husband, a Dante fan. The lemons were confiscated and she turned left to find her next plane to San Francisco and I turned right, leaving the dry, stagnant air of the airport for two hours. My friend and former student Bill Addison picked me up for a short visit. What's near an airport? He managed to take me to a bleak, grey neighborhood with faded clapboard houses, cracked sidewalks, and crumbling asphalt.

"Ohh, I love this," and I meant it. I was in the unflashy under-belly of my own country.

Grant Park dated back to the 1800s. We settled into seats at the Little Tart Bakeshop late in the afternoon with little selection left. I had a bowl of yogurt and granola and we snagged the last chocolate-caramel tart. I sipped chamomile. Bill had a macchiato and we settled across the table from each other the very day Atlanta dropped into fall weather.

His friend Leon had suddenly died two days earlier. Having just climbed over the hump of forty, this was Bill's first close death. In a way he was lucky, but it didn't hurt less. I listened— his waking this morning in stunned shock, the details of Leon's physical problems, visits in his last weeks. A thin black time-out-of-mind headache was forming over my left eye and my shoulders were concrete blocks. At the same time I was jittery from the plane ride and happy and amazed to be in this on-the-spot, face-to-face connection with my long-distance friend.

"Bill, remember Kobun Chino, the Zen teacher I've told you about?"

He nodded. Where was this going out-of-the-blue?

"Wendy just told me this last week. Years ago a whole rash of important teachers had died and her friend was freaked out.

"She went to Kobun, a bit hysterical. 'I can't take it Kobun, I don't know what I'll do when you die.'

"'Who say I die first?' Kobun flashed back in his ungrammatical English."

The fork traveling to Bill's mouth stopped. My water glass froze in hand. Kobun's comment was falling through Bill's body and reverberating through mine. We tumbled through space, up for grabs, free for the moment, defending nothing, drenched with a cutting truth. The sad tale of teaching in Italy, a friend's death— it all splashed with a crystal clarity. We both burst out laughing.

"Oh Nat," Bill shook his head.

"Nothing like Zen," I concluded.

How happy I am that Sean Murphy has spent a year and a half of his life gathering these stories of crazy Zen American teachings, stories that rivet the mind and turn things upside down—a searing push into awakening. And he did such a thorough, beautiful job, mixing in his own journey to these stories and teachers, which takes the book to another whole, rich level.

I remember him sitting—and sleeping—on my old yellow couch in St. Paul at one point while he was interviewing Midwesterners on one of his journeys, traversing the country, digging out any crag or corner, angle or tale he might have missed. At the time I commiserated: it was hard work, taking determined concentration. Think of the koans from 8th, 9th, 10th century China: what are they but interactions between teacher and student, teacher and teacher, student and student, and a few reveal transactions in heavenly realms—but all well-digested, at this point through so many years whittled down to bare sticks of raw teaching for us to decipher. Someone had to collect them.

This is what Sean has done in *One Bird, One Stone*, begun the large job of collecting wisdom created on American soil, keeping the lineage alive, carrying it over seas. Who knows how terse, arrow-like our tales will become, continuing the resounding bell, calling all to their true home. Maybe even the bad girls in my Italy class, seen from a thousand years from now, may hold the germ of a new beginning.

In the way of books, *One Bird, One Stone* disappeared, went out of print. Now with the foresight of Hampton Roads, they are calling back these stories, making them thankfully visible again.

The process of turning them over, composting them for future generations has begun. I loved this book when it came out over a decade ago, but now with hindsight I appreciate even more what important work Sean Murphy has done and I thank him. Stories are the most vibrant way to pass on the teachings.

Natalie Goldberg
Santa Fe, NM
November 21, 2012

part one

ORIGINAL FACE: EARLY ENCOUNTERS

There was a fisherman in China who for forty years used a straight needle to fish with. When someone asked him, "Why don't you use a bent hook?" The fisherman replied, "You can catch ordinary fish with a bent hook, but I will catch a great fish with my straight needle."

Word of this came to the ear of the Emperor, so he went to see this fool of a fisherman for himself. The Emperor asked the fisherman, "What are you fishing for?"

The fisherman said: "I am fishing for you, Emperor!"

—Reported by Sokei-an Sasaki, first Zen master to "bury his bones" in America.

BEGINNINGS: THE IRON BULL

When the Indian monk Bodhidharma, the First Ancestor of Zen Buddhism, brought his realization of the Buddha's teachings to China in the sixth century C.E., there followed a legendary encounter with the Chinese Emperor Wu, which I'll retell here in my own words for those unfamiliar with it.

Having heard that a monk of great wisdom had arrived in his country, Emperor Wu, who was a devout Buddhist, commanded an audience.

"I have built many monasteries and erected temples to honor the Dharma," the Emperor greeted his guest. "Is there not great merit in this?"

"No merit whatsoever," answered the ragged monk.

"Is that so?" replied the Emperor, who was no doubt a bit flustered at having received such a bold response. "What then, is the meaning of the holy truth?"

"Vast emptiness," replied Bodhidharma. "Nothing holy."

"Well then who are you," demanded the Emperor, "who stands here before me?"

"I do not know," said Bodhidharma; with this he walked off and spent the next nine years in a cave meditating, facing a wall.

Thus began the school of Buddhism known as Zen (or Ch'an, in China), as well as the tradition of Zen stories—mind-to-mind encounters on the Great Matter of the dharma, the Buddhist teachings of enlightenment. For the roughly 1,500 years that have passed since this snaggle-toothed monk went into his cave, such stories have succeeded in delighting, bewildering, and occasionally awakening those who have heard them. Beginning, it seems, with the unfortunate Emperor Wu, who, it is said, wrote the following verse on the occasion of Bodhidharma's death:

I saw him without seeing,
Encountered without meeting.
Now, as before,
I regret and lament.

The teachings of Zen Buddhism have continued to travel since the time of Emperor Wu, passing through Vietnam, Korea, and Japan, and finally coming ashore in America and Europe. This book, in recording the sayings and doings of American teachers and students, is intended as a small addition to the literature of this tradition which, ironically, calls itself:

A special transmission, outside the scriptures;
No reliance upon words and letters;
Direct pointing to the mind;
Seeing into one's own nature, and the realization of Buddhahood.

The idea of compiling a collection of American Zen stories has been with me for some time, nearly from the beginning of my own introduction to formal practice in the 1980s. I'd been inspired early on by the book *Zen Flesh, Zen Bones*, by Nyogen Senzaki and Paul Reps, which introduced many Americans to the seemingly eccentric and paradoxical world of the Chinese and Japanese Zen masters. I was particularly drawn to the first part of that book, a collection of 101 traditional Zen stories from Chinese and Japanese sources, which preserved the oral tradition of mind-to-mind transmission of the dharma, teacher to student, across the centuries. As the years went by, I noticed these stories and similar traditional tales cropping up again and again in other books—but where, I began to wonder, were the new ones? I was certainly hearing them from my teachers and fellow practitioners, both at the Zen centers where I practiced, and at the Naropa Institute, the Buddhist-inspired university where I pursued my MFA in writing. While a few of the collections coming out included some contemporary Eastern and Western sources, and others featured the teachings of a particular Western teacher, I had yet to see a volume of stories that dealt with a broad range of what seemed to me a remarkable phenomenon: the migration of the ancient tradition of Zen Buddhism to the New World.

When I spoke to my own teacher, Abbott John Daido Loori of Zen Mountain Monastery in upstate New York about my idea for this book, he offered guarded encouragement. "It seems to me," he said, "that some of the recent attempts at these sorts of collections have missed the point, the heart of the practice." He admonished me to be thorough, and to make the writing of the book an extension of my own Zen practice. More than that: to make it inseparable from practice itself.

Heeding my teacher's call to practice has included, over the past year and a half, sitting zazen and listening to talks at a variety of Zen centers; meeting, interviewing, and occasionally being challenged by nearly a hundred Zen teachers and long-time practitioners; trying to remain present while dealing with rental cars and airports, getting lost in major cities, and tussling with deadlines; and struggling with my own difficulty in articulating a tradition based on an experience—seeing into one's true nature—that is beyond words. As always, the practice continues.

I feel, as is sometimes said in Zen training, "like a mosquito trying to bite an iron bull."

chapter one

THE LAND OF THE WHITE BARBARIANS

To be awake is to be alive. I have never yet met a man who was quite awake. How could I have looked him in the face? We must learn to reawaken and keep ourselves awake, not by mechanical aids, but by an infinite expectation of the dawn.

—HENRY DAVID THOREAU

I was pleased to rediscover in the course of my research that there is a lineage of sorts in American Zen practice that extends all the way back to the Transcendentalist writers and poets of the 1800s. Ralph Waldo Emerson printed extracts of Buddhist texts in his magazine, *The Dial*, in the 1840s, while Henry David Thoreau published segments of Elizabeth Palmer Peabody's translation of the *Lotus Sutra*, finding encouragement there for the contemplative life he would later adopt at Walden pond. Indeed, as Thoreau lay upon his deathbed in 1862, a friend asked whether he had made his peace with God. The poet responded, in Zen-like fashion: "I was not aware we had quarreled."

The earliest known Zen master to arrive in America was Soyen Shaku, abbot of a prominent Rinzai temple in Japan. Ignoring warnings from his peers that "the land of the white barbarians is beneath the dignity of a Zen master," Shaku first traveled to the U.S. in 1893 to speak at the historic World Parliament of Religions in Chicago. Shaku felt privately that the formalized Zen of Japan had largely hardened into stylistic ritual; but his personal vision, as presented at the World Parliament, was of a Buddhism still capable of evolution, "an idealistic universal religion based on the law of cause and effect (the law of nature), and appropriate for the twentieth century." Afterward, Shaku spent a week at the home of Paul Carus, a noted author and publisher in the fields of religion and science, who agreed that Buddhism was uniquely suited to close the gap that had opened between these two areas, as it did not "depend on miracles or faith." Influenced by these encounters, Shaku returned to Japan with the resolve to introduce modern Buddhism to America.

Twelve years later, Soyen Shaku revisited the U.S. as the guest of Mr. and Mrs. Alexander Russell of San Francisco. In 1906, he again addressed an American audience—this time in a more cryptic vein: "I have studied Buddhism for more than forty years . . . but only very recently have I begun to understand that . . . after all, I do not understand anything."

Shaku's enigmatic presentation of the absolute basis of reality went unappreciated by most of the audience members, whose reactions ranged from disappointment to outright laughter. But the master spent nine months at the Russell home, instructing their family in Zen, during which time Mrs. Russell became the first American to undertake *koan* study (the examination of seemingly paradoxical Zen questions or stories such as "what is the sound of one hand clapping?" as part of meditation practice). Afterward, he set off on a lecture tour of the States. Thus was the first seed of Zen planted in America.

Two of Soyen Shaku's disciples, D.T. Suzuki and Nyogen Senzaki, as well as Shaku's dharma "grandson"—Shigetsu Sasaki, better known as Sokei-an—would later take up residence, at Shaku's urging, in the United States. While the contribution of D.T. Suzuki to Zen in America is widely recognized and will be addressed later, that of Nyogen Senzaki and Sokei-an is not so well-known.

Nyogen Senzaki arrived in San Francisco in 1905 as attendant monk to Soyen Shaku; but after the Russells' housekeeper decided he was "too green" for his proposed position as houseboy, Shaku sent him off on his own. "Just face this great city and see whether it conquers you or you conquer it," Shaku instructed his disciple, adding that Senzaki should wait twenty years before attempting to teach Zen. True to his teacher's instruction, Senzaki spent the next twenty-three years working as a farm hand, houseboy, waiter, and language tutor, before founding the Western world's first successful Zen practice centers in San Francisco and, later, Los Angeles.

Never formally sanctioned as a Zen master, Senzaki always referred to himself as a simple monk. "I have never made any demarcation of my learning," he said, "and so do not consider myself finished at any point." Nevertheless his influence was enormous. He was the co-compiler of the teaching stories collected in *Zen Flesh, Zen Bones,* as well as a number of other texts which brought the dynamic and idiosyncratic teachings of Zen to a popular American audience for the first time. Many early American Zen students began their study with him; best known among these was Robert Aitken, the pioneering American who discovered Zen in a Japanese prisoner-of-war camp in the 1940s and went on to become one of the first U.S. teachers. Aitken reports:

(Senzaki) studied English and Western philosophy diligently, particularly the works of Immanuel Kant. "I like Kant," he once said to me. "All he needed was a good kick in the pants!"

Senzaki wrote the following on his hopes for establishing an authentic practice of Zen in America:

Americans in general are lovers of freedom and equality; for this reason, they make natural Zen students. There are eight aspects of American life and character that make America fertile ground for Zen:

American philosophy is practical.
American life does not cling to formality.
The majority of Americans are optimists.
Americans love nature.
They are capable of simple living, being both practical and efficient.
Americans consider true happiness to lie in universal brotherhood.
The American conception of ethics is rooted in individual morality.
Americans are rational thinkers.

"Zen is not a puzzle," said Senzaki. "It cannot be solved by wit. It is spiritual food for those who want to learn what life is and what our mission is."

The Most Beautiful Vow (1)

In 1929, Nyogen Sensaki left San Francisco to come to Los Angeles. During this time, he was extremely poor and often went hungry. For a time, he cared for the severely retarded and physically handicapped son of a neighbor, Shubin Tanahashi, so that she would be free to work. Although her son, Jimmy, was considered unable to speak, Sensaki somehow managed to teach him to repeat the first of the Four Great Bodhisattva Vows of Zen: "Shujo muhen seigando" ("Sentient beings are numberless, I vow to liberate them"). Mrs. Tanahashi became Sensaki's close student and friend, and saw to it that he always had enough to eat for the rest of his life.

Many years later, Eido Shimano, dharma heir to Sensaki's friend Soen Nakagawa, visited Jimmy in the hospital. Jimmy was nearly forty years old at the time, but on seeing Shimano's shaved head, he immediately put his hands together in prayer position and repeated "*Shujo muhen seigando.*"

Eido Shimano said it was the most beautiful vow he had ever heard.

The True Meaning of Cleanliness (2)

For a time, Nyogen Sensaki was a manager for an apartment house. Whenever a tenant moved out, Senzaki would clean the vacant apartment thoroughly—but once the new tenants arrived, he reported, they would inevitably clean it all over again. The newcomer would then often take him aside and say that the former tenant must have been a poor housekeeper as the place had been left in such bad condition.

Sensaki spoke about these incidents in this way: "Such actions are piling dust in the room instead of cleaning to make it pleasant to live in. No matter how carefully and repeatedly you have cleaned a room, when the sun's rays flood into it, you will see millions of dust particles flying in the air. Of course, I approve of cleanliness, but if there is no harmony in your mind, you will never see the true meaning of cleanliness."

It is also reported that Sensaki worked for a time at a motel, but could never understand why a man and woman would rent a room and then only stay for two hours.

DHARMA WORDS FROM NYOGEN SENZAKI

In Zen meditation we think non-thinking—that is, we think nothing. What this means is that our whole psychological mind ceases to function, and as a result, our whole being becomes united with the essence of mind. You call this essence the God within you, Absoluteness, Ultimate Reason—it doesn't matter. No matter what you call it, to unite with this essence is the very reason we meditate together.

I have been asked to explain what Realization is, but if it could be explained it would not be Realization. While you are kneading the dough of your thoughts, you cannot enjoy the bread of Realization . . .

Walking through the forest of thoughts, just keep on walking until you find yourself cornered in a place that admits neither of advance nor retreat. Here your knowledge will be of no avail. Even your religion will be unable to rescue you. If you are really eager to enter Realization, just go straight ahead, holding tenaciously to the question "What is Realization?" March on bravely.

Use your own sword . . . carve out a way for yourself. There will come a time when all of a sudden you will lose hold of your sword and at that moment—behold! You will have gained your true self.

Nyogen Senzaki's dharma "nephew," the young layman Sokei-an Sasaki, who studied with a disciple of Soyen Shaku named Sokatsu Shaku, arrived in San Francisco in 1906 at Soyen Shaku's urging, along with his teacher and six other disciples. The group made several abortive attempts to establish themselves in the U.S.—most notably, a failed zendo/strawberry farm on a tract of barren land sold to them in a swindle. The "farm" brought forth such poor produce that local farmers laughed at them. Sokei-an's teacher, along with the other disciples, soon sailed back to Japan. Sokei-an, however, who remained behind, was to play a key role in years to come in the establishment of Zen in the United States.

Sokei-an spent most of the following twenty years wandering America. He lived for a time in New York City, where he frequented Greenwich Village, and became known as a writer and artist. As Alan Watts described him, he was during this period "very much the bohemian, with long swirling hair, the original Dharma Bum of America." Sokei-an's American writings, published back in Japan, made him something of a literary figure in Tokyo, and provided him with some income. But after seeing a dead horse on the street one day in New York and suddenly being reminded of life's impermanence, he realized it was time to complete his Zen training. Sokei-an went back to Japan, where he was sanctioned as a teacher by Sokatsu Shaku in 1928. He returned to New York to found, in 1931, what was to become the First Zen Institute of America. Here he proceeded to lead the first groups of Americans in koan study. "I had a house and one chair," reported Sokei-an, "and an altar and a pebble stone. I just came in here and took off my hat and sat down in the chair and began to speak Buddhism. That is all."

Carve Me a Buddha (3)

Before Sokei-an came to America, when he was just beginning his study of Zen, his teacher arranged a meeting for him with Soyen Shaku. The master, having heard he was a wood carver, asked, "How long have you been studying art?"

"Six years," replied Sokei-an.

"Carve me a Buddha," said Soyen Shaku.

Sokei-an returned a couple of weeks later with a wooden statue of the Buddha.

"What's this?" exclaimed Shaku, and threw it out the window into a pond.

It seemed unkind, Sokei-an would later explain, but it was not: "He'd meant for me to carve the Buddha in myself."

Long Time Dead (4)

In the late 1920s, while searching for a place to establish a Zen practice center, Sokei-an visited Dr. Dwight Goddard , editor of one of the earliest English-language Buddhist compilations, *The Buddhist Bible*. Sokei-an arrived in Vermont however, to find that Dr. Goddard was looking for a hired hand for his 300-acre potato farm, not a Zen teacher—much less a Zen master.

In the center of the property was a big dry area of woodland which had been dead for a long time. The doctor, while showing Sokei-an around, told him: "I always come beneath this tree to meditate."

Sokei-an said: "Then you must know this tree? This woods [sic]?" Sokei-an struck the tree with a stick and exclaimed again: "Then you must know this tree!"

Sokei-an's question did not penetrate the doctor's mind. The doctor looked at the sky and replied. "Yes, this has been dead a long time." Sokei-an observed that the doctor would never understand.

The next morning Goddard took Sokei-an to the potato field. Another man was working for four dollars a day. The doctor said: "If you can plow, you can stay as long as you like."

Sokei-an replied: "This ground has no trees. Where there are no trees Zen will not grow. I will return to the city."

A dynamic and dramatic teacher, Sokei-an "was utterly transported out of himself when he sat in the roshi's chair," wrote Ruth Fuller Everett, who was later to become Ruth Fuller Sasaki. "You had the feeling . . . this was not a man, this was an absolute principle that you were up against." Fellow Institute member Mary Farkas added: "His way of transmitting the Dharma was on a completely different level . . . it was his *silence* that brought us into *it* with him. It was as if, by creating a vacuum, he drew all into the One after him."

Sokei-an once told Alan Watts, who was married for a time to Everett's daughter Eleanor, that it had been reading Ralph Waldo Emerson's essay "Self-Reliance" that triggered his first experience of *satori*, or *kensho*—insight into his true nature—a fitting repayment for what the Transcendentalists owed the East.

According to Watts, however, Sokei-an's unconventionality was still apt to surface occasionally, in sometimes startling ways. One evening, Watts reported, Sokei-an, dressed in his formal brown and gold brocade robes, was delivering a lecture on the *Sutra of Perfect Awakening* before a distinguished New York audience, when he made the statement: "In Buddhism purposelessness is fundamental. No purpose anywhere in life itself. When you drop fart you do not say, 'At nine o'clock I drop fart.' It just happen."

The response of his listeners has gone unrecorded.

After Japan's attack on Pearl Harbor in 1941, Sokei-an and his students were placed under round-the-clock surveillance by the FBI. The following year, Sokei-an was sent to an internment camp. Although he was eventually released through the efforts of First Zen Institute, the experience ruined his health. He married Ruth Fuller Everett in 1944, but died the following year, having asked her to carry on his work.

"I have always taken nature's orders," said Sokei-an, "and I take them now."

He had been, in the words of Mary Farkas, "the first master to carry Zen to America, to speak his mind in English, and to bury his bones here."

I Am from Missouri (5)

Sokei-an went to Boston three times in an attempt to explain Zen to Dr. Tupper, President of the Japan Society of Boston.

Feeling he had failed on the first two attempts, Sokei-an finally framed his explanation in the simplest words he could muster:

"Zen is: 'I am from Missouri'."

DHARMA WORDS FROM SOKEI-AN

One day, when I was traveling through Idaho, I went into some woods. There I found a spring and a little pond covered with autumn leaves. The water [appeared] red because of the red foliage. I was very thirsty, so I knelt down and scooped some water into my hands. The water was clear. It had not been stained or tinted by the autumn leaves. Our mind, I realized, must be pure like this pond. The original nature of mind is not so far away. It can be attained immediately. Purity is the nature of this original mind.

When you go to Riverside Drive and sit beside the Hudson River your thoughts come and go like sailing boats. Finally, they go away—the mind becomes blank—and you do not see the sailing boats. Then the blank mind goes away, and you are absolutely not there. But you still see the river and the green trees; you are expanded into the universe; and your heart beats in the rhythm of nature.

Then, "Oh!" and you come back.

Nyogen Senzaki was also interred for the duration of the war, at Heart Mountain Relocation Center in Wyoming. There he established a zendo called "The Meditation Hall of the Eastbound Teaching" for the benefit of the 10,000 or so dispossessed Japanese-Americans detained there. Re-dubbing Heart Mountain "The Mountain of Compassion," Senzaki went so far as to speculate that the massive relocation of so many Buddhists might even have some positive outcome in supporting "the eastbound tendency of the teachings." Beat Poet Albert Saijo, who was interned in the camp as a teenager, remembers Senzaki from those years: "Even as a kid seeing him in camp I could see he walked different & stood different—I did not have to talk to him to know he was in some other space from us others—he was living out of a different place than average & conventional—obviously there was an aura of quiet around him at all times—I'm just beginning now to fully appreciate him."

Parting

Thus have I heard:
The army ordered
All Japanese faces to be evacuated
From the city of Los Angeles
This homeless monk has nothing but a Japanese face.
He stayed here thirteen springs
Meditating with all faces
From all parts of the world,
And studied the teaching of Buddha with them.
Wherever he goes, he may form other groups
Inviting friends of all faces,
Beckoning them with the empty hands of Zen.

—Nyogen Senzaki, May 7, 1942

Over the years Senzaki sent a number of his American students, including Robert Aitken, to study in Japan with his friend, Soen Nakagawa, Abbot of Ryutakuji Monastery. In 1949 he hosted the first visit to the U.S. by Soen Roshi, who was later to become a key figure in the development of Zen in America. A few years later Senzaki returned as Soen Roshi's guest to revisit his homeland for the first—and last—time in fifty years.

One evening in 1957, Senzaki announced that he would be with his students for just one year longer; and as he predicted, it came to pass. Nyogen Senzaki died the following year at the age of 83. In what was perhaps the first use of modern technology to preserve a Zen teacher's parting words, Senzaki tape-recorded his final message, so that his students were able to hear his voice one last time:

Friends in Dharma, be satisfied with your own heads. Do not put any false heads above your own. Then minute after minute, watch your steps closely. Always keep your head cold and your feet warm. These are my last words to you.

Then, says Aitken: "He added, 'Thank you very much, everybody, for taking such good care of me for so long. Bye bye.' And the tape ended with his little laugh."

In his will, Senzaki wrote:

Do not erect a tombstone! The California poppy is tombstone enough . . . friends of the Dharma, please accept my selfish request. Forget about me as quickly as possible.

The Fifth Patriarch told a new monk
Southern monkeys have no Buddha-nature
The monk proved he had Buddha-nature
By becoming the Sixth Patriarch;
In any part of the globe
Where there is air, fire can burn.
Someday my teaching will surely go to the West,
Led by you.

    —Soyen Shaku, written to his American student, Mrs. Alexander Russell

Bringing Zen to America is as uncertain as
holding a lotus to a rock, hoping it will take root.

—Sokei-an

chapter two

THE MYSTERY OF THE BAMBOO:
EARLY STUDENTS AND TEACHERS

"What makes a man in his middle years give up a secure job and comfortable income, family, and friends for the austere rigor of a Zen monastery and the uncertain life of a 'homeless one'?" wrote Philip Kapleau, speaking of his own path in *Zen: Dawn in the West*.

Particularly, one might add, when the land he was leaving was the staid, self-satisfied America of the 1950s, where to drop one's career and set off on a spiritual quest to an Asian country was hardly in vogue—and the destination was a nation that, less than a decade before, had been considered a mortal enemy.

Perhaps, as Kapleau, who went on to become one of the earliest Americans to complete his training and become a Zen teacher, has variously written, it was his "painful tensions and . . . exhausting restlessness," "painfully felt inner bondage," or the "need to understand the appalling sufferings . . . witnessed in Germany, Japan, and China, just after World War II."

Or simply, as he later referred to it: "that damn 'nothing' feeling."

I can well remember the sense of exhilaration that came with my first reading of Kapleau's *The Three Pillars of Zen*, which was first published in 1967, the earliest book on Zen training written by an American teacher. With its mix of fiery lectures by Kapleau's teacher, Hakuun Yasutani, in which the roshi exhorted his students to see their true nature for themselves, along with contemporary descriptions of enlightenment experiences by Westerners and Kapleau's accounts of his own rigorous training (the American ex-businessman, known only as P.K. in the book, is actually Kapleau), it could not have been more distinct from the other best-selling American Zen practice manual of that period, Shunryu Suzuki's gentle *Zen Mind, Beginner's Mind*. But *Three Pillars* fired in a generation of U.S. spiritual seekers a conviction uniquely suited to their American upbringing: that one did not have to settle for simply reading about the religions and philosophies of the East and the possibilities for enlightenment they offered— one could *do* it, and see it, for oneself. Kapleau's own sense of conviction, as articulated in this and subsequent books, made the experience seem, in fact, almost mandatory.

As a court reporter for the war-crimes trials, Kapleau had witnessed the aftermath of World War II in both Germany and Japan, but was struck by the different response exhibited by the two nations. The German leaders, Kapleau reported, seemed to remain predominantly self-justifying and unrepentant for the atrocities they'd committed, while in Japan it was not uncommon to hear statements in the news media like this: "Because we Japanese have inflicted so much pain on others, we are now reaping the painful harvest."

When Kapleau asked Japanese acquaintances about this difference, he was told that it was due to their acceptance of the "law of karmic retribution." When he inquired further, they told him he would have to study Buddhism if he wanted to understand it. Kapleau sought out D.T. Suzuki at his home in Kamakura, but, although he found the scholar's presence remarkable, his discourses on the philosophy of Zen were too technical to be of much use to him. Something more seemed to be required, but for the moment he didn't know what it was.

Kapleau returned to the United States after the war in "a mood of black depression." He established a prosperous business, but worldly success brought no satisfaction. Suffering from ulcers and allergies, unable to sleep without medication, and, by his own account, "in bondage to the joyless pursuit of pleasure," Kapleau felt, by the age of forty, that he was at a dead end. "My vacuous life no longer had meaning," wrote Kapleau, "yet there was no other to take its place."

Kapleau continued to attend lectures by D.T. Suzuki, who was then teaching at Columbia University, but again found simply studying the philosophy of Zen to be of limited benefit. Finally, in 1953, a Japanese friend advised him to forget the theory and take on the practice, telling him: "If you really want to learn Buddhism and not just talk about it, your whole life will be transformed. It won't be easy, but you can rely on this: once you enter upon the Buddha's Way with sincerity and zeal, Bodhisattvas will spring up everywhere to help you. But you must have courage and faith, and you must make up your mind to realize the liberating power of your Buddha-nature no matter how much pain and sacrifice it entails."

This, says Kapleau, was "the transfusion of courage" he needed. "After several months of agonizing," he wrote in *Zen: Dawn in the West*, "I gave up my work, disposed of my belongings, and set sail for Japan, determined not to return until I became enlightened."

His friend's summation of the difficulties involved proved to be entirely correct. For the next thirteen years, Kapleau struggled with physical pain, language barriers, fatigue, and his own mind— although his previous ill health, sleeplessness, and depression cleared up entirely. At last, while studying with Yasutani Roshi in 1958, Kapleau passed the koan "Mu" and experienced his first glimpse into his true nature.

The experience, he wrote, left him feeling "free as a fish swimming in an ocean of cool, clear water, after being stuck in a tank of glue."

First Lesson (6)

After traveling around Japan for some time, looking without success for a Zen teacher who might be willing to work with Western students, Philip Kapleau and his traveling companion, Professor Bernard Phillips, received a letter from Abbott Soen Nakagawa Roshi of Ryutakuji Monastery, saying they could stay there for a short time.

Excited at the prospect of finally meeting a teacher with whom they could communicate in English, the two Americans spent the six-and-a-half-hour train ride formulating a variety of philosophical questions they hoped he would answer for them.

On their arrival that evening, Soen Nakagawa greeted them, asking if they were tired from their long trip and might like to rest for a bit.

"We're a little tired," they admitted, "but we've prepared a number of questions on the subject of Zen that we—"

"Stop!" the roshi commanded. "After you do zazen, you can ask whatever you want. Meanwhile, I have some business to attend to." Ignoring the protests of the Americans, who had never been instructed in how to meditate and weren't even sure they could sit crosslegged, the roshi told them, "Do it any way you want. Just sit on the floor and remain silent." With that, he left them to their own devices.

Until the roshi had concluded his "business," wrote Kapleau, the two "sat—no, wriggled—wordlessly for two miserable hours in the dark hall . . . concentration impossible, thoughts chasing each other like a pack of monkeys, excruciating pain in legs, back, and neck . . ."

At last, the roshi sent for them, and proceeded to offer a simple meal of rice, which they devoured. He then asked cordially, "Now—what would you like to know about Zen?"

"Not a thing," responded the Americans, who were by this time so exhausted they could scarcely remember their questions.

"Then you'd better go to sleep," said the roshi, "because we get up at 3:30 in the morning. Pleasant dreams!"

"That was the worst sitting I've ever sat in my life!" said Kapleau, looking back on the experience during a conversation at the Rochester Zen Center. "One look at me and he had me pegged. *That* was my first lesson in Zen."

You Spit, I Bow (7)

The morning after Philip Kapleau and Professor Phillips arrived at Ryutakuji Monastery, they were given a tour of the place by Abbot Soen Nakagawa. Both Americans had been heavily influenced by tales of ancient Chinese masters who'd destroyed sacred texts, and even images of the Buddha, in order to free themselves from attachment to anything. They were thus surprised and disturbed to find themselves being led into a ceremonial hall, where the roshi invited them to pay respects to a statue of the temple's founder, Hakuin Zenji, by bowing and offering incense.

On seeing Nakagawa bow before the image, Phillips couldn't contain himself, and burst out: "The old Chinese masters burned or spit on Buddha statues! Why do you bow down before them?"

"If you want to spit, you spit," replied the roshi. "I prefer to bow."

In 1934 Nyogen Senzaki's friend and student, Shubin Tanahashi, whose son Jimmy he had often cared for, ran across some writings in a Japanese magazine by a then-unknown young poet-monk named Soen Nakagawa. She was so impressed she passed them on to her teacher. The writings so moved Nyogen Senzaki that he wrote a letter of appreciation to the monk, initiating a correspondence that was to last for the next twenty-four years, until Senzaki's death.

Soen Nakagawa, who would later come to be regarded by many as one of the great haiku poets of his time, had always felt a kinship with the West. He credited Schopenhauer, whom he read in high school in the 1920s, with being an important inspiration in his decision to pursue the spiritual life. A few years earlier, he and some fellow classmates from Hiroshima Junior High School had pooled their money to buy a recording of Beethoven's Ninth Symphony. He found the experience of hearing it so moving that he "shivered for three days afterward." Soen was left with a life-long love of European composers. In college, where he majored in Japanese literature, he read the Bible and many Western classics. By the time he became a monk in the early 1930s, Soen had already developed the vision of establishing an international Zen practice center. He even spent a brief, if unsuccessful, period prospecting for gold on an offshore island, in hopes of funding it.

Known as an eccentric even in his youth, Soen had limited patience for institutionalized Zen, and his teacher, Gempo Roshi, recognizing his brilliance, gave him a lot of leeway in his training. Soen spent long periods sequestered in his hermitage on Dai Bosatsu Mountain, where he fasted or scavenged for wild edibles, practiced zazen, wrote poetry, and chanted "Namu Dai Bosa," a liturgy of his own invention. Thus, Soen Nakagawa was as surprised as anyone when just after Gempo Roshi's 85th birthday in 1950, his teacher named him his dharma heir and Abbot of Ryutakuji Monastery.

Soen Nakagawa's first experience of America had been the year before, in 1949, when wartime tensions eased enough for him to make a long-awaited visit to see Nyogen Senzaki. The two had been corresponding at this point for fifteen years and, despite the fact that they had never met in person, they considered one another to be the closest of friends. The visit cemented Soen's link to the United States. Senzaki began to send American students to study with Soen Nakagawa; and when word got out that there was an English-speaking roshi at Ryutakuji who was sympathetic to Westerners, American and European seekers began to show up in increasing numbers for instruction in Zen practice. Most notable among these, in the early years, were Philip Kapleau and Robert Aitken.

It's Not What You Say … (8)

During a retreat at Ryutakuji Monastery, Soen Nakagawa pulled Westerners Philip Kapleau and Bernard Phillips aside and asked them:

"What did Christ say as he was dying upon the cross?"

"He said," replied Kapleau, "'My God, why hast thou forsaken me?'"

"*No!*" shouted Soen Roshi. He turned to Phillips. "What did Christ say when he was dying on the cross?"

"Well, I think that's right," answered Phillips. "He said, 'My God, why hast thou forsaken me?'"

"No!" corrected Soen Roshi again.

"Well then," asked the Westerners, "What *did* he say?"

Soen Roshi spread his arms to the sky and cried in agony: *"My God, why hast thou forsaken me?!!"*

The Point of Zen (9)

Soen Nakagawa first addressed an American audience on the subject of Zen at the San Francisco Theosophical Library in 1949, during a visit to see Nyogen Senzaki. He began by quoting Soyen Shaku's infamous line: "Only very recently have I begun to understand that after all, I do not understand anything," from the master's 1906 talk.

"Nowadays," said Soen Roshi, commenting on Shaku's statement, "there is no one capable of being dumbfounded . . . . Everyone knows everything and can answer any question."

The roshi illustrated his point by quoting from Wolfgang von Goethe's *Faust*:

> *. . . Already these ten years, I lead,*
> *Up, down, across, and to and fro,*
> *My pupils by the nose—and learn*
> *That we, in truth, can nothing know!*

"This 'we in truth, can nothing know,'" said Soen Roshi, ". . . is exactly the point of Zen. We Zen monks apply ourselves day after day, year after year, to the study of the Unthinkable."

Meanwhile, back in New York, responsibility for the activities of the First Zen Institute had fallen largely, in the wake of Sokei-an's death, to two of his closest students, Ruth Fuller Sasaki (formerly Ruth Fuller Everett) and Mary Farkas. The two had first encountered Sokei-an when they joined what was then known as the Buddhist Society of America on the same day in 1938. After Mary Farkas paid her first $5 membership fee, Sokei-an told her, "Now you are a pillar of this temple." Her donation was at the time enough to pay one month's rent.

Ruth Fuller Everett, a prominent society woman, was by that point already an experienced practitioner, having received zazen instruction from D.T. Suzuki while on a trip to Japan in 1930. In 1932, at the age of 40, she'd returned to Japan and petitioned Nanshinken Roshi, a fierce Rinzai master known for not allowing women in his zendo, to enter training with him. The roshi, apparently believing that Westerners were inherently unable to sit cross-legged, provided her with an enormous plush chair which, as Everett later described it, was "upholstered in bright green velour . . . with pearl buttons which if pushed . . . sent the back down with horrifying speed, and caused arm and footrests to spring out suddenly from the least expected places!" The roshi told her that the chair, unfortunately, could not be permitted in the zendo, but that she would be welcome to sit in his house. Within several weeks, however, Everett had prevailed in her wish to practice in the zendo—without the chair. She stayed for several months, becoming perhaps the first American to complete a daunting Rohatsu sesshin—a week-long retreat in which participants sit excruciatingly long hours of zazen from long before dawn until late into the night.

Everett had found her true teacher, however, back in America, in the person of Sokei-an Sasaki. After moving to New York, she'd become a key supporter of Sokei-an's group and editor of their journal, *The Cat's Yawn*. During the early years, Sokei-an rarely asked his students to sit zazen, limiting his instruction to talks and the private meetings with students known as sanzen. Everett eventually confronted him for trying to offer Zen without sitting meditation, to which her teacher replied: "If I put them down on cushions and made them do zazen, I would have no roof over my head!" After this, however, he encouraged Everett to begin instructing members in sitting practice, and a core group began to gather for daily zazen.

Several years later, Everett funded the acquisition of new quarters for the group, which at that point took the name First Zen Institute of America. Somewhere along the way, a romance had begun to bloom between her and Sokei-an and, in 1944, she married her teacher to become Ruth Fuller Sasaki. Following Sokei-an's death, she took on many of the responsibilities of the Institute, then returned to Japan in 1949 to continue her Zen studies and to carry on the translation work her husband had begun. She would remain there for the next eighteen years, until her death in 1966, studying koans under Sokei-an's dharma brother, Goto Zuigan Roshi, and overseeing the translation of a number of important texts.

In 1956, Ruth Fuller Sasaki became the first American to be ordained as a Zen priest. She went on to restore Ryosen-an Temple in Kyoto, becoming its Abbess, and established a zendo there for the purpose of "making traditional Zen study available to Western students."

A Letter from Japan
Ruth Fuller Sasaki wrote the following to members of the First Zen Institute in 1958:

The appointment of myself, an American, as priest of a Rinzai Zen temple is unique in the history of that sect. The fact that I am a woman is not of such importance, for there have always been, at least in Japan, some temples presided over by nuns, to which category, of course, I now belong . . . [upon ordaining as a priest] the postulant takes the monks' vows from his teacher and usually his head is shaved. No, do not fear. My hair has not been cut off, nor will it be. There are rules for exceptional cases . . .

In the course of the very simple ceremony I was taken to the hondo—"main hall"—of the monastery . . . and allowed to burn incense before the figure of Daito Kokushi, founder of the line of Daitokuji teaching . . . . This life-sized figure carved of wood has been placed deep within the main shrine of the hondo. The Kokushi sits, as he must often have sat in life, full of power, his eyes—of glass—glaring in the light of the candles, his real stick uplifted ready to strike. It is quite an experience to walk into that shadowy place and stand face to face with the old man . . .

Alone at the altar of the Founder of Daitoku-ji, I bowed three times, fore-head on the ground, then entered into the deep recess of the altar, where only disciples in Daito Kokushi's line may enter, and, bowed again and burned incense before the life-sized figure seated in its depths.

Walter Nowick first encountered Zen while he was a music student at Juliard in the late 1940s. As he told the story during a conversation we shared at his farm in Maine, he'd picked up a copy of a publication called *The Cat's Yawn* while waiting to see his teacher for a piano lesson at her home. Flipping through it, he came upon a poem that caught his eye. As he remembers, it read:

The Forest of Zen
All night long
the shadow of the bamboo sweeps the stairs
but not a particle of dust is stirred.
All night long
the moonbeams penetrate the pool
But not a trace is left.

"What *is* this?" Nowick inquired of his teacher.
"Zen," she replied.
"I want to study this," Nowick said.
The Cat's Yawn turned out to be a publication of the First Zen Institute, of which Nowick's teacher was a member; the poem was a translation by Sokei-an [Nowick's version from memory is somewhat different from the original]. His teacher subsequently took him along to several of the Institute's meetings.

After the first gathering, Nowick recalls, he was so eager to try zazen on his own that after he got off the train on his way back to his parents' home on Long Island, he sat down in a field to meditate, believing he would achieve enlightenment in a short while. Interrupted some time later by the sound of his mother's worried voice calling his name, he rose to his feet to discover himself the same as ever; and he realized that this was not going to be as easy as he'd thought.

Several years later, Nowick found himself en route by train from Tokyo to Daitokuji Monastery in Kyoto. The First Zen Institute had helped him acquire a visa and passport. This was a difficult matter at the time, for with the U.S. occupation still in force, a request to do anything as odd as spending time in a Zen monastery was viewed with the utmost suspicion. As Nowick recalls, he was finally issued a visa stamped "For Compassion-ate Purposes." He remembers watching from the window as his train passed great bamboo forests, calling to mind the lines of verse that had brought him here; and at that moment, as though in reflection of his thoughts, a Japanese student sitting beside him leaned over and whispered: "Do you understand the mystery of the bamboo?"

The train's sound system was playing Schubert. Nowick dug through his bags and, to the amazement of the Japanese stu-dent and his companions, extracted a book of sheet music that included the piece that was playing. He and the students spent the rest of the trip singing Schubert.

When Nowick arrived in Kyoto, and stepped at last through the gates of Daitokuji Monastery, having no idea at the time that he was to spend the better part of the next sixteen years here, he remembers thinking to himself: "Here you are. The place you've been dreaming about these last few years—you're here."

"What a thing," he says, looking back on the experience. "What an amazing feeling it was."

The year was 1950. He was twenty-four years old.

Ready or Not . . . (10)

On Walter Nowick's first meeting with Goto Zuigan Roshi in Kyoto, the Master, who had lived briefly in the United States as part of Sokatsu Shaku's ill-fated strawberry farm in the early part of the century, told the young American he would "take his English out of mothballs" in order to teach him Zen. *Sanzen*, the private meetings with the master in which the student attempts to present his or her understanding of a particular koan, were to commence the following morning.

Nowick nodded in response, perhaps a bit apprehensively, and added, "I *am* a little slow."

"Slow or fast," intoned the roshi, "—we will examine."

Poet Gary Snyder ended up at Daitokuji too, after Alan Watts introduced him to Ruth Fuller Sasaki, who secured him a grant from the First Zen Institute to study and work with her translation team. A mountaineer, environmental activist, and scholar of Oriental languages, Snyder's interest in Asian culture was sparked when, as a boy growing up in Washington state, he saw an exhibition of Chinese landscape paintings. Their mountains struck him as bearing a remarkable resemblance to his own beloved Cascade Range. Snyder later taught himself to meditate by studying statues of Buddha figures and reproducing their sitting posture.

Associated with the West Coast wing of the Beat movement (of which more will be said later), Snyder was one of the poets featured at the famous Six Gallery poetry reading in San Francisco in 1955, which brought the "San Francisco Renaissance" to the attention of the nation. On the same evening Allen Ginsberg debuted "Howl," which was to change American poetry forever. The following year, on May 15, 1956, Snyder set sail for Kyoto. For most of his time in Japan, Snyder studied at Daitokuji with Sesso Oda Roshi, dharma heir to Walter Nowick's and Ruth Fuller Sasaki's teacher, Goto Zuigan.

Of his teacher, Snyder wrote:

[Oda Roshi was an] especially gentle and quiet man—an extremely subtle man, by far the subtlest mind I've ever been in contact with, and a marvelous teacher whose teaching capacity I never would have recognized if I hadn't stayed with it, because it was only after five or six years that I began to realize that he had been teaching me all along. . . . Oda Roshi delivered teisho lectures in so soft a voice nobody could hear him. Year after year, we would sit at lectures—lectures that only roshis can give, spontaneous commentaries on classical texts—and not

hear what he was saying. Several years after Oda Roshi had died one of the head
monks, with whom I became very close, said to me, "You know those lectures that
Oda Roshi gave that we couldn't hear? I'm beginning to hear them now."

Snyder was to continue his rigorous training and koan study at
Daitokuji for the next twelve years.

What Is Serious? (11)

When Gary Snyder first went to Japan to study Zen, he asked his teacher
Oda Roshi whether it was all right that he wrote poetry.

Oda Roshi laughed and replied: "It's all right as long as it truly comes
out of your true self."

Nevertheless, feeling that he needed to be completely serious in his
practice of Zen, and uncertain whether poetry was serious enough, Snyder quit writing almost completely for a number of years.

Just before Oda Roshi died, Snyder went to visit him in the hospital.

"So Roshi," Snyder asked, still seeking clarification, "it's—Zen *is* serious, and poetry is not serious?"

"No," corrected Oda Roshi. "Poetry is serious. Zen is *not* serious."

Says Snyder: "I'd had it all wrong!"

In Ruth Fuller Sasaki's absence, the First Zen Institute was largely
held together by the efforts of Mary Farkas, who would serve for
more than forty years until her death in 1992. Farkas, by her own
account, believed in the early Zen of ancient China, a "Zen of
eccentrics, loners, scholars, isolated monks and small groups . . . a
Zen without rules, regulations, money, dogma, priests, titles, or
ranks." Although she never referred to herself as anything other
than the Institute's Secretary, she had been presented with the
purple robes of an Abbess by a Zen master, though she rarely
wore them. A fellow member reported an incident that illustrates
the esteem in which she was held, which took place while Farkas
was away in Japan in the 1950s, trying to find a teacher to succeed
Sokei-an:

Many visitors would arrive expecting to be greeted and given audience by the act-ing head of the First Zen Institute. I remember one Japanese scholar who arrived ready to do [dharma] battle with Herself . . . he came early and was seated in a suitable location in the front row. When the informal tea time commenced, he asked for Mrs. Farkas and was told she was in Kyoto. He immediately became exercised and began an adversarial exchange with the senior members . . .

According to reports, the senior students politely, but effi-ciently, saw the scholar to the door, thus ending the aborted "dharma combat."

For many years, Farkas collaborated with Institute founding members Audrey Kepner and Edna Kenton in the compiling and editing of Sokei-an's talks, which she published first in the Insti-tute's monthly magazine, which by this time had been renamed simply *Zen Notes*, and later in the first book-length collection of Sokei-an's teachings, *The Zen Eye*.

On a visit to Japan in the 1950s Farkas asked Goto Zuigan Roshi, "Don't you think we've made some progress in this last half century?"

"Yes," replied the roshi, encouragingly. "You could say you have taken a step."

What Is "Spiritual"? (12)

Mary Farkas always disliked the use of the word "spiritual" as applied to Zen practice, for she believed it created a false distinction between prac-tice and daily life. Once she heard D.T. Suzuki use the term in a lecture on Zen, and approached the scholar afterward, asking his true opinion of the term.

Suzuki paused for a time and finally responded: "It is a great obscenity."

Farkas nodded her head in agreement.

Worthwhile to Help (13)

Once when a Zen master came to teach in New York, Mary Farkas, who knew he didn't like the city, asked why he kept returning. He didn't answer at the time; but, Farkas reported, "he later said that 'he would remain as long as there was a person here or even half a person who was worth-while to help.'"

"There is an initial experience of finding oneself on the path that can be very profound," writes Robert Aitken. "In my own case, while I was in a Japanese internment camp during the war, sick as a dog with asthma, I found R.H. Blyth's *Zen in English Literature and Oriental Classics*. I must have read that book ten times, finishing it and starting again . . . the world seemed transparent, and I was absurdly happy despite our miserable circumstances."

Aitken, who later founded the Diamond Sangha in Hawaii and went on to become one of the first American Zen teachers, came to Zen practice after he was captured while working as a civilian on the island of Guam when the Pacific war broke out in the 1940s. "We climbed to the highest peak [on the island]," says Aitken, "We could see the whole island ringed with Japanese ships, so we knew that we had to give ourselves up." He was taken back to Japan, and interred as an enemy alien. There, one of his guards loaned him a copy of Blyth's book.

"All my work," wrote Aitken, "comes from the profound vow that was made for me on reading it: that I would devote my life to Zen Buddhism, no matter what the difficulty."

In 1944, Aitken's camp was combined with the camp where Blyth, an expatriate Englishman, was interred, and Aitken began an apprenticeship and friendship that was to last twenty years, until his mentor's death in 1964. "If we had not met," he later wrote, "I might well have spent my life mundanely, saying and doing trivial things."

Aitken went on to practice with nearly all of the teachers avail-able to Westerners at the time: Nyogen Senzaki in Los Angeles and D.T. Suzuki in Hawaii, and Asahina Roshi, Soen Nakagawa, Hakuun Yasutani, and Koun Yamada in Japan. "They were all as different as could be," Aitken said recently, in a phone interview from his Hawaii home. "Each one was totally himself. I'm very grateful to have had the chance to study with all of them."

Aitken underwent extended periods of traditional monastic training, despite severe and recurrent bouts of ill health and knees that became so swollen with hour upon hour of sitting that he could scarcely walk. During his first intensive meditation retreat, or sesshin, with Asahina Roshi in 1950, Aitken says, he was appalled to realize that the morning service began and ended with nine full bows—prostrations—to the altar. "It was as though," says Aitken, "all the beliefs that I had about the righteous importance of the individual were suddenly just snatched. And I thought, my God, what am I doing?" He resolved to suspend judgment, however, and to concentrate on his zazen. In time, Aitken came to appreciate such formal aspects of the practice, and later wrote, "(Bowing) is a sign of throwing everything away . . . . All our self-concern, all our preoccupations are thrown away completely. There is just that bow."

Despite all of his difficulties, Aitken says, he never felt any doubt about continuing. "It was the only thing I could do," he says. "I can't explain that."

In 1959, Aitken and his wife Anne started a sitting group in Honolulu, where they hosted sesshins by several of the teachers with whom they'd studied in Japan. Finally, at a retreat with Soen Nakagawa, Aitken, as the roshi described it, "got a little bit of light."

"I knew he was referring to my experience," Aitken later wrote, "but I did not treat it very seriously. However, I found the ceiling of my mind to be infinitely spacious. Everything was bright and new."

Just Like Riding a Bicycle (14)

"Zazen," says Robert Aitken, "Is just like learning how to ride a bicycle. You have to steer, pump, keep your balance, watch out for pedestrians and other vehicles—all at once. You are riding a pile of parts with your pile of parts. After you learn to ride, however, what then? You are free of those parts, surely. You are one with the bicycle, and the bicycle keeps its own balance. It steers and pumps itself, and you can enjoy your ride and go anywhere, to the store, to school, to the office, the beach. You have forgotten sprockets and handle bars. You have forgotten that you have forgotten."

A True Person of Zen (15)

Yamada Koun Roshi, the cigar-smoking layman and hospital administrator who became dharma successor to Yasutani Roshi, and with whom Robert Aitken eventually completed his Zen study, has been quoted as saying: "If one is a true person of Zen, no one would be able to pick you out on the Tokyo subway."

Hakuun Yasutani Roshi was the teacher of a number of Western students in the 1950s and 1960s, including Philip Kapleau and Robert Aitken. At more than eighty years old, he continued to travel throughout Europe and America to conduct rigorous week-long Zen retreats, renowned for their vigor and discipline. A "skinny hawklike man," with a piercing gaze, and prominent ears that stuck out "like teacups," Yasutani, according to Kapleau, "could often be seen trotting about Tokyo in a tattered robe and a pair of sneakers on his way to a zazen meeting, his lecture books in a bag slung over his back, or standing in the crowded second-class interurban trains." Robert Aitken's first impression of him, at a retreat he attended in Japan when the roshi was already more than seventy years old was "a distillation of pure energy."

"He devoted himself fully to us," said Aitken, who described his teacher as "like a feather, but full of passion."

Yasutani Roshi once asked one of his Western students, "When you die, does everything around you die too?"

"I don't know," replied the student. "I haven't had that experience yet."

"When you disappear," the roshi stated, "the entire universe disappears. And when the universe vanishes, you vanish with it."

On another occasion, a Western student said to Yasutani, regarding his practice of a particular koan, "I know what I'm *supposed* to do, but I can't do it."

Yasutani answered: "There is nothing you are supposed to do . . . . You only have to grasp the fact that when it rains the ground gets wet, that when the sun shines the world becomes bright."

A number of Yasutani Roshi's students went on to become prominent figures in the development of American Zen, including Robert Aitken, Philip Kapleau, Taizan Maezumi, and Eido Shimano.

"The fundamental delusion of humanity," Yasutani used to say, "is to suppose that I am *here*—" at this, he'd point to himself, "—and you are out there."

More Things in Heaven and Earth . . . (16)

During one of Yasutani Roshi's first American Zen retreats, held at a Quaker center in Pennsylvania, a graduate student in philosophy from Temple University left after the first day. The note of explanation he'd left on his seat read: "If I were to stay for the [full] five days, my philosophy would be crushed."

DHARMA WORDS FROM YASUTANI ROSHI

An electric news screen has a lot of light bulbs and shows letters by lighting some of them up . . . . When you look at it from afar, it certainly seems as though the letters are flowing, but when you go up close and look at it, it is just some light bulbs going on and off, and there is not a single flowing letter. In the same way as that, everything in the universe seeming to exist and seeming to be active is completely untrue . . .

Everything in the universe is like that.

It was left to Jiyu-Kennett, an Englishwoman who later established the Shasta Abbey in northern California, to assemble the most astonishing array of "firsts" in the history of Zen in the West. After ordaining as a priest in the *Ch'an* [Chinese Zen] tradition in Malacca, Malaysia in 1962, she entered into training at Sojiji Monastery in Japan, becoming the first woman to be admitted to a major Soto sect training center since the 14th century. The following year, Kennett became the first Westerner to receive dharma transmission in the Soto sect from her teacher, Keido Chisan Roshi, a Japanese pioneer in seeking equality between the sexes. Kennett later received the title roshi and full authority to teach, becoming one of the few women in the history of Zen to attain this rank. After serving as abbess of her own temple in Japan, she moved to San Francisco in the 1960s, to become the first fully sanctioned woman Zen teacher in the U.S.

Kennett went on to found the Shasta Abbey, which at its peak in the 1970s and 1980s had some one hundred Zen monastics in training.

Kennett's approach to teaching, according to one senior student, was "not to lighten the load of a disciple, but to make the load so heavy that he or she would put it down."

The Next Best Thing (17)

When Jiyu-Kennett was training at Sojiji Temple in Japan in the early 1960s, she was surprised one day by the arrival of an important visitor.

As Kennett tells it, she had just come back from an outing to find a large contingent of priests and ladies in the Abbot's guest department, "and in the center, one middle-aged [lady] who looked rather kind." The woman smiled as Kennett approached, and since introductions did not seem to be forthcoming she says, "I held out my hand. [The woman] shook it with great glee, obviously enjoying herself and thoroughly pleased . . . I noticed that everyone seemed to be startled but, since nobody explained who she was, I felt that I had done the right thing . . . To my delight, she began speaking in English, telling me how delighted she was that I was there and hoping to see me again on her next visit."

Shortly thereafter, Kennett returned to her quarters, where the Director of the temple soon called on her.

"I want you to shake hands with me," he announced.

"May I ask why, Reverend Director?" Kennett responded.

"You shook the hand of the Empress of Japan. No living person has touched that hand other than the Emperor. You do not realize what a great thing you have done!"

A moment later, her door swung open again to reveal the entire staff of temple officers, waiting with outstretched hands, and an even larger group of junior trainees behind them.

"I suppose," wrote Kennett later, "that shaking the hand of ... her who shook the hand is the next best thing to shaking the hand!"

In the early 1950s Asahina Sogen, Abbot of Engakuji Temple in Japan, visited the First Zen Institute of America in New York City. He corrected the zazen posture of the Institute's members, for whom this was the first visit of a Zen master since the death of Sokei-an nearly ten years before.

"Suppleness is very important," said the roshi, speaking of the correct position of the spine. "We say, if it is supple, it is alive. If it is rigid, it is dead."

After zazen, while eating ice cream and drinking tea, he demonstrated Master Rinzai's famous shout of "Ho!"—the purpose of which was to bypass all thinking and return those who heard it to the present moment of experience.

"To give a 'Ho!'" said the roshi, "is agreeable in the quiet night air of New York."

With that he departed, leaving the Institute's members on their own again.

chapter three

NEW MIND AND EYEBALL KICKS: THE ZEN BOOM OF THE FIFTIES

1958 will be great year, year of Buddhism, already big stir in NY about Zen, Alan Watts big hero of Madison Avenue now, and Nancy Wilson Ross big article about Zen in Mademoiselle mentions me and Allen and knows her Buddhism good, now with Dharma Bums I will crash open whole scene to sudden Buddhism boom and look what'll happen closely soon . . . everybody going the way of the Dharma, this no shit . . . then with arrival of Gary (Snyder), smash! Watch, you'll see. It will be a funny year of enlightenment in America . . . everybody reading Suzuki on Madison Avenue . . . that in itself mighty strange . . .

—JACK KEROUAC, FROM 1957 LETTER TO PHILIP WHALEN,
JUST BEFORE PUBLICATION OF THE DHARMA BUMS

I remember vividly, as a twenty-two-year-old undergraduate, first encountering Jack Kerouac's novel *The Dharma Bums*. While my college roommates clanged around the kitchen making dinner and playing music I closed myself in my room, utterly absorbed in Kerouac's lunatic world of spontaneous religion—so different from the stuffy, gloomy Protestant churches I'd visited with my grandmother at Christmas and Easter. Why, you could *live* and still be spiritual! I was reading the part where the Kerouac alias, Ray Smith, meditates alone in the woods every night. At one point, he spits into a puddle and watches the stars reflected there vanish—begging the question that if those stars, so apparently solid, were not, how could we know *anything* was? This was my first encounter with Buddhism—or Kerouac's idiosyncratic version thereof—and the effect was as though a door I'd never known existed suddenly swung open before me. Such a notion—that what we think of as the external world might at least in part be a projection of our minds—had never occurred to me before with such clarity and force. I put down my book and left my room, moved past my oblivious roommates eating their unreal hamburgers and drinking their unreal beers, and stepped out into the night. There, I stood out on the lawn, looking at ground and sky, touching trees, fence posts, a fire hydrant: all seemed equally unreal, equally an imposition of the mind, with its labels of name, color, and form, on some vast, unimaginable reality.

What I'd experienced, without knowing it, was a lingering echo of the Zen boom of the 1950s.

The second wave of Zen in America was led by three very different men: a Japanese scholar named D.T. Suzuki; an expatriate English philosopher, Alan Watts; and American novelist Jack Kerouac, the co-founder, with Allen Ginsberg, of the Beat movement.

Of the three, D.T. Suzuki was the one most grounded in formal practice, and therefore most qualified to speak of it. As a young man in Japan, he had trained under Soyen Shaku for some years, finally achieving *satori*, or *kensho*—insight into his true nature—under the tutelage of the master. Shaku had presented him with the name "Daisetsu," meaning "Great Simplicity" or even, as Suzuki liked to translate it, "Great Stupidity"—a backhanded compliment in the world of Zen. Suzuki used the name for the rest of his life. Though he chose not to ordain as a monk, and was never formally sanctioned as a teacher, Suzuki became a formidable scholar of his tradition. With over one hundred books on Zen, including some thirty titles in English, in addition to a relentless program of lectureships, speaking engagements, and conferences all over the world, Suzuki is often credited with establishing Zen, almost single-handedly, in the West.

Poet Gary Snyder writes:

I clearly remember when I first read a book by D.T. Suzuki; it was September of 1951, and I was standing by the roadside in the vast desert of eastern Nevada hitchhiking the old Route 40. I had found his book a few days earlier in a "metaphysical" bookshop in San Francisco. I was on my way to enter graduate school in Indiana, and here by the highway in the long wait for another ride I opened my new book. The size of the space and the paucity of cars gave me much time to read Essays in Zen, First Series. It catapulted me into an even larger space; and though I didn't know it at the moment, that was the end of my career as an anthropologist . . . D.T. Suzuki gave me the push of my life and I can never be too grateful.

Suzuki lived in the U.S. at various points throughout his life; but his most influential period began in 1950 when, at the age of eighty, he returned from Japan to begin his well-known series of lectures on Zen at Columbia University, which were to attract the interest of artists, intellectuals, and seekers of every stripe. Despite Suzuki's soft-spoken, unassuming manner, the lectures were said to have had a remarkable air about them; and one professor at Columbia might have spoken for many when he said: "When I am listening to Dr. Suzuki's lectures, everything seems alright and certain, but when the lecture is over and I leave, the old confusion returns."

That Suzuki was no ordinary academic is a fact attested to again and again by those who knew him. An attendee at a European conference reported how, at the end of the final meeting, the participants "hurried off in all directions to every continent"—all except Dr. Suzuki, who "delayed his departure by one day because the following night was the August full moon, and he wanted to enjoy calmly contemplating it over the Ticinese Mountains, and its reflection in Lake Maggiore."

"In meeting him," wrote Thomas Merton, "One seemed to meet that 'True Man of No Title' that the Zen masters speak of."

Psychoanalyst Erich Fromm remarked on Suzuki's "ever-present interest in everything around him":

He gave life to everything through his interest . . . (in) Mexico he visited the house of a friend . . . and admired the beautiful garden, with its many old trees. Two years later, when he returned . . . he looked at one of the trees and asked: "What happened to the branch that was here last time?" Indeed, a branch had been cut off, but Dr. Suzuki remembered that branch and missed it.

One day Miss Okamura and my wife were looking for him; they could not find him anywhere, and just as they began to become a little worried they saw him, sitting under a tree, meditating. He was so relaxed that he had become one with the tree, and it was difficult to see 'him'.

Supreme Spiritual Ideal? (18)

During a much-heralded World Congress of Faiths, held at the Queen's Hall in London, Zen scholar D.T. Suzuki was asked to speak on the theme of "The Supreme Spiritual Ideal." After listening to various other dignitaries hold forth on the subject, it was Suzuki's turn to take the platform.

"How can a humble person like myself talk about such a grand thing as the Supreme Spiritual Ideal?" he began. "Really, I do not know what Spiritual is, what Ideal is, and what Supreme Spiritual Ideal is."

With that he proceeded to spend the rest of his speech on a description of his house and garden in Japan, and how life there differed from life in a big city.

The audience gave him a standing ovation.

Who's in Charge Here? (19)

Theologian Paul Tillich delivered a talk at Union Theological Seminary on the subject of religious authority. Afterward, he asked D.T. Suzuki, who was in attendance at his invitation, where he thought religious authority might ultimately reside. Suzuki raised himself up on his toes, leaned forward, and placed his index finger lightly against the chest of his much larger host.

"You, Dr. Paul Tillich, are the authority," Suzuki responded.

"Yes," replied Tillich, after a moment. "I thought you might say something like that."

Know Your Own Mind (20)

D.T. Suzuki, in a question-and-answer period after one of his American lectures, was pressed by a psychic who insisted that he must have developed some clairvoyant abilities as a result of his Zen training.

Having fended off her questions a number of times, Suzuki finally responded: "What's the use of knowing the mind of another? The important thing is to know your own mind."

Suzuki's eloquent writings about the freedom inherent to Zen, its iconoclasm, distrust of authority, and absence of ritual or dogma, sent a compelling message to an American society whose spiritual traditions appeared to be running out of steam. Some of these statements however, have turned out to be, strictly speaking, not entirely accurate—as many of the Zen Boomers discovered when they went on to train with traditional masters and discovered form and hierarchy were very much in place. And Suzuki frequently neglected to mention the essential practice of zazen. Why?

I once asked an American Zen priest, a vocal admirer of Suzuki, what he thought the reason was for these omissions.

"He was trying to invent a new tradition," replied the priest. "He felt the Asian forms had grown stale and the spirit had gone out of the practice. He was trying to save it by creating a new Zen for the West—a Zen westerners could handle. That *he* could handle. And he probably thought trying to get us to actually sit still and be silent was a hopeless mission!"

Suzuki died in 1966 at the age of 96. His assistant, Miss Okamura, reported that she "did not feel any great change occurred between him alive, and him in death." Although she saw his body lying there motionless, she said, it seemed to her as though his life would continue on.

The scholar's parting words, in keeping with his unassuming demeanor, were simply: "Don't worry. Thank you! Thank you!"

Change We Must (21)

While attending a symposium hosted by psychoanalyst Dr. Karen Horney on the changeability of human nature, D.T. Suzuki was asked to respond to the question of whether human beings could change.

"The question is not 'can human nature change,'" responded Suzuki. "Human nature *must* change. Thank you very much."

DHARMA WORDS FROM D.T. SUZUKI

Man is a thinking reed, but his great works are done when he is not calculating and thinking. "Childlikeness" has to be restored with long years of training in the art of self-forgetfulness. When this is attained, man thinks yet he does not think. He thinks like showers coming down from the sky; he thinks like the stars illuminating the nightly heavens; he thinks like the green foliage shooting forth in the relaxing spring breeze. Indeed, he is the showers, the ocean, the stars, the foliage.

"It is said, perhaps with truth," wrote Alan Watts in his autobiography *In My Own Way*, "that my easy and free-floating attitude to Zen was largely responsible for the notorious Zen boom . . . in the late 1950s." This is a statement with which anyone who traveled in circles with an Eastern bent in the Fifties, Sixties, or even Seventies would find it hard to disagree—for when the word Zen was heard to cross anyone's lips at that time, the name Alan Watts was likely to follow.

Despite his position as a teacher and administrator for the Academy of Asian Studies in San Francisco, and the vigorous publishing and speaking schedule he maintained as the nation's leading exponent of Zen philosophy, Alan Watts, like Jack Kerouac, had never at that point actually visited Japan. Nor had he undertaken any formal Zen training beyond a few abortive weeks of koan study with Sokei-an, which he broke off after deciding that trying to find the answers to the koans was like "trying to find a needle in a haystack." Nevertheless Watts, whose religious background included a Doctorate in Divinity and several years as an Anglican priest, had a knack for re-interpreting the wisdom of the East in a way that made it seem as though any Westerner could grasp the heart of Zen, if only they'd loosen up a bit and open their eyes.

"From the beginning," wrote Watts, "I was never interested in being 'good at Zen' in the sense of mastering a traditional discipline . . . What I was after was not so much discipline as understanding . . . To sit hour after hour and day after day with aching legs, to unravel Hakuin's tricky system of dealing with koan . . . was not what I needed to know."

There were sometimes uneasy relations between Watts and the Beats—Watts' 1958 essay, "Beat Zen, Square Zen, and Zen" was, by his own admission, "somewhat severe" in its assessment of Jack Kerouac and his associates, and he was quoted elsewhere as saying that Kerouac had "Zen flesh but no Zen bones." But they all eventually mended their differences, and Watts later wrote in glowing terms of Gary Snyder, one of the few original Beats to undertake formal Zen study: "My only regret is that I cannot formally claim him as my spiritual successor . . . I can only say that a universe which has manifested Gary Snyder could never be called a failure."

Though it has become fashionable to dismiss Watts as a popularizer, this ability to popularize was part of what brought so many Americans to Zen practice. As Gary Snyder said, "Whether or not his books are 'real Zen' is beside the point. You meet people all the time who say, 'I owe so much to Alan Watts' writings. They helped me lead my life.'"

And when Shunryu Suzuki Roshi of the San Francisco Zen Center overheard one of his students criticizing Watts, he admonished him, saying: "You completely miss the point about Alan Watts! You should notice what he has done. He is a great Bodhisattva!"

Beyond Words (22)

When Alan Watts finally did get to Japan, in the early 1960s, he spent a pleasant evening with Morimoto Roshi, in the village of Nagaoka, while a ceaseless rain drummed upon the roof of the temple.

"There's no real point," Morimoto told Watts, during a prolonged but relaxed conversation, "of going to the trouble to translate all our old Chinese texts—not if you're serious about understanding real Zen. The sound of rain needs no translation."

Jack Kerouac, the most famous of the Beat writers, made his discovery of Buddhism independently, through stumbling upon various texts, including Dwight Goddard's *The Buddhist Bible*, in a public library. Shortly thereafter, in 1954, Kerouac wrote to poet Allen Ginsberg about his "discovery . . . of sweet Buddha . . . I always did suspect that life was a dream, now I am assured by the most brilliant man who ever lived, that it is indeed so . . ."

Kerouac wasn't afraid to reinterpret Buddhism to suit his Beat ethos. He wrote Gary Snyder at the monastery where Snyder was practicing in 1956, in a letter true as ever to his idiosyncratic style of spelling and punctuation: "I'm really humbled now before the spectacle of these magnificent men forsaking alcohol and tobacco to just watch cows in the hazy moon and make it off what is there, the objective beautiful sad ungraspable world as it is . . . Altho really frankly I think an American zendo with no rules and all the cats talking all day when they feel like it and orgies at night with shaktis would be the best thing . . ."

Kerouac went on in the same letter:

O what a dream or vision . . . I had of [Zen poet] Han Shan! He was standing in the marketplace in China on a Saturday morning, with a little peaked hat . . . and a seamed and weatherbrowned face, and very short, and hopelessly tangled rags hanging from him all over, and a small . . . bindlestiff bundle, he looked very much like you but smaller and he was old. Cant you find someone like that in Japan? Well I went to Chinatown alone one night at 2 and while eating I drummed on the table to every beat of the pots and voices in the kitchen, quietly, and when I

left all the cooks came to look at me . . . But a week later I went to another res-
taurant and saw the old blue-aproned chinaman sitting in the kitchen door and
askt him, "Why did Buddha come from the west?" Answer: "I'm not interested."
My answer: "Because Buddha came from the West." And left. And was almost
crying."

For all Kerouac's willing manipulation of Buddhist truths, he
managed to capture a certain spirit of freedom at the heart of
the practice. And *The Dharma Bums,* published in 1957 (whose
main character, Japhy Ryder, is based on Gary Snyder) is remarkable for its prophetic vision of a "rucksack revolution" to come,
in which America would be thronged with hitchhiking seekers,
youthful, ragged, "beat" but free—legions of Dharma bums, turning to the East for spiritual guidance.

It would be less than a decade before it would all, in a sense,
begin to come true.

Today, the lineage established by Kerouac and the other Beats
is carried on at the Jack Kerouac School of Disembodied Poetics at Naropa University (formerly the Naropa Institute) in
Boulder, Colorado, the Buddhist-influenced college founded by
Allen Ginsberg and Chogyam Trungpa, a Tibetan Lama. While
revisiting Naropa in order to interview several of my former
teachers who had frequented the American Buddhist world for
many years, I stumbled to my great delight upon several vol-
umes of Kerouac's selected letters in the Allen Ginsberg Library.
These contained correspondence exchanged over a number of
years between Kerouac and fellow Beats Gary Snyder and Philip
Whalen on the subject of Zen. Included was Kerouac's original
account of his famous meeting with D.T. Suzuki, which is better
known in a later version Kerouac wrote for a Bay Area magazine,
as well as the author's original dust-jacket copy for *The Dharma
Bums.* Later, in my small home-town library, (in case anyone
should doubt the ongoing influence of the Beats), I miraculously
discovered a copy of the long-out-of-print *As Ever,* a collection of

correspondence between Allen Ginsberg and the legendary Neal Cassady, which yielded an account of Ginsberg's first investigations into Zen. There I also discovered *Big Sky Mind*, an anthology of Beat writings on Buddhism, which featured Philip Whalen's "Weird Satori." Together, they provide a glimpse into the spirit and enthusiasm of both the Beat scene and the American Zen world as it existed at the time.

Don't Forget the Tea

On the day his novel *The Dharma Bums* was published, Jack Kerouac was on his way to a party in his honor, accompanied by poets Allen Ginsberg and Peter Orlovsky. On impulse, he stepped into a phone booth and phoned Zen scholar D.T. Suzuki, who was then living in New York, and had recently sent word that he wanted to meet him. Kerouac's 1958 letter to Philip Whalen, who had served as the model for the Warren Coughlin character in *The Dharma Bums*, and later became a Zen teacher in his own right, contains this version of the encounter:

Word came out that DT Suzuki wanted to see me so I called him on the phone, a woman answered and said (as Allen and Peter waited outside phonebooth listening with big serious faces of Dharma), ". . .When can we arrange the appointment with Dr. Suzuki?" and I said, "Right now," and she said, "I'll go tell Doctor Suzuki" and was gone into big back secret whispering chambers and came back and said, "Half an hour all right?" I said "Yes" . . . [we] came to a door with a nameplate with his name on it and rang a long, long time. Finally I rang three times deliberately and he famously came, walking downstairs, a small bald Japanese man of 80 and opened the door. Then he . . . led us upstairs to a room where he picked out special chairs and made us just sit there and picked his own chair facing us behind a huge bookpiled desk. So I wrote him out my Koan, "When the Buddha was about to speak a horse spoke instead," and he had a funny look in his eye and said, "The Western mind is too complicated, after all the Buddha and the horse had some kind of understanding there."

. . .Then he said, "You young men sit here quietly and write haikus while I go and make some powdered green tea." And we told him all about you and Gary

[Snyder] and drank the tea in black bowls and he said it was weak . . . so he made another batch real strong and Allen said, "It tastes like shrimps" . . .he said "Don't forget that it's tea." . . . then we all got high on that green tea . . . [he] said he drank it every day, something has happened to me since then I think . . . I wrote a haiku for him:

> *Three little sparrows*
> *on the roof.*
> *Talking quietly, sadly*

and they wrote some too, Allen and I both wrote the same haiku in fact, in different words . . .

> *Big books packaged*
> *from Japan—*
> *Ritz crackers*

Because of his big box of Ritz crackers on the shelf under big books packaged from Japan, and so finally I told him I'd had some samadhis lasting a whole halfhour or 3 seconds and o yes, the great thing . . . as we were leaving I suddenly realized he was my old fabled father from China and I said, "I would like to spend the rest of my life with you, sir," and he said "Sometime." And he kept pushing us out the door, down the stairs, as tho impatient, tho was me instituted the idea of leaving . . . then when we were out on the street he kept giggling and making signs at us through the window and finally said "Dont forget the tea!" And I said "The Key?" He said "The Tea."

In a second letter to Whalen later that month Kerouac added:

> *Dear Phil,*
> *A golden giant has finally pulled the Dharma out of my eyebrows.*

Whalen, according to Kerouac, later wrote back in response to Suzuki's remarks about the Western mind:

Tell Mr. Suzuki that I had no idea there was such a thing as a Western mind. In Buddhism, there's only a universal mind.

A New Kick—2500 Years Old

Allen Ginsberg describes his earliest explorations into Zen Buddhism in a letter to Neal Cassady dated May 14, 1953:

I am on a new kick 2 weeks old, a very beautiful kick which I invite you to share . . . I am now spending all my free time in Columbia Fine Arts library and NY Public leafing through immense albums of asiatic imagery. I'm also reading a little about their mystique and religions . . . if you begin to get a clear idea of the various religions, the various dynasties and epochs of art and messianism and spiritual waves of hipness . . . you understand a lot of new mind and eyeball kicks. I have begun to familiarize myself with Zen Buddhism thru a book by one D.T. Suzuki . . . Zen is a special funny late form with no real canon or formal theology, except for a mass of several hundred anecdotes of conversations between masters and disciples. These conversations are all irrational and beguiling . . . [they] are given to the Zen novitiates, and made up as they go along sometimes, until the novitiate is completely beflabbered intellectually and stops thinking . . . then finally one day he gets the Big point and has what is known as SATORI, or illumination. This is a specific flash of vision which totally changes his ken . . .

They refuse to have a theology or admit that one exists, or anything verbal at all. That's the point of these anecdotes, to exhaust words. Then the man sees anew the universe.

A Weird Kind of Satori

Beat poet Philip Whalen, who later went on to become a Zen teacher, described during an interview with writer Aram Saroyan a "visionary experience" he'd had while on his way to spend the summer working as a fire lookout in Washington state:

It was a big guard station that was built on a raft on Ross Lake, way up by the Canadian border. And we used horses to pack people into the lookouts from that raft, and one night all the horses were on a raft that was tied up next to ours, and in the middle of the night one of the horses fell off, with a great splash, because they had all been jumping around—I don't know what got at them, the moon or something—and the horses were all dancing and singing, and one of them got excited and went overboard. And so I got up out of bed . . . we were all rushing around trying to find the horse that had fallen overboard. Well, I was the one that found her. She was a horse with one eye called Maybelle, and here she was in the water, so that people yelled at me, and I said, "I found it." And they said, "well, hold up her chin, and we'll get a rope on her." . . .I was kneeling over the edge of this raft in my underwear, and holding this horse under the chin, and the rope in the other hand, and the sense—you know, it was two o'clock in the morning, and it was a beautiful summer night, and the mountains were all around, and the lake, and this horse, and me—and I suddenly had a great, weird, kind of satori, a sort of feeling about the absolute connection between me, and the horse, and the mountain, and everything else . . .

The City Will Not Listen

Text from Jack Kerouac's original dust jacket copy for *The Dharma Bums*, early July 1958:

"The Dharma Bums" is a surprising story of two young Americans who make a goodhearted effort to know the Truth with full packs on their backs, rucksack wanderers of the West Coast hiking and climbing mountains to go and meditate and pray and cook their simple foods, and down below living in shacks and sleeping outdoors under the California stars.

Although deeply religious they are also spirited human beings making love to women, relishing poetry, wine, good food, joyful campfires, nature, travel and friendship. The hero is young Japhy Ryder, poet, mountaineer, logger, Oriental scholar and dedicated Zen Buddhist, who teaches his freight-hopping friend Ray Smith the Way of the Dharma Bums and leads him up the mountain where the common errors of this world are left far below and a new sense of pure material kinship is established with earth and sky. Yet it is the ancient way of all the wild prophets of the past, whether St. John the Baptist in the West or the holy old Zen Lunatic Han Shan in the East. Japhy and Ray adventure in the mountains and on the trails, and then they come swinging down to the city of San Francisco to teach what they have learned, but the city will not listen. "Yabyum" orgies, suicide, jazz, wild parties, hitch hiking, love affairs, fury and ignorance result but the Truth Bums always return to the solitude and peaceful lesson of the wilderness.

In this new novel, Jack Kerouac departs from the "hipster" movement of the Beat Generation and leads his readers towards a conception of "continual conscious compassion" and a peaceful understanding truce with the paradox of existence.

The Dharma itself can never be seen, but it is felt in this book. It is the strangest of tales, yet an honest, vigorous account depicting an exciting new Way of Life in the midst of modern despair . . .

Read slowly and see.

Perhaps the most influential artist to emerge from the 1950s Zen boom was avant-garde composer John Cage. Cage encountered Zen, in the form of D.T. Suzuki's lectures at Columbia University, at a time when he felt so confused about his personal life and the role of art in society that he was seriously considering giving up composition and entering psychoanalysis instead.

The encounter with Suzuki not only radically altered his world view; it overturned his approach to his art. "[Since my] study with D.T. Suzuki," said Cage, "I've thought of music as a means of changing the mind. Of course my proper concern first of all has been with changing my own mind. Through Buddhism . . . I saw art not as something that consisted of a communication from the artist to the audience, but rather as an activity of sounds in which the artist found a way to let the sounds be themselves. And in being themselves, to open the minds of the people who made them or listened to them to other possibilities than they had previously considered."

In the early 1950s, the composer delivered his famous Zen-influenced lecture on the subject of "Nothing" at the Artists' Club in New York. "Our poetry now," said Cage, "is the realization that we possess nothing. Anything therefore is a delight, since we do not possess it, and thus need not fear its loss."

For the rest of his life, Cage sought to create an ego-free, intentionless approach to musical composition. He is perhaps most famous for his explorations into what Alan Watts called "the melodies of silence"—the most infamous example being a composition called 4'33," in which the performer sits for four minutes and thirty-three seconds before the piano without ever laying fingers to the keys, and the only sounds heard by the audience are those that naturally occur in the room. "After a while," wrote Watts, "one hears [these] sounds emerging, without cause or origin, from the emptiness of silence, and so becomes witness to the beginning of the universe."

"In connection with my study of Zen . . ." says Cage, "I have used . . . chance operations in all my works . . . in order to free my ego from its likes and dislikes." He explains, "I attempt to let sounds be themselves in a space in time. There are those . . . who find this attempt on my part pointless. I do not object to being engaged in a purposeless activity."

The Sleep of Babes (23)

Alan Watts tells the story of an example he witnessed of John Cage's often cited choiceless awareness of sound, which occurred one evening when Cage slept on the philosopher's living room couch. There was a hamster cage in the room, equipped with a squeaky exercise wheel, and Watts offered to move it to another location if it was bothersome.

"Oh, not at all!" replied the composer, who apparently had been enjoying the performance already. "It's the most fascinating sound, and I shall use it as a lullaby."

Isshu Miura Roshi, a Rinzai Zen master who came to New York in the late 1950s at the invitation of the First Zen Institute of America, went on to quietly lead a small group of ten or so Zen students in his New York apartment for some years. He was once asked what the most important element of Zen was.

"Mind your own business," replied the roshi.

part two

THE NEW BODHIDHARMAS

I feel Americans, especially young Americans, have a great opportunity to find out the true way of life for human beings . . . You begin Zen practice with a very pure mind, a beginner's mind. You can understand Buddha's teaching exactly as he meant it.

—Shunryu Suzuki Roshi

JUST IN TIME

Starting in the late 1950s and into the Sixties and Seventies, like legions of Bodhidharmas, they began to arrive: Shunryu Suzuki, founder of the San Francisco Zen Center; Taizan Maezumi, of the Zen Center of Los Angeles; Ch'an (Chinese Zen) Masters Hsuan Hua of Gold Mountain Monastery in San Francisco and Sheng-yen of the Ch'an Meditation Center in Elmhurst, New York; Korean Master Seung Sahn; the Vietnamese monk Thich Nhat Hanh; and many more. For the first time Americans, on a large scale, had access to the actual practice of Zen, rather than just its philosophy. This era marked as well the return of the first wave of Westerners who had gone to study overseas: Philip Kapleau, Walter Nowick, Jiyu-Kennett, Gary Snyder, and others. Many of these went on to establish practice centers in the U.S., where they began the daunting work of interpreting a 2500 year old Asian tradition for the 20th-Century Western world. Thousands flocked to the new Zen centers—particularly members of the youth culture which had, in fulfillment of Kerouac's "Dharma Bums" prophecy, succeeded the Beats as the most visible representatives of America's counterculture. If the Fifties brought the "Zen boom," the Sixties and Seventies brought a full-scale Zen explosion.

Although many of the figures presented in Part One of this book are no longer with us, I was fortunate, in the course of my research, to speak with many of the individuals in this and subsequent sections, including Philip Kapleau and the elusive Walter Nowick, who like one of the legendary Zen masters of old, has always resisted being sought out by the curious. And although I was not able, partly because of his age and declining health, to formally interview Philip Whalen, one of the last original Beat poets and later a Zen teacher, there is nonetheless a bit of a story to my brief meeting with him.

It happened that I was visiting the San Francisco Zen Center and other Bay Area practice centers just in time to attend the memorial service commemorating the tenth anniversary of the death of Issan Dorsey, the pioneering Zen teacher who, together with a handful of students, founded the Hartford Street Zen Center's Maitri Hospice at a time when AIDS hysteria was at such a peak that hospital staff sometimes refused to touch patients for fear of infection. For most of the decade following Dorsey's death Philip Whalen had been Hartford Street's abbot. I'd been trying to contact him without success since I'd arrived in the Bay Area, and this seemed likely to be my final chance.

On the afternoon of the service, I drove over the Golden Gate Bridge into the city from the apartment where I was staying at in Mill Valley. I was running late, and barreled down Divisadero Street in my rented Geo Metro into the crowded Castro District to find, on that busy Saturday afternoon, not a single parking space left within a ten block radius of the Zen center—not even an illegal one. I cruised helplessly past the Hartford Street zendo, watching through the front window as visitors milled about inside; the three o'clock starting hour approached, then passed.

At last, I managed to squeeze my Geo into a spot that miraculously opened in front of a Chinese laundry—karma?—and sprinted up tiny, one-block-long Hartford Street to the Center. I found the front room empty, the door locked. I could hear drums and bells coming from somewhere—perhaps the basement zendo or back garden, inaccessible behind the row houses. After jiggling the knob a few times in the hope that it might change its mind, and eyeing the doorbell which, considering the ceremony had clearly already begun, I didn't feel bold enough to use, I gave up. I was halfway down the front walk when something made me turn back.

Mounting the steps again, I put my face to the glass of the door at exactly the right moment to glimpse a procession of dark-robed figures descending the stairs, carrying bells and drums and incense burners. The leader, a man wielding a ceremonial fly whisk who had—uncharacteristically, for a Zen priest—a beard and long brown hair spilling down past his shoulders, paused before the door long enough to open it for me.

"You're just in time," he announced—and, in a perfect moment of Zen spontaneity, plucked a vase of flowers from the mantelpiece and handed it to me. With that, I suddenly became a member of the procession, which wound its way through the front part of the house, into the kitchen and down the back stairs into the garden, filled with visitors who had come to honor the memory of Issan Dorsey.

The priest with the fly whisk, I would later discover, was Steve Allen, Issan Dorsey's only dharma heir. Remarkably, I would also find out that he and his wife Angelique were living in Northern New Mexico, no more than a half hour's drive from my home.

I won't go through all the details of what followed: the offering of incense, the prostrations and memorial poems, and my own stumbling foray to the altar to offer up the vase of flowers, which I'd clutched through the beginning of the ceremony, shifting my weight from one foot to the other while wondering what it was I was supposed to do. However, several of the anecdotes I heard about Dorsey that day, from the story-telling session that followed in the meditation hall, have made their way into later portions of this book.

At the reception that followed, I finally got the chance to talk to Philip Whalen, who I'd noticed earlier as an elderly priest with a shaved head. He was clearly having trouble with his vision, and was being assisted by an attendant.

"Mr. Whalen," I said, pulling up a chair alongside his, as his eyes turned in a rather heart-wrenching attempt to focus on me.

"I'm the writer who called you last week, wondering if I might interview you for the book I'm researching."

"Ah yes," said Whalen. "I haven't called you back." He sighed an old man's raspy sigh. "I've done so many interviews, you know," he said, reaching moodily for a stuffed mushroom h'ors d'oeuvres. "I find them terribly irritating."

chapter four

THE GREAT MIGRATION

This kind of group practice, such as at a Zen center, can be of real ben-
efit to a world such as ours. Perhaps it is not so irrelevant to a world in
which harmony is scarcer than diamonds, and in which the realization
of Truth is widely regarded as an impossible dream.

—Taizan Maezumi Roshi

Three features of the San Francisco Zen Center remain fixed in memory from my visit there. The first is a set of stained glass windows with two images on them: one, a pair of young, strong hands in perfect gassho—prayer position—white against the deep, purple-blue of stained glass. These are said to represent those of Dainin Katagiri, who as a young man served as assistant to the temple's founder, Shunryu Suzuki Roshi. Beside Katagiri's are another pair of hands, also in gassho, but with one finger bent over, crooked and broken, the result of a stone-working accident at the Zen Mountain Center in Tassajara. These hands remain forever slightly cupped, as though holding a small bird: Suzuki Roshi's broken-fingered gesture of appreciation to the universe, all the more perfect for its imperfection.

Then, in the dim hallway behind the zendo, there is the verse inscribed upon the *han*, the hanging wooden block that is struck with a mallet to call the residents to zazen. Sometimes known as the Evening Gatha, common to many schools of Zen, this is a verse with which I am well acquainted; but finding it here unexpectedly, in this shadowy, narrow hallway, sends the proverbial chills up my spine:

Life is fleeting,
Gone, gone—
Awake,
Awake each one!
Don't waste this life!

Finally, and most powerfully, there is the life-sized screen print of Suzuki Roshi, standing in silhouette on the landing of the center's main staircase with Zen stick upraised, as his students must often have seen him, stalking along behind the rows of sitters in the zendo. You mount the stairs and there at the landing his form looms suddenly, as through his ghost, which still dominates this place, has remained substantial enough to cast a shadow. As in fact it has, not only over the San Francisco Zen Center, but the entire face of Zen in America.

Shunryu Suzuki (who bears no relation to D.T. Suzuki, the scholar) came to the United States at the age of fifty-three, at the behest of the Zen Soto sect headquarters in Japan, to lead the congregation of Sokoji temple in San Francisco's Japantown. The year was 1959. Although the move was the fulfillment of a life-long dream, the new priest—not to mention his conservative, mostly middle-aged and elderly Japanese-American congregation—must have been taken somewhat aback when shortly after his arrival an increasing stream of bohemians, nonconformists, and other representatives of America's counterculture, having heard that a Zen master had arrived in town, began showing up for zazen instruction. Suzuki, like Soyen Shaku, had always felt it his mission to spread the Dharma to America, as far-fetched a notion as that must have seemed to the Soto Zen establishment at the time. He'd even studied English in his youth in preparation for the move. Now, without planning it, he'd landed at one of the key focal points of America's Beat movement and Zen Boom, as well as the soon-to-be-epicenter of the Hippie phenomenon.

A member of the First Zen Institute of America who was then living in San Francisco described the new wave of practitioners in a letter to the folks back home: "[There are] boys that look like beatniks with beards, sweat shirts, and some with sandals, but I must say they seem sincere."

As Eido Tai Shimano, Soen Roshi's dharma successor, has observed, 1960 was the point where the emphasis of Zen in America shifted from the intellectual to the practical. For not only San Francisco, but the U.S. as a whole, Shunryu Suzuki was a primary agent of this change.

"He was just very present," says Jakusho Bill Kwong, one of Suzuki Roshi's earliest students, now the resident teacher at Sonoma Mountain Zen Center. "And ordinary. That was his special quality. The projection [of his students and others] made him a superhuman being. But actually he was just present and just ordinary and no more and no less. And that's why I say that he was the first *person* I ever met."

"By the time I started to practice," says Sojun Mel Weitsman, Abbott of the Berkeley Zen Center, "I'd been looking around for a long time. And I said to myself, 'I have to do this. This sort of opportunity might not come by again. I have to take this all the way.'"

"When I began to practice," says Zenkei Blanche Hartman, Abbess of San Francisco Zen Center, "it was sort of like grabbing a life preserver in a stormy sea. Before I came to practice, what I'd thought I wanted was for everyone to love me. What I discovered was that I'd had it backwards—my *real* deep desire was to be able to love everyone. Which, when I met Suzuki Roshi, seemed to be a real possibility. Because he seemed to be able to do that."

Before her first private interview with Suzuki, Hartman says, she was instructed in how to perform the formal series of prostrations used to begin a meeting with a Zen teacher:

"But I was so full of gratitude I didn't want to stand way back and do some formal bow. I wanted to bow *to* him. So I went around the mat and bowed so that my head touched the floor right where his left knee was. He'd been sitting there when I bowed, but when I lifted my head, he'd jumped up and was head to head with me on the floor. I was amazed. He wasn't a young man, and he would've had to move very fast to do something like that!"

Absolute Freedom? (24)

In the early Sixties, an aspiring Zen student confronted Suzuki in his office at Sokoji, the Japantown temple in San Francisco where Suzuki was then head priest.

"If you believe in absolute freedom," demanded the student, indicating a cage in the corner of the room, "then why do you keep a bird in a cage?"

In response, Suzuki walked over to the cage, opened the door, and let the bird fly out.

The story was reported in the San Francisco Chronicle, and attracted many people to Suzuki's fledgling San Francisco Zen Center. There is, however, a lesser-known sequel to the tale. A short time after the newspaper article, a new student, Bill Kwong (now Kwong Roshi) visited the temple to inquire about Zen. Remembering the story about the bird, Kwong asked what had happened to it—was it still in the building or had it flown off?

As David Chadwick tells it in his biography of Suzuki, *Crooked Cucumber*:

Everyone looked down. Had [Kwong] said something wrong?

"The cat," Suzuki said softly.

"The cat?" Kwong repeated, looking at the feline comfortably curled on Della's lap.

McNeil leaned over to Kwong and said softly, "The cat ate the bird."

"[Roshi] felt so bad about it," added Della.

Suzuki said nothing. They drank their tea.

Not Two (25)

Someone once asked Suzuki Roshi: "What is Zen?"

Suzuki held up his hand with two fingers spread open. "Not two," he said. Then he brought them together. "One."

Every Day Is Important (26)

Elsie Mitchell of the Cambridge Buddhist Association reports an early visit from Suzuki Roshi, in 1964. He'd written that he would be arriving on Wednesday night, and they planned to have someone meet him at the airport.

On Tuesday afternoon, a number of the members set to work housecleaning. That evening the meditation room was in the process of being scrubbed down when the doorbell rang. There on the front step, a day early, was Suzuki Roshi, wearing a big smile on his face, and highly amused to find everyone in the midst of preparations for his arrival.

Ignoring their protests, he tied back the sleeves of his robes and insisted on joining in "all these preparations for the important day of my coming!"

The next morning, says Mitchell, after she'd left the building to run some errands, "He found himself a tall ladder, sponges, and pails. He then set to work scrubbing Cambridge grease, grime, and general pollution from the outside of the windows in the meditation hall. When I returned with the groceries, I discovered him on the ladder, polishing with such undivided attention that he did not even hear my approach. He had removed his black silk kimono and was dressed only in his Japanese union suit. This is quite acceptable attire in Japan. Nevertheless, I could not help wondering how the sedate Cambridge ladies in the adjoining apartment house would react to the sight of a shaven-headed man in long underwear at work right outside their windows!"

Follow the Yes (27)

When Katharine Thanas, who is now resident Zen teacher for the Santa Cruz Zen Center, was struggling with whether to make a deeper commitment to Zen practice, she came before Suzuki Roshi during *shosan* (a formal public encounter with the teacher), and without preamble, simply said, "Inside me there is a yes and a no."

"Follow the yes," Suzuki told her.

Before you attain enlightenment, enlightenment is there. It is not because one attains enlightenment that enlightenment appears. Enlightenment is always there and if you realize this, that is enlightenment. If you think, however, that enlightenment is some particular thing you can reach, which you can attain sometime, you will be discouraged because you are seeking for it.

But if you feel that it is not possible to attain enlightenment, you will also be discouraged . . . Whether or *not* you realize your true nature, or attain enlightenment, is a minor problem and not the big one. It is all the better if you do, but even if you don't there is no need to seek for some other special teaching, because the teaching is always right here.

The most visible Soto Zen teacher in the U.S., as founder of the San Francisco Zen Center and the Zen Mountain Center at Tassajara—the first Buddhist monastery established in the Western hemisphere in the 2,500 year history of the religion—Suzuki Roshi was also America's most active proponent of *shikantaza*, or "just sitting" practice. This form of Zen meditation discourages self-conscious seeking after enlightenment, in the trust that zazen itself is the perfect expression of one's true nature. "To take this posture is itself to have the right state of mind," said Suzuki Roshi in *Zen Mind, Beginner's Mind*, which was first published in 1969, and remains a seminal text of Zen Buddhism in America to this day. "If enlightenment comes, it just comes."

What's here right now? Delusion is yesterday's dream—
enlightenment, tomorrow's delusion.

—Taizan Maezumi Roshi

My first encounter with Hakuyu Taizan Maezumi, founder of the Zen Center of Los Angeles, came when I returned to my then-home in Santa Barbara in the mid-1980s, following a long absence. Having just gone through a period of crisis and spiritual confusion, I'd determined to find a Zen teacher as soon as possible after my arrival. As I stepped off the plane the friend who picked me up handed me a copy of Peter Matthiessen's *Nine-Headed Dragon River* saying, "Here, you've got to read this!" The book is Matthiessen's account of his many years of Zen practice, in which Maezumi Roshi features prominently. I'd often run across the phrase, "when the student is ready the teacher appears"—a common enough saying in Zen literature. But I'd never expected to have his name and precise location handed to me when my search had scarcely begun. Within a couple of weeks, I found myself headed toward the Zen Center of Los Angeles, ninety miles to the south, to participate in an Introduction to Zen seminar.

The morning section of the workshop was, to say the least, unimpressive. Not only was the center located in a particularly crowded and seedy section of Los Angeles, with drug deals happening openly on the corners, but the session was led by a single uninspired monk who would clearly have rather spent the day doing something else. And what could be the purpose, I wondered, of all these black robes, shaven-headed monks, and Buddha statues—ritual elements I had conveniently overlooked in my extensive readings on Zen practice? I knew that it was not fair to judge the center until I'd met the teacher, but as the day wore on, marked by a series of increasingly dull expositions on the Buddha's teachings, which made realizing one's true nature sound as appealing as drinking a tub of dishwater, I was feeling more and more inclined to find another place to pursue my spiritual investigations.

After lunch, we were led on a tour of the grounds, which were admittedly lovely, replete with flower gardens and twisted, Zennish trees that looked as though they'd been transplanted from an old scroll painting. The tour ended in the library. I was standing in the corner of the room furthest from the door, look-ing at a volume of Master Dogen's writings, when the door swung open and in walked a mild-looking, middle-aged Japanese gen-tleman with a shaved head.

"Hello, everybody," he said in a soft-spoken, accented but articulate English. "I am so pleased you could all come to visit Zen Center. I am sorry that because of many obligations I have not been able to spend more time with you, but I wanted to take this opportunity to welcome you personally."

Somewhere during the course of the greeting, I realized that this must be Maezumi Roshi—though I couldn't reconcile this polite, smiling figure with the commanding presence I'd imag-ined from Matthiessen's account. The roshi ended his speech by inviting us all to come back for one of the center's weekend pro-grams, in which we would be entitled, as part of our introductory seminar, to attend a *dokusan* [private interview] with him.

That would have been the end of the encounter, and very likely the end of my involvement with the Zen Center—except that in moving to exit the roshi paused, for no apparent reason, and turn-ing his head with a calm deliberateness, shot me the clearest, purest glance from across the room I'd ever received. The event might not have seemed so unusual, if not for the fact that of the fifteen or so people scattered about I was the furthest away, and during the course of his brief address he hadn't so much as cast an eye in my direction. I don't know how long he held the look—perhaps it was only a second or two. Then, with the same calm deliberation, he turned, stepped across the threshold, and was gone. But the elec-tricity of that glance coursed through my body for hours.

It was one of the few truly uncanny acts I ever saw Maezumi Roshi—or any Zen teacher—perform.

Better Not to Ask (28)

A student asked three different teachers, early in his practice, about re-incarnation.

"Better to say 'could be' than to say 'no,'" replied Eido Shimano Roshi.

"It's a nice story," answered Sochu Roshi.

"Better not to ask," was the answer given by Maezumi Roshi.

On another occasion a Los Angeles Zen Center donor asked Maezumi Roshi during a lunch meeting: "All that reincarnation stuff—it's just symbolic, isn't it?"

Maezumi slammed his fist on the table so hard the glasses leapt in the air. "It is a fact!" he exclaimed.

What Is It Like? (29)

Maezumi Roshi was sitting on the front porch of the Zen Center of Los Angeles one evening with one of his students when a disheveled, extremely inebriated man staggered up to them.

"Whaarsh it like," the man slurred, ". . . to be enlightened?"

Maezumi looked at the man quietly.

"Very depressing," he answered.

Never Mind That (30)

A professional dancer, who'd been forced to abandon her career after being pushed in front of a subway train and injuring one of her feet, attended a retreat with Maezumi Roshi. Self-conscious about the appearance of her injured foot, she always kept it covered with a sock.

In her first interview, she asked Maezumi a question about Zen practice, but he answered, "Never mind that. Tell me about your foot." She told him the story, and when her tears began to come she looked up to find that the roshi was crying too.

This went on for most of the week. Every day she'd come in and ask Maezumi about her practice, he'd ask about her foot instead, and they'd cry together. Finally the day came when she walked into the interview room and began to tell him about her injury, but it summoned no tears from her.

"Never mind about that," Maezumi interrupted. "Let's talk about your practice."

We're Responsible (31)

Gerry Shishin Wick, who is now resident Zen teacher for the Great Mountain Zen Center in Lafayette, Colorado, was assisting Maezumi Roshi during a meditation retreat in Mexico City. The sesshin was held in a neighborhood home that had just been built and was not yet inhabited. During the retreat the next door neighbor's dog ran out into the street and was killed by a car.

Maezumi insisted on holding a funeral, saying, "We're responsible for that dog."

Wick responded, "What do you mean Roshi? How could we be responsible?"

Maezumi said, "There was an empty house here, and now there are all these people, ringing bells and walking around. Maybe the dog sensed that, became disturbed, and ran out into the street. We have to have a funeral for that dog."

Everyone at the retreat, as well as the neighbors, who'd never before been exposed to any Eastern practices, went on to participate in a proper Buddhist funeral, with chanting and offering of incense.

A Matter of Life and Death (32)

When John Daido Loori was a monk at the Los Angeles Zen Center, he remarked one day to Maezumi Roshi: "I have resolved the question of life and death."

"Are you sure?" replied Maezumi.

"Yes," replied Loori.

"Are you really sure?"

"Absolutely," Loori answered.

With that, Maezumi threw himself violently upon Loori and began to strangle him.

Gasping for breath, Loori struggled to escape, tried to push him off, but to no avail.

Finally he swung back his fist and struck his teacher, knocking him aside.

Maezumi rose to his feet and brushed himself off. "Resolved the question of life and death, eh?" he laughed, and walked off.

Later Loori, still bearing the marks of his teacher's fingers on his throat, passed a senior monk, Genpo Sensei.

On seeing the bruises, Genpo did a double take. "Told Roshi you'd resolved the question of life and death, did you?" he said, and strode away laughing.

Our practice rests on a physical base, just as our lives begin physically. First we learn to bring our bodies into harmony—we learn to sit physically. Once that happens, our breathing naturally settles into a harmonious cycle—we start to breathe easily, smoothly, and naturally. And as body and breath settle down . . . we find that the mind itself is given the opportunity to settle into its own smooth and natural functioning. The racket and babble of our noisy minds gives way to the clarity and naturalness of our true selves. In this way we come to know who we really are and what our life and death really is. Once we begin to establish this direct physical harmony between body, breath, and mental activity, we have a chance to extend such benefits to one another. We can learn to live together in the best way, leading to the realization of everyone's true nature, not only on an individual but also a group level as well.

Taizan Maezumi's first encounter with Americans occurred while he was still an adolescent, just after World War II, when the grounds of his family temple were made into an anti-aircraft battery. The American soldiers, he later said, taught him "to drink beer, smoke cigarettes, and cuss!"

Ordained as a monk at age eleven, Maezumi came from a family of Zen priests. Like Suzuki Roshi, he had always wanted to come to America; in 1956, with assistance from a Japanese loan shark, he procured the means to do so. He worked first as a priest for Zenshuji Temple in Los Angeles, the American headquarters of the Soto sect. Like Sokoji in San Francisco, the temple catered mainly to the area's large population of Japanese-Americans, focusing largely upon ceremonies and public events, and placing little emphasis upon zazen. Maezumi also worked as a translator for Mitsubishi Bank, and for a time, even wrote fortunes for a Chinese cookie company.

Like many of the more compelling Zen teachers throughout the history of the tradition, Maezumi always felt drawn to a broader approach to Zen than that offered by any single sect. Although he first received the Dharma transmission in 1955 from his father, Kuroda Roshi, in the Soto school, by the age of sixteen he'd also commenced koan study with Koryu Osaka, a lay Rinzai Master; and in the early 1960s, during one of Yasutani Roshi's trips to America, Maezumi began koan study with him, too. Maezumi eventually received *inka*, or full sanction of awakening and authority to teach Zen, from both teachers, becoming one of the few Zen masters to hold the dharma transmission in three lineages. By 1967, the small zazen group he'd begun at Zenshuji had rented their own quarters and moved out to establish what would later become the Zen Center of Los Angeles, with some 200 resident trainees at its peak in the 1970s. Maezumi Roshi, who died in 1995, is notable for his unique synthesis of the Rinzai and Soto training approaches—and his White Plum lineage of American teachers has gone on to become one of the largest and most influential in the West.

Perhaps the best demonstration of Maezumi's hard-yet-soft synthesis of the Rinzai and Soto schools is illustrated by the following series of interactions that took place during my first five day *sesshin*, or intensive practice retreat with him:

On the first day, distracted by thoughts and feelings for a woman I'd been dating, I went in for my private interview with the roshi despondent about my inability to keep my mind on my practice. I was expecting to be scolded for my poor efforts, but Maezumi responded: "You're in love! That's wonderful! Don't worry so much about your practice. Just relax and enjoy your sitting."

On the second day, troubled by serious pain in my back and knees, I was considering dropping out of the retreat entirely. I went to dokusan, expecting to be admonished to sit through the discomfort. Instead Maezumi said: "Don't try so hard! Practice is not asceticism. Take the next period off and rest yourself. Now, I'll give you a back massage." With that he directed me to turn around, and proceeded to rub my back and shoulders.

By the third day I was struggling with constant sleepiness, since a painting crew had mixed up the screens on the buildings, and mosquitoes from the center's koi pond swarmed nightly into the dormitories past the ill-fitting frames, keeping everyone awake. But when I tried to tell the roshi about these difficulties, he cut me off, saying: "Stop feeling sorry for yourself! Make some effort. You're not trying hard enough!"

To get this chance (to practice the Dharma) is very difficult. To be born as a human being is very difficult. Among uncountable sperms and eggs . . . you are here. Wonderful chance. Congratulations.
—Soen Nakagawa Roshi

From the 1960s through the early Eighties Soen Nakagawa, who had been influential in Japan in the training of such early American Zen students as Philip Kapleau and Robert Aitken, began to come regularly to the States to lead sesshins, or sitting retreats, when his responsibilities as Abbott of Ryutakuji Monastery in Japan would allow it. Soen Roshi, as his American students called him, was famed for his unconventional teaching methods, which were eccentric even by Zen standards. One often-reported trick was the time he placed a pumpkin on his sitting cushion in the interview room during sesshin. He then called participants in for private interviews and hid behind a screen, watching while the baffled students did their customary prostrations before the impassive gourd. Or he might don a mask and appear out of nowhere, then drop it to pronounce: "I've taken off my mask. When will you take off yours?"

Soen loved to walk around New York City. He'd stare at the lighted skyscrapers; at their tops, he claimed, he saw Buddha figures in the lights. "Look at the Buddha," he'd point, "Shining Buddha!" He'd fill the sleeves of his robes with nuts and berries from Central Park, or herbs growing in the sidewalk cracks, and add them to his bowl at the next meal. He loved the musical "Fiddler on the Roof," and when asked a question about why some particular point of ceremony needed to be performed in a certain way, he might burst into song, responding: "Tradition!"

Soen even made up a new koan in response to the Apollo missions: "Without getting in a spaceship, bring me a rock from the moon." It is not known if any of his students ever managed to pass it.

Despite being the abbot of a major temple, Soen Roshi had an uneasy relationship with traditional forms, and had earned a reputation as an eccentric even in Japan. Known for his love of green tea, powdered and whisked in the traditional fashion, he might sit down anywhere, if the mood stuck him, to conduct an impromptu tea ceremony. He claimed that once, on a visit to Israel, he'd floated, unsinkable, on the salt-saturated surface of the Dead Sea, serving tea to a group of friends. In an airport one of his students asked if Roshi might conduct a tea ceremony; in answer he extracted a tin from his sleeve, dipped his finger into it, and instructed the student to open her mouth.

"There," he announced, dabbing a fingertip of powdered green tea onto her tongue. "Now you make the water!"

Once, at Dai Bosatsu Monastery in upstate New York, Soen asked a student who had just returned from studying tea in Japan to perform a ceremony for him, but she protested that she did not have her supplies. The roshi must have persisted in his request, for a short while later the two were seen sitting on the dock at the edge of Beecher Lake, pouring non-existent tea into non-existent bowls and sipping at them, in a perfect pantomime of the formal ceremony.

Soen once invited the teachers from the New York branch of a prominent tea school to join him for tea at his New York Zendo—a great honor, considering that he was abbot of an important Japanese temple. Soen proceeded to conduct a traditional ceremony, flawless in every detail but one: with characteristic wry humor, what he whisked into their bowls was not green tea, but instant coffee.

Does a Dog Have Buddha Nature? (33)

American writer Wendy Johnson, a long-time resident at Green Gulch Farm Zen Center in California, remembers a retreat she attended with Soen Roshi at a Trappist monastery on the outskirts of Jerusalem in the early Seventies. The group included a rabbi, an Israeli draft resister, and a number of Americans, as well as a number of participants from orthodox Jewish and Christian backgrounds. One evening, Soen found the chanting service to be rather spiritless, so he ordered all present to meet him outside after the final sitting period. He proceeded to take them on a long walk through the darkened hills.

The monastery was just outside Jerusalem, surrounded by Arab villages, and at the time, shortly after the Six Day War, it wasn't generally considered advisable to wander about the countryside. Still, Soen led the group off into the darkness, loudly chanting the Kannon Sutra. At one point they rounded a bend to find the entire valley spread out below them. Calling the group to a halt, Soen Roshi demanded, "What is the true nature of mind?" He answered himself: "MU is the true nature of mind!" [literally meaning "no," "nothing," or "emptiness," but referring to the koan in which a monk asks Joshu, "Does a dog have Buddha nature?" and Joshu replies: "Mu!"].

Soen admonished the group to chant Mu until their small selves fell away. They chanted with such ferocity that the tears ran down their faces. Soen's booming baritone voice, strikingly deep for his tiny frame, rang out as loudly as the rest. And as they stood there, shouting Mu at the top of their lungs in the dead of night, the dogs of the surrounding villages began to join in, yapping and baying in a wild cacophony of affirmation—as though they, at least, knew the answer.

Nobody Home (34)

Soen Roshi used to tell the story of how in London, as he was about to enter a bathroom, someone informed him it was in use. As Zen teacher and author Peter Matthiessen tells it, in *Nine-Headed Dragon River:*

The roshi waited there politely for a long time before he became concerned, after which he knocked, then opened the door.

"Nobody there!" He laughed delightedly. "Wait as long as you like! Never anybody there! From the beginning!"

Shaking Hands with Essence (35)

On a visit to Israel, Soen Nakagawa Roshi called upon Jewish philosopher Martin Buber.

During the conversation Soen Roshi's American traveling companion remarked, "There are many religions: Christianity, Buddhism, Judaism—but the essence is the same."

"Where *is* essence?" responded Buber.

"Let us shake hands with essence," replied Soen Roshi, extending his hand. "Okay?"

At this Buber laughed heartily.

Wonderful Costumes (36)

One Sunday morning, Soen Nakagawa, together with shakuhachi flute master Watazumi Doso and Doso's wife, was invited to visit the New York City home of painters Harvey Konigsberg and his wife, Patricia. The visit came at a time when Harvey and Patricia were going through a particularly difficult period in their lives. On entering their loft in Little Italy, Soen paused before a painting Harvey had done of Bill Walling, one of the founders of the Bioenergetics Institute, who'd been an important teacher to him. "There's something incomplete about this," Soen Roshi said.

As it turned out, Walling had recently died. The Konigsbergs had felt dissatisfied with the memorial service, and lacked a sense of closure. On hearing the story, Soen Roshi improvised a memorial service on the spot, an event the couple found extremely moving.

Afterward, to shift the mood, Soen Roshi began randomly opening closets; inside he found a variety of martial arts attire and other articles of clothing. "Ah!" exclaimed Soen. "Wonderful! Costumes!" He began pulling out items and handing them to the other guests, and within a short time had created an impromptu costume party. Then, to the amazement of his hosts, he proceeded to rearrange their living room furniture.

Later there was a performance by Doso's wife, a dance master, to an accompaniment of pounded pots and pans, arranged by Soen. Then Watazumi Doso announced that, since the Konigsbergs seemed to have a lot of pets about, he was going to perform a special "Song for Beasts." No sooner had he begun to play—on a pennywhistle, as he did not have his shakuhachi with him—than their three cats and dog began to filter into the room. Ignoring the assembled human beings, they padded about Watazumi Doso as he played. After the piece was finished, reports Konigsberg, "he began a different song for human beings, and the animals all left." Although Soen Roshi had planned to spend only an hour or so, he ended up staying the entire day.

"The whole experience," remembers Konigsberg, "was like a bombardment of light."

And the furniture? "The change lifted the feeling of the place entirely," Konigsberg says. "We never put it back."

DHARMA WORDS FROM SOEN ROSHI

Most people think that we live in the actual world while we are alive, and that after we take the last breath we somehow wander into a vague realm of the spirit. It is a great mistake to see two separate realms. Instead, where we live is in fact the spiritual realm, a realm of many billion worlds, which goes beyond three, four, or even infinite dimensions. Then the danger is that we might think that this is a realm that is empty and boundless. Watch out! It's all manifested right here at this moment. It is alive and kicking!

There is a wonderful Buddha statue at the Metropolitan Museum. There are national-treasure bodhisattvas and many statues. They are wonderful, of course . . . But, you are living bodhisattvas, each of you, living! Not bronze or wood. Sometime, something bad may happen. "Oh, I will pray to Buddha." No, no, no! There is no such Buddha. Realize this and every human being becomes wonderful . . . Open your own eyes! . . . Don't think, "Oh, I am not yet enlightened. Some day I'll get enlightenment." From today, forget such! From the beginning, we are the Enlightened One. Believe this with definite faith . . . So with this mind, please, let us bow to each other . . .

Without exception, each of you is a living Buddha . . . Without exception, okay?

In the late 1960s, Soen Roshi sustained a head injury, which some say was caused by falling out of a tree in which he'd been meditating—an event often pointed to as the cause of his increasingly eccentric behavior. It is said that he suffered from pain at various times in his life, but this worsened in his later years to the point where, in the late 1970s, he shut himself away in his quarters at his Japanese monastery, grew his hair and beard long, and refused to see anyone.

Soen Roshi came out of his self-imposed retirement in 1982 to pay a last visit to his American students. As Peter Matthiessen reports it, he left them with these words: "Cooking, eating, sleeping, every deed of everyday life is nothing else than this Great Matter. Realize this! So we extend tender care with a worshipping heart even to such beings as beasts and birds—but not only to beasts, not only to birds, but to insects too, okay? Even to grass, to one blade of grass, even to dust, to one speck of dust. Sometimes I bow to the dust . . ."

Soen Roshi died at Ryutaku-ji Monastery in Japan in 1984; half of his bones are buried there, and half in America.

Meditation is not an escape from life . . .
but preparation for really being in life.
—Thich Nhat Hanh

I first saw Thich Nhat Hanh speak at the closing event for a retreat in Southern California in the 1980s. All I had heard beforehand was that a Vietnamese Zen monk, who had been politically active in helping victims on both sides of the war in Vietnam and had been exiled by his government for these activities, was now leading reconciliation retreats between Vietnamese monastics and American veterans, and that I shouldn't miss the chance of attending the final evening. I later found out Thich Nhat Hanh been nominated by Martin Luther King for the Nobel Peace Prize, for the same activities that had led to his exile. I wasn't prepared however, for how moving the evening would prove to be—beginning with the spectacle of a number of enormous American ex-GIs, some of them in combat fatigues, sharing the stage with a group of diminutive brown-robed monks and nuns.

Thich Nhat Hanh spoke first, and then the veterans and monastics came up one by one to tell their stories—how they'd suffered during and after the war, the nightmares and paranoia, the regret and fear many had faced in coming here, and the healing they'd experienced during a week of practicing sitting and walking meditation and sharing their experiences of the war with one another. The evening ended with an exchange of embraces between the participants, many of whom were in tears at reconciling with their former enemies.

In a conversation from Jerry Brown's book, *Dialogues*, Thich Nhat Hanh said:

During the war in Vietnam, we suffered so much, but as a monk I continued to practice in order not to lose track of reality. In the situation of war one might be carried away by despair or anger. But if you are caught by despair or anger, you lose the insight you need to bring people out of danger. I was living very deeply each moment of my life, and the life of my people, and was [able to see] that the war created suffering not only for the Vietnamese people, but also for the American people. I was able to see that the young Americans who went there in order to kill were also victims of the war, victims of a notion, a policy. And I had compassion to offer to them, because I was able to see them as victims.

Not Taking Sides (37)

Thich Nhat Hanh, when asked whether he supported North or South Vietnam in the ongoing conflict, responded:

"I'm for the center."

Don't Just Do Something . . . (38)

Thich Nhat Hanh, a pioneer in the field of Buddhism and social action, has nonetheless been quoted as saying: "Don't just *do* something. Sit there!"

The True Secret of Mindfulness (39)

An American student asked Thich Nhat Hanh how she could be more mindful in her daily work.

"Do you want to know my secret?" replied Thich Nhat Hanh, with a smile. "I try to find the way to do things that is most pleasurable. There may be many ways to perform a given task—but the one that holds my attention best is the one that is most pleasant."

Touching the Present Moment (40)

Thich Nhat Hanh was leading a reconciliation retreat between Vietnamese monks and nuns and American veterans of the Vietnam War. One of the American vets confessed during the retreat that he had killed five Vietnamese children in an ambush, and since then could not bear to be alone in a room with children.

Thich Nhat Hanh responded: "At this very moment there are many children who are dying in the world. There are children who die just because they lack a single pill of medicine. If you are mindful, you can bring that pill to that child, and you can save his life. If you practice like that for five times, then you will save five children. Because what is to be done, is to be done in the present moment. Forty thousand children die every day because of lack of food. Why do you have to cling to the past to think of the five who are already dead? You have the power to change things by touching the present moment."

DHARMA WORDS FROM THICH NHAT HANH

In 1976, I went to the Gulf of Siam to help the boat people who were adrift at sea. We hired three ships to rescue them and take them to a safe port. Seven hundred people were on our ships adrift at sea when the Singapore authorities ordered me to leave the country and abandon all of them. It was two o'clock in the morning and I had to leave within twenty-four hours.

I knew that if I could not find peace in that difficult moment, I would never find peace. So I practiced walking meditation all night long in my small room. At six o'clock, as the sun rose, a solution came to me. If you panic, you will not know what to do. But practicing breathing, smiling, and walking, a solution may present itself.

If I had supernatural powers, I would take you to the Pure Land of Amitabha Buddha, where everything is beautiful. But if you bring your worries and anxieties there, you will defile it. To be ready to enter the Pure Land, you have to learn to make peaceful, anxiety-free steps. In fact, if you can learn to take peaceful, anxiety-free steps on the Earth, you won't need to go to the Pure Land. When you are peaceful and free, the Earth itself becomes a Pure Land, and there is no need to go anywhere else.

Despite Thich Nhat Hanh's world-wide teaching activities and his more than thirty books in some twenty languages, making him the most visible exponent of Engaged Buddhism in the West, this humble, soft-spoken monk has continued to live quietly and simply at his retreat center, Plum Village, in rural France. He teaches by example, stressing the Buddhist basics of mindfulness, following the breath, and walking meditation. "Just the way he opens a door and enters a room demonstrates his understanding," remarked Trappist monk Thomas Merton. "He is a true monk." Nhat Hanh's Tiep Hien Order of Interbeing, with its precepts of simplicity, pacifism, and non-accumulation of wealth, has sparked a broad-based popular movement in Buddhism that has proved enormously influential in the United States and Europe.

Through his teaching of "inter-being," Thich Nhat Hanh constantly reminds his students of the interrelatedness (and therefore lack of independent "self") of all things. In another talk I attended, he held up a sheet of paper and invited the audience to consider the many elements that had brought it into being. The page was not simply composed of wood pulp, Thich Nhat Hanh explained, but of the sun, water, and nutrients that nourished the tree, as well as the people that harvested and processed it, and many other elements in an endless chain of causation. The same goes for human beings. Thus Thich Nhat Hanh tells his students: "We may like to use the word 'self,' but if we are aware that self is always made of non-self elements, we are safe . . . It is like a flower—it is made of non-flower elements; like America—it is made of non-American elements. The moment we see ourselves in this deeper way, we begin to realize that we 'inter-are' with other people, and the feeling of distinction, the feeling of discrimination in us, vanishes. Then we begin to have peace."

"When you are guided by compassion and loving-kindness," says Thich Nhat Hanh, "you are able to look deeply into the heart of reality and to see the truth . . . Serenity helps. We have to learn that. Calm helps. To be serene, to be calm, does not mean to be inactive. You can be very active and calm at the same time."

Wendy Johnson reports on a Peace Walk with Thich Nhat Hanh, from her *Gardening at the Dragon's Gate: At Work in the Wild and Cultivated World*

It was early summer 1982 in New York City. Peter and I . . . planned to join the International Peace March that would be the culmination of an ecumenical conference called Reverence For Life. The march would pass through the streets of New York to the United Nations. Thich Nhat Hahn was a primary member of the conference . . .

On the streets of New York City that June day, close to one million people had assembled. There was an electric spirit of revival meeting, an Independence Day parade, coursing through the crowd. A surge of humanity roared for peace all along the emptied avenues of Manhattan. Thich Nhat Hanh stood quietly in the street with a throng of delegates and participants . . . he was still and slightly somber, somewhat grave and watchful . . . a contingent from Zen Center was with him in the street. Silently the group joined hands and began to walk with excruciatingly slow steps. Thich Nhat Hanh led the march and set the pace. He knew what he was doing. "To really make peace, first slow down," he said to us. "Be aware of your every step. You moved through my country with great haste. We could not slow you down. Today, please walk in mindfulness. Life itself depends on awareness of your pace and steps."

Behind us the crowd was stacked up for blocks. People called out in irritation and impatience. Thich Nhat Hanh moved with regal sovereignty. Unfazed, measured in pace, he walked with them. Baker Roshi described this slight, brown-robed Zen monk as "a cross between a tractor and a cloud." The impatient crowd thronged around him, gesturing and blowing red-faced on shrill whistles. Undistracted, adamantine, the Zen group inched on, pressing peace with every step into the heat-softened pavement of New York.

Moment to moment, how do you help others? Not only human beings, but this whole world. When enlightenment and correct life come together, that means your life becomes truth, the sufferng world becomes paradise. Then you can change this suffering world into paradise for others.
—Seung Sahn

When Seung Sahn, the first Korean Zen master to teach in the West, came to America in 1972, as Stephen Mitchell puts it in his preface to Seung Sahn's *The Whole World Is a Single Flower*, "his young hippie students, with their acid trips and casual nudity, must have seemed to him like creatures from another planet: fascinating, barbaric, full of potential."

After obtaining employment in a laundromat in Providence, Rhode Island (the owners likely having little idea of their employee's true range of talents), Seung Sahn was soon sought out by students from Brown University. Soen-sa-nim, as he is known to his students, shortly afterward established the Providence Zen Center, which would eventually become the head temple for his Kwan Um School of Zen, with some three dozen centers worldwide. "I just loved Soen-sa-nim's humor and his wild attitude," says Joan Halifax, now a Zen teacher in the Buddhist Peacemaker Order. "He didn't take everything so heavily and seriously . . . he had an outrageous attitude towards life. Everything struck him as wildly funny, and I appreciated that." Known for his dramatic teaching style, incisive insight, and unbounded sense of humor, Seung Sahn has become one of the most influential teachers in the West, and his uniquely phrased directives for practice have entered the general American Zen vocabulary: "Try mind"; "Don't make anything"; "Only don't know."

By the time he arrived in the U.S., Soen-sa-nim had already established a reputation in his home country. Ordained a monk at the age of twenty-one, following a period of World War II resistance activities, and a thorough study of philosophies West and

East, he entered into a solitary one hundred day retreat. During this period he ate only powdered pine needles, which eventually caused his skin to turn green. For twenty hours a day, he chanted the Great Dharani of Original Mind Energy, while beset by a variety of fears, doubts, and visions both beautiful and terrifying. On the hundredth day, while chanting and hitting a *moktak* (percussion instrument), he suddenly felt his body vanish and sensed himself to be in infinite space. When he returned he understood everything to be his true self.

After some months of further practice, including a one hundred day retreat at Su Dok Sa Monastery, Seung Sahn went to visit Chun Song, a master known for his unconventional and idiosyncratic actions. As Stephen Mitchell reports it:

"Soen-sa bowed to him and said, 'I killed all the Buddhas of past, present, and future. What can you do?'

"Chun Song said, 'Aha!' and looked deeply into Soen-sa's eyes. Then he said, 'What did you see?'

"Soen-sa replied, 'You already understand.'

"Chun Song said, 'Is that all?'

"Soen-sa said, 'There's a cuckoo singing in the tree outside the window.'

"Chun Song laughed and said, 'Aha!' He asked several more questions, which Soen-sa answered without difficulty. Finally Chun Song leaped up and danced around Soen-sa, shouting, 'You are enlightened! You are enlightened!'"

Seung Sahn subsequently had interviews with three more masters, each of whom gave him Inka, or authentication of his awakening. In January 1949, at age twenty-two, he received the dharma transmission from Master Ko Bong, the most prominent Zen master of his time. This was the only transmission Ko Bong ever gave.

Zen Master Seung Sahn instructs his students: "Only go straight, don't know: try, try, try for ten thousand years, nonstop. Then you attain the Way, the Truth, and the Life."

Already a Corpse (41)

A student of Korean Master Seung Sahn was attending her first retreat at his newly acquired center in Providence. The building was a former funeral home on a busy corner; its pink floral-patterned carpeting was still in place. On the third day the student awoke and looked in the mirror to see herself as a corpse, with blackened face and teeth falling out. Deeply affected by the vision, she hurried to tell Seung Sahn about it in her morning interview.

On hearing the story the teacher burst out laughing and tapped her on the shoulder with his Zen stick. "Don't worry," he laughed. "You're a corpse already!"

No More Reading (42)

After seeing Seung Sahn speak for the first time, Hawaiian American Su Bong Soen Sa asked if he could have a private meeting with the teacher, to which Seung Sahn agreed. Su Bong Soen Sa showed up with a big volume of Zen sayings, which he had been studying, and hoped the master might clarify for him. Seung Sahn made him wait for a long while before he would see him. Finally Seung Sahn invited him in for the interview. Su Bong Soen Sa, heart pounding at being before a master for the first time, turned the book toward Seung Sahn and pointed with his fingertip, saying, "There's a line in this book by the Sixth Patriarch that I wonder if you would explain for me . . ."

In a flash, Seung Sahn leapt at the book and slammed it shut on his finger, shouting, "No more reading! Who are *you*?"

Subong Soen-sa couldn't answer. He decided at that moment to become Seung Sahn's student, and eventually went on to become one of his dharma heirs.

An Old, Old, Thing (43)

When Zen teacher Bobby Rhodes was just beginning her practice with Master Seung Sahn during the hippie era, she had a reputation for being fond of things that were old: clothing, jewelry, and other such items.

One day her teacher came to her and said: "I have a present for you. It's something that's really, really old."

Seung Sahn dropped the gift into her outstretched palm. It was a stone.

But Why? (44)

Once Su Bong Soen Sa did a hundred-day solitary retreat in California. Perhaps two thirds of the way into it he began to feel rather bored and uncertain about why he should continue such an intensive schedule all by himself. He left the cabin where he was practicing and hitchhiked to the nearest phone booth to call Master Seung Sahn.

"I've got a question for you," he said when his teacher answered.

"Yes?" came back the suspicious voice of Seung Sahn, who knew he was supposed to be in silent retreat.

"I see clearly now that I can accomplish this retreat. But still I'm wondering—why? If I already know I can do it—why continue?"

"For All Beings!" Seung Sahn shouted, and slammed down the receiver.

Su Bong Soen Sa went back to his cabin and finished the retreat.

Very Good Demonstration (45)

A senior student who had been practicing with Seung Sahn for many years was walking with his teacher along a hallway. When the Master, in response to some item in the conversation, advised him for the umpteenth time, "Only don't know," something in the student snapped.

Grabbing his teacher and shoving him up against the wall the student shouted, "If I hear you say that one more time I'm going to scream!"

Seung Sahn looked at him and nodded. "Very good dharma demonstration!" he said.

DHARMA WORDS FROM MASTER SEUNG SAHN

Human beings understand too much. But what they understand is just opinion. Like a dog barking. American dog say, "Woof, woof." Korean dog say "Mung, mung." Polish dog say, "How, how." So which dog barking is correct? That is human beings' barking, not dog barking. If dog and you become one hundred percent one, then you know sound of barking. This is Zen teaching.

What we call "world" is only an opinion. Take away your opinion, then what? What is left? That is the point. Take away your opinion—your condition, situation—the mind is clear like space. Clear like space means clear like a mirror. A mirror reflects everything: the sky is blue, tree is green, sugar is sweet. Just be one with the truth—that's Zen style. If your mind is clear like space, then you see clearly, hear clearly, smell clearly—everything is clear. That is dharma. That is truth.

chapter five

ANYWAY, DO ZAZEN:
THE WIDENING CIRCLE

Katagiri Roshi said, in a talk some ten years after he came to America:

I have been reading your Descartes. Very interesting. "I think, therefore I am." He forgot to mention the other part. I'm sure he knew; he just forgot to mention: "I don't think; therefore I'm not."
—Reported by Natalie Goldberg

Dainin Katagiri and his contemporary Kobun Chino have much in common. Both came from Japan to the United States in the 1960s and assisted Suzuki Roshi at the San Francisco Zen Center. After Suzuki's death, each went on to found centers of their own, becoming important and influential teachers in their own right. Many students who initially trained with Suzuki Roshi went on to study with one or both, finding the same emphasis on shikantaza, or "just sitting" style zazen, and creating an intricate practice network between these primary members of the Soto Zen "family" in the U.S. Although Dainin Katagiri passed away some years ago, Kobun Chino, at the time of this writing, was still alive and teaching, in his own idiosyncratic fashion—a fashion that some say requires the student to stand squarely upon their own feet and make their own decisions, and others say can scarcely be called "teaching" at all. During a retreat at Hokoji Temple in Northern New Mexico, I had a chance to spend some time with him.

Kobun is here, the reluctant roshi, and the tiny temple of Hokoji, a bit of old Japan perched on the flanks of El Salto Mountain in Northern New Mexico, is packed to the gills for the first time in years. On the high seat at the center of the zendo he sits, a study in grey: grey in his grey outer robe, grey with his close-cropped hair, grey-faced in the dim zendo light. The blue muffler wrapped around his neck against the Rocky Mountain chill, the unshaven scalp, and the fact that his students all call him simply "Kobun," are all marks of his unconventionality. He speaks quietly, wanderingly, like a bird flitting from one branch to the next; and it is only after the movement is complete that it becomes apparent there is any pattern to it: "I feel very blessed to have all of you here today for this Founders' Ceremony. You might say, actually, that I am 'blessed out'! . . . Hello Barbara, how are you? How is Paul? He must be, let us see, fourteen by now—ah, yes . . . Actually, this entire mountain is a temple, but this place [indicating the room]. . . this place is a factory of Buddhas!"

Originally sent as a young monk in the 1960s by Japan's Soto church to assist Suzuki Roshi in San Francisco, Kobun Chino went on in the 1970s to found several centers of his own, then seemingly abandon them, then return erratically, only to vanish again. He has raised one family and, in his sixties, started another. A true eccentric in the manner of many a Zen man before him, Kobun is renowned for fleeing from seekers, avoiding even those who call themselves his students, and shunning all outward show of rank. Now, for the first time in four years, for this Rohatsu retreat commemorating the Buddha's enlightenment, he has returned to Hokoji, the temple he founded some fifteen or more years ago while living in New Mexico.

I've been able to attend only the last couple of days of Rohatsu. I did, however, stop by earlier in the week to hear one of his talks, as did a number of other visitors—several of whom, between Kobun's poetic, wandering manner, his Japanese accent, and his soft-spoken delivery, emerged more than a bit baffled by the experience.

"I very much like your roshi," remarked a visiting monk, "but I can't understand a word he says!"

Still, there is much that is charming and illuminating about Kobun's verbal meanderings—and every so often, if you're patient enough to sit through long stretches of puzzlement, there emerge small jewels of great, idiosyncratic beauty:

"Inside your skin and the skin of a dog, it is exactly the same."

"Past and future do not exist without you. Everything you need for your life and your practice are directly in front of you in the present moment."

"Those who die wrapped in Buddha's great cloak die a beautiful death."

Kobun, who spent many years in the San Francisco Bay area, delights in referring to the long, narrow meditation hall, converted from a carport, as "this cable car zendo"; and he goes off on long riffs about where it might be headed and when it might stop. This never ceases to amuse him, so that his talks are peppered with laughter.

Diane, the center's caretaker, calls him "our poet Zen master."

On the last morning of the retreat, in the middle of one of the final sitting periods, I am settled deeply into my zazen when Kobun's voice emerges abruptly from his seat in the zendo, breaking the deep, dark silence that has grown here. "The moon is high . . ." he begins—apropos of what, I can't imagine, as it is currently 11 o'clock in the morning—"and it gleams upon the roof of the temple, and in the depths of the temple pond, with its many swimming koi . . ."

Amid the communal aching of backs and legs, I can feel the minds beginning to shift—minds that have been sitting in silence for six days, struggling with the pain in the knees and back that comes from extended sitting, minds emerging from silence to wonder: "Where on earth is he going with this?"

"Beside the pond," continues the roshi's soft voice, "stand two figures, one tall and one short. The tall one is the temple priest, my father; the short one is a burglar who the priest has just surprised in the act of robbing the temple. 'I will gladly bring you the temple riches,' says the priest, while the robber holds him at knifepoint. 'But if you are such a master thief, perhaps you can first solve for me one question: can you catch one of the koi in this pond without getting your hands wet?'"

To make Kobun's long story short, the robber is unable to respond, and leaves without taking anything. As one might expect, three months later he returns and presents the priest with an answer. Kobun's father takes the burglar as his disciple, and sets him up in the village with an honest business—a shoe shop, of all things.

The story, delivered in a far less linear version than that presented here, is interspersed with long pauses, and is spoken in such a low voice that those at the far end of the zendo are surely unable to hear it all. It is offered with no explanation, and when it is finished Kobun ends as suddenly as he began, leaving the zendo again ringing with silence.

In the break between the end of the retreat and the Founders' Ceremony that afternoon, I interview my friend Bob Krueger, a longtime student of first Katagiri Roshi, and now, Kobun.

"There's a tradition in Zen," Bob says, "that your first teacher is a supportive, fatherly figure, but your second teacher is supposed to be more challenging. That's certainly the way it's been with me. A friend once said that Katagiri was hard on the outside but soft on the inside, while Kobun was soft on the outside and hard on the inside. That's been my experience. Katagiri always supported and encouraged me, but Kobun—well, I never know what he's going to do. I sometimes get nervous being around him, especially after a retreat, because I never know what he's going to come up with!"

Truer words were never spoken. No sooner do we step back into the caretaker's house to prepare for the Founders' Ceremony than we're greeted by an exuberant Kobun, eyes flashing like a child's, who immediately turns all planned activities upside down. "All right," he announces. "It's time for . . . *koan theater!* You—" he points to me, "You're the tall one, the priest. And you—" he singles out Bob, who's been doing his best to recede, chameleonlike, into the background, "You're the short one, the robber. You'll need a hat—" At this, everyone points to an odd sort of black fedora on the head of one of the participants, "—and a dagger." Someone grabs a huge knife from the kitchen and hands it to Bob, and someone else plops the hat upon his head.

"There," shouts another participant, tossing some crumpled up papers into the center of the room. "That's the ransacked temple."

"All right," nods Kobun, grinning. "Go ahead."

"Go ahead with what?" we ask.

"The koan. You know: 'The moon shines from on high into the depths of the koi pond . . . beside it stand two figures, one tall and one short . . .'"

I can't pretend to remember all the details of his talk that morning, but there's nothing to do but dive in.

"All right," I accost Bob, who points his kitchen knife menacingly at me. "I'll gladly bring you the temple treasures. But first, if you're such a master thief—show me how to catch one of the koi in this pond without getting your hands wet!"

"I can't do that," responds Bob, sensibly.

For a moment we're at a standstill.

"How about doing the earlier part of the story," someone suggests, "in the temple, when he first discovers the thief."

"Okay," we agree. People strew more wreckage about the living room to make the ransacked temple more believable. I step into the space and all at once Bob lunges out at me. "Bring me the temple treasures!" he demands, brandishing his kitchen knife. Everyone is laughing, blowing off steam from the sesshin.

"Wait a minute," I turn to look at Kobun. "Isn't the priest supposed to be your father?"

I never had gotten clear whether this was an old Zen story into which he'd just added his father—who was in fact a temple priest—or whether it had actually happened that way.

"Yes," agrees Kobun. "You are my father."

I turn back to Bob. "Begone thief," I cry, "—or I'll call my son Kobun to give you a good thrashing!"

The room breaks up. Kobun is slapping his hands against his knees in glee at the spectacle he's created. Meanwhile, either Bob's really settled into his role, or the twist I've thrown him arouses genuine fear, for his eyes grow wide and he steps back a pace. Now we're both at a loss.

"Okay, it's three months later," coaches Kobun. "You're sitting beside the pond when the thief returns with his answer."

I'm waiting there in the living room moonlight, sitting beside the coffee table koi pond, when Bob sidles up again out of the darkness and plunks himself down beside me.

"Well thief," I greet him. "You've returned. Did you bring an answer?"

At that moment, as though on cue, Diane's little white terrier comes running up. By this time we're both seated on the floor, and Bob reaches out automatically to pet it.

I stare at the dog, who actually *is* about the size of one of those huge temple goldfish, in a long moment of amazement. "You've done it!" I cry. "Here is the koi. You've caught it without getting your hands wet!"

The room dissolves. Kobun, on the couch, is rocking back and forth in his grey robes, slapping his hands against his knees, while the dog prances about, delighted to be the center of so much attention.

After it all settles down a bit Bob asks, "So what next? This is where I become a shoe salesman, right?"

"Oh yeah." I plop my bare foot into his lap, feeling loose with that crazy energy that sometimes comes after sesshin, "I'll set you up in an honest business, thief—if you can measure this foot, which fills the entire universe!"

Later, there's the traditional Zen work, updated for the 21st century—chopping wood, carrying water, and vacuuming—to make the place presentable for the ceremony. Then the event itself, attended by various spouses, children, and members of the community—and at last, as dusk falls over El Salto Mountain, with its great walls of granite, comes the celebratory potluck. At some point during the proceedings, Kobun explains to a group of us that the reason he'd brought up the story of the thief that morning was in response to the prevailing Western attitude that one is supposed to "get something" from the practice of Zen. What we "thieves" end up getting, says Kobun, is only what we had all along.

Through it all, I've been watching for the right moment to ask Kobun, who generally says "no" to such things, whether he might have time while he's in town to do an interview. Finally, after the crowd has dwindled, I find him sitting alone on the couch, looking surprisingly small, even a bit frail, in his grey robes.

"Excuse me, Kobun," I say. "I know you're very busy, but I'm working on a book on Zen in America, and I've been wondering if you might have the chance in the next couple of days to do a brief interview."

The answer I receive is pure Kobun—for he grins broadly, nodding his head in apparent assent, while clearly enunciating: "No."

The two responses are so conflicting that for a moment I'm unable to process the information.

"Excuse me?" I say.

"No," repeats Kobun, still nodding. "I have no time. But tell them—" he pauses for a moment to consider. "Tell them we know nothing of Zen." He smiles once more. "Tell them we only know just sitting." With that he folds his hands in his grey-robed lap and looks up at me. "Tell them that." He nods again. "It was very nice to practice with you."

"And you," I respond.

The interview is over.

Changing the World (46)

A student once asked Kobun Chino Roshi about the significance of prostrations in Zen practice. Kobun told the story of how, when he was ten or eleven years old and his father passed away, he'd dropped to the floor weeping in an uncontrollable expression of grief. When he rose to his feet both he and the world seemed irrevocably changed.

"I think of bowing that way," he said. "You go down, and when you come back up again, you're a different person. The world has changed."

No Thought Required (47)

A student who worked with learning disabled children asked Kobun Chino Roshi what the best way was to help them.

Her teacher's answer was simple: "No thought of helping."

New Tricks? (48)

Zen teacher Angie Boissevain recalls an incident that took place when she was studying with Kobun Chino Roshi in Los Altos, California. One day when Boissevain arrived for a meeting, explaining that she had an important question to ask him, Kobun suggested they step out into the park next to his office, and grabbed a bag of cookies to take along. They sat down on a bench and Kobun took out a cookie for each of them. No sooner had Boissevain launched into her question however, than they were descended upon by an enormous dog, who tried to take hers away.

"Go away, dog," Boissevain said, "we're busy." The dog persisted. "Get lost!" she said, pushing it away. The dog crossed to her other side, where it tried to nuzzle open the cookie bag. "Go away!" Boissevain repeated, shoving it away again. "We're talking about something important!"

At this point, Kobun leaned over and opened up the bag of cookies. He took out three and handed them to the dog, who happily trotted off. It didn't bother them again.

Form Is Emptiness (49)

During a shosan (a formal public question-and-answer session) Angie Boissevain came before Kobun Chino Roshi with a question that had been burning within her all morning. But after she made the customary three bows and knelt before him she found her mind utterly blank, the question gone.

She sat before him in silence for a long time before finally saying: "Where have all the words gone?"

"Back where they came from," replied her teacher.

I'm not sitting only for me, or you, or the Minnesota Zen Center. I'm sitting for all sentient beings, all over the world, forever.

—Dainin Katagiri Roshi

In *Writing Down the Bones,* Natalie Goldberg describes how her teacher, Dainin Katagiri of the Minnesota Zen Center, used to say "Have kind consideration for all sentient beings." Once she asked him, "What are sentient beings anyway? Are they things that feel?"

Katagiri told her, Goldberg reports, "that we have to be kind even to the chair, the air, the paper, and the street. That's how big and accepting our minds have to become."

Wendy Johnson reports a similar encounter during a retreat at Katagiri's country center in southern Minnesota, which was used only for several months each summer:

"The night before I'd been in the zendo by myself. It was sesshin and I'd had this experience where I imagined all the *zafus* (sitting cushions) being there through all the seasons without us on them . . . how there was a kind of continuity. It was a very vivid experience. The next day during a talk Katagiri said, 'if you can't break the frame around your life, maybe you should not pretend, and keep going in this lineage as if you're doing that, because everything depends on breaking the frame.'

"Somebody had asked the head student a couple of weeks before what real effort was, and she hadn't been able to answer. On this day, Katagiri said, 'Effort, effort—you always think about effort in terms of human effort. But what about the effort of a zafu practicing night after night? They keep going every season and there's no comment about their effort—the effort it takes them to hold you up, or the effort that an animal makes when it's hungry, the effort of a deer . . .' He just went on and on and on like that, and I remember beginning to weep . . . He'd brought it up, that same experience I'd had the night before! Often times Zen students will say it seems like the teacher was entering their mind, reading their mind. It was very powerful . . . I had a visceral experience of the frame around my life dissolving and cracking open. I'm very grateful to Katagiri Roshi."

Katagiri stories abound, illustrating the broad and lasting influence he and his dharma heirs have exerted on Zen in America; some of these, as with many of the first Asian teachers, involve cases of cultural or linguistic misunderstanding. One of my favorites, a version of which also appears in Natalie Goldberg's memoir of her training with Katagiri, *Long Quiet Highway*, was told to me several times in different forms during the course of my research for this book. As one of Katagiri's dharma heirs, Yvonne Rand, tells it:

"Some of the leaders of the community of practitioners wanted to do some fund-raising and they decided to have an afternoon tea party. So they got all their grandmothers' linen tablecloths, and silver and tea cups, and made sandwiches with the crusts cut off. They invited what were described as the 'Minneapolis/St. Paul Swells'— all the people of wealth and prestige, none of whom had ever gone to the Zen Center, or were ever likely to.

"At a certain point, after the guests had arrived, Katarigi Roshi came down the stairs, looking radiant, as he could in his robes. He looked at everyone, welcomed them, and began, 'You know, of course, we all will die.'"

The guests, it is reported, left early, and the center netted scarcely a penny.

In another case one of Katagiri's monks, while editing a book of his teacher's talks, was looking at a transcription made by another Zen student when he ran across the phrase: "It's like war, coming up from the ground, filling the battle of your life. Your life is really a big battle . . ."

"Hmm," he thought. "That doesn't sound like Katagiri." He went back to the original tape, which sounded similar to the transcription. On listening carefully however, he realized what Katagiri had actually said was, "It's like water coming up from the ground, filling the bottle of your life. Your life is really a big bottle . . ."

Dainin Katagiri first came to the U.S. in 1963, and worked for five months at Zenshuji in Los Angeles, the same temple where Maezumi Roshi was based, before being transferred to Sokoji in San Francisco to assist Suzuki Roshi. Katagiri's English was poor enough at the time, it is said, that his language tutor back in Japan had told him he had "infinite potential, for anything would be an improvement." In the early Seventies, after Suzuki's death, Katagiri moved to Minneapolis to found the Minnesota Zen Center, where he taught until his death in 1990. There, away from Suzuki's shadow, he came into his own as a teacher.

There was much speculation as to why he chose such a remote and frigid location, where Buddhism was still considered—if it was considered at all—a strange and alien religion. One of his long time students explained it this way:

"Katagiri wanted the challenge of being a pioneer on the frontier of Zen, and he was impressed with the people who came from Minneapolis to San Francisco and asked him to come there. He hoped to have normal working class American students instead of just hippies—but much to his dismay, hippies came from all over the Midwest to study with him!"

Katagiri himself said that the cold was good for practice, as it forced people to turn inward. Practitioners remember traveling to the Zen center in mid-winter for dawn zazen, when the temperatures might stay twenty degrees below zero, or colder, for weeks on end. But they came, some from hundreds of miles, some of them for every retreat.

Letting students figure things out for themselves was a hallmark of Katagiri's style. "If you showed up for dawn zazen," says Natalie Goldberg, "Katagiri didn't say anything. And if you didn't come he didn't say anything either. After a while I realized I wasn't going to get any praise for showing up. Zazen was there for us, if we wanted it."

One of Katagiri's dharma heirs told me a story about a ceremony he performed with Katagiri, which illustrates something of his teacher's approach:

"I was the Ino [chant leader and instrumentalist] and we'd just gotten a statue of Avalokitesvara, the Bodhisattva of Compassion. Katagiri wanted to have an eye-opening ceremony for it. So he had me come upstairs the day before, and he handed me a script for the ceremony. I had my copy and he had his copy, and we went over it and I made notes. There were certain times where I had to ring a bell or hit something or other while he would do this or do that . . . so we'd gone through the whole thing, and I thought I understood it.

"So the next day the ceremony begins. I've got the script in front of me, and Katagiri comes in and bows and makes offerings. At some point though, he breaks with the script and just starts winging it. I'm going into a panic—what are we going to do next? He's moving things around and I'm trying to hit bells when I'm supposed to, and at a certain point I look at him and I realize, he's not following this thing at all. The script is useless. And I suddenly realized, he wasn't attached to this in the least. So I just relaxed and tried to follow him. It ended up being completely improvised, and after it was over people were coming up and saying, 'What a nice ceremony.' But I learned something there. On the one side you have form. On the other, freedom. You can have both at once."

Zen priest Paul Courtney, who was sitting in on our conversation, added, "You could see it, watching Katagiri bow. Bowing was the heart of his practice. He was just so present. When Katagiri bowed, the whole room bowed."

But Katagiri Roshi didn't always take such a hands-off approach, particularly with his long-time students. Zen priest Jodo Cliff Clusin remembers a time in his Zen practice where, "I was working for an insurance company, and I wasn't that into it. I told Katagiri Roshi I had this bad attitude, and I remarked, 'Why don't they just fire me?'"

Katagiri, as Clusin recalls, "really laid into me about how I couldn't be a priest with that kind of attitude. He gave me a talk about being whole-hearted at work. So I went back, and I started paying more attention, walking faster between the desks, working harder. People noticed it, my boss noticed it, they offered me a raise, and I found a better job in a new field in a month! It turned my life around." Says Clusin: "You know, you sit there during a lecture and you think, 'this is great, I'm learning so much'. . . but until you spill your guts to your teacher about what you actually think about something, it doesn't really hit you."

Paul Courtney also shared with me a collection students had gathered of Katagiri's favorite phrases, some of which I remembered from his book, *Returning to Silence*:

In Zen, you let your frontal lobe rest.
Whatever you think is delusion.
The moment between before and after is called Truth.
Anyway, do zazen.

Although Katagiri Roshi passed away too soon, at the age of sixty-two, his influence continues to grow through the work of the twelve dharma successors he left behind, the writings of former students such as Wendy Johnson and Natalie Goldberg, and the broad circle of lives he impacted, both in San Francisco and the Midwest.

"Katagiri Roshi," says Natalie Goldberg, "gave me a vision of what it was to be human—the possibility of what it could be to be a human being."

No Matter Where You Go, There You Are (50)

After several years of practice, a student came to Dainin Katagiri Roshi, saying; "I used to think I knew what you were saying in your lectures. But lately, I just don't understand at all."

A grin spread over his teacher's features. "Finally," Katagiri said, "you're getting somewhere!"

Yeah, So What Good Is It? (51)

Katagiri Roshi was invited to give a seminar at a yoga conference in Chicago. In order to counter the typical American concern regarding what one was going to "get" from a certain practice—an attitude he imagined might be prevalent at the conference—Katagiri titled his topic "Zazen Is Useless."

He was surprised when no one showed up for the talk.

An Unpaid Debt (52)

Jodo Cliff Clusin and some other students were talking with Katagiri Roshi about how much psychotherapists charge in America for their services. "Hoji-san," joked Clusin to his teacher, "that's why I always go to you for advice. You're free."

Katagiri first joked back, saying, "I will get you a bill, no problem." Then he turned serious. "When I die," he told Clusin, "I will give you a very big bill."

Gathering No Moss (53)

Zen priest Jean Leyshon was working as Katagiri Roshi's personal attendant, or "Anja," during the annual four month training period at his country center in southern Minnesota. Her responsibilities included keeping his house and clothing clean and orderly, and in general, being on call for anything he needed.

One day, Katagiri Roshi seemed upset about something, and the residents in training were concerned about him. He liked to drive the center's old tractor during the work period, mowing the back fields, and on this particular day he was driving it somewhat erratically, mounting the hills at such a steep angle that the students looking on were worried for his safety.

Leyshon thought, "I'm going to do something about this." For some reason, she decided that playing a joke on him might help.

Arriving back at his cabin, she looked around for an object that would suit her purposes and noticed a large, beautiful stone marked with quartz from the stream bed at Tassajara Monastery, which the students had presented to Katagiri as a memento of his time there. Katagiri had a Japanese style bath on the second floor of the cabin—an upright fiberglass basin with a cover—and one of the responsibilities of his attendant was to draw and heat the water so that he could bathe when he came back from work practice. Leyshon drew the bath, then put the cover in place and hauled the stone, which weighed twenty or thirty pounds, up the stairs and placed it on top of the cover, pinning it down.

Some time later, she was working around the cabin when she heard Katagiri come in, muttering to himself. She heard the sound of his feet ascending the stairs, then his voice saying, "What is this?" and the clunk of the stone being placed upon the floor.

The roshi was in the bath for some time. Leyshon busied herself with trimming candles and other work that needed to be done, sitting at a table at the bottom of the stairs. Finally she felt tired from her long hours of work and put her head down on her arms to rest.

After a while, she heard Katagiri get out of the bath and the sound of movement from above as he dried and dressed himself. By this time Leyshon was feeling apprehensive about her teacher's response, so when she heard his footsteps coming down the stairs she remained in place with her head upon her arms, too nervous to look at him. She heard his steps halt at the bottom of the stairs.

"Jean," Katagiri asked, "Is there something wrong?"

She lifted her head and looked at him. "No, Roshi," she answered. "I'm just tired." With that she got up and came over to him. His face, she said, looked like it was broken into a thousand pieces.

Katagiri patted her on the shoulder. "Take it easy," he told her. "Get some rest."

Leyshon took the night off at the roshi's request.

Later, in the early fall, she took to placing the stone on top of the wood stove, as there was a loose plate on the top she feared might come off. One day a group of workmen came to replace the stovepipe.

"Have her move the stone," Katagiri said to the men, nodding in the direction of Leyshon. "She's a strong woman, very strong woman."

Then, with a hint of a smile he added, "This stone moves around the cabin on its own."

Buddhism, the real Buddhism, is practice. Any moment
must be practice. Any moment must be true.
—Ch'an Monk Tsung Tsai

"The most fascinating thing about Tsung Tsai," says writer George Crane of his teacher and friend, the Ch'an (Chinese Zen) monk who escaped communist China in 1959 during the "Great Leap Forward" era of religious persecution, "is that he spends his whole life, till he's thirty-one years old, living in this mountain monastery at the edge of the Gobi Desert. For him the twentieth century doesn't exist. He lives a thousand years ago. He's a tenth century man. All the things of the twentieth century, electricity, automobiles, he knows nothing about.

"Sixteen months later he slips under the barbed wire into Hong Kong. That three thousand mile trip is amazing—but what he really does, is he walks through time. He walks into the twentieth century. And he does it with complete ease, with complete relaxation, and total acceptance."

Although revered as a dharma master in Hong Kong, Tsung Tsai lived the quiet life of a hermit monk for much of the time since his arrival in the U.S. in the 1960s, until his story recently came to light in Crane's book *Bones of the Master*. The book describes Tsung Tsai's flight from China, and a later expedition he and Crane undertook back to Mongolia, to find the grave of Tsung Tsai's teacher and erect a shrine in his honor.

Having built his own cabin in upstate New York, Tsung Tsai writes, meditates, and translates traditional Chinese poetry, while trying to avoid seekers and the curious. A doctor of Oriental medicine, he also performs occasional healings, as the editors of several publishing houses discovered when he and Crane went to pitch the first four chapters of *Bones of the Master*, in hopes of funding their expedition to China. Tsung Tsai was dressed for the occasion in his many-times-patched orange monk's robe he'd acquired in Hong Kong thirty years before, a straw hat fixed with duct tape, and a pair of battered Tai Chi shoes. Perhaps to reassure them that he could withstand the rigors of the journey which awaited them, he began at one of the publishing houses to demonstrate his youth and vitality. As Crane tells it:

"As it turned out, sixteen publishers had expressed interest . . . I remember we were sitting at one publishing house. The editor-in-chief was there with her new publisher. Tsung Tsai began to show them how young he was. 'Look at the skin on my arm. Very young. Very pretty!' Then he said to the editor, 'You touch.' So she touched it. Then he touched *her* skin, took her arm, and felt her pulse. 'You need my help,' he announced. 'You are very weak.'"

Although the editor didn't take Tsung Tsai up on his offer of a treatment, she later made an offer on the book. The two continued their tour of publishing houses. In a later meeting, Tsung Tsai was talking about his old teacher when he burst into tears in the conference room. "The whole room got silent," says Crane: "He sat there and cried and cried. Nobody said anything. We were around this table with the publicist, the publisher, the editor-in-chief . . . he cried for what seemed like a half hour—probably it was just a few minutes, but it seemed like forever because the room became absolutely silent. Then all at once he stopped crying and broke into laughter. He said: 'My teacher would laugh at me.'"

In yet another meeting Tsung Tsai took a woman's pulse and announced, "You bleeding now. But you soon be over. Day or two, you be done."

"That's Tsung Tsai," says Crane. "You never know what he's going to do. There's no filter. There's never anything going on beneath the surface. What you see is what you get. It's 'this is it. This is who I am'."

All of the publishers ended up making offers on the book.

Who's the Boss? (54)

Tsung Tsai, in addition to living the life of a simple monk, is a doctor of Oriental medicine and acupuncture. He once did a healing consultation with a Rabbi's son, who had been very ill. As George Crane tells it, Tsung Tsai proceeded to examine the boy, and gave him a prescription for Chinese herbs. At one point during the interaction, the Rabbi and his son left to pray. Tsung Tsai watched with interest. When they came back he remarked to them, "Very nice. I just talked to your boss today, too!"

When the consultation was over the Rabbi asked if they could give him any money in exchange for the treatment. Tsung Tsai proceeded to open the pins on the many pockets of the rain jacket he'd scavenged from a dust bin in New York City. He found two dollars crumpled up in one pocket and a handful of change in another.

"No," he concluded. "Today my pockets are full."

Tsung Tsai watched as the two got back into the Rabbi's Cadillac. As they drove off he looked at Crane, then back at the Cadillac, then back at Crane. "This Rabbi business must be pretty good, eh?" he said.

A Little Advice (55)

Like many Ch'an monks, Tsung Tsai has also trained in the martial arts, although he refuses to discuss it. Once, George Crane was walking with him along Houston Street in New York City. Tsung Tsai was dressed in his usual patched robe, and a big teenage street tough came up and accosted them, saying "Kung Fu monk, huh?" With that he began throwing a series of vicious kicks at them. The two just stood there for a while but the kid wouldn't stop, and refused to let them pass. All of a sudden, in the midst of one of the

ONE BIRD, ONE STONE

kicks, Tsung Tsai reached out and with a movement so swift Crane couldn't see it, the kid hit the ground, winded but unhurt—seeming more amazed than anything that this sixty-nine-year-old man could lay him out that quickly.

Tsung Tsai leaned over him and said, "Boy, I give you little bit advice. When fighting, keep two feet on ground. One leg in the air—no balance!"

Sparse Plum

In the yard
a couple of
>*graceful*
>>*twigs*

dot dot
>*flower petals*
like stars
>*disperse*

insomnia
midnight on
>>*the gloomy*
>>>*verandah*

upon window panes
the moon
>*moves*
>>*shadows*

—"Hermit Crazy About Plum," Zhou Lu Jing,
From A Thousand Pieces of Snow, Ming Dynasty China.
Translated by Tsung Tsai and George Crane

In an interview with the two in *Tricycle Magazine,* Crane was asked how his association with Tsung Tsai and Ch'an Buddhism had changed his life.

"I became legal," explained George. "I got my drivers license, I paid my taxes."

"More! More please!" put in Tsung Tsai. "You pay your family debt, your friend debt, your neighbor debt. Now only keep one wife, no more keep girlfriend. No more eat bad food. Now almost vegetable!"

The interviewer asked Tsung Tsai how he felt about *Bones of the Master*.

"So special book," answered Tsung Tsai. "Georgie do very good job, put lots of energy into this book. You begin to understand Chinese mind, Chinese culture. And then you understand Buddha mind. Chinese mind is very close to Buddhist mind."

When asked about monasticism, Tsung Tsai concluded: "Monk, no monk, doesn't matter. People need to learn compassion, first for self, then neighbor, then country. Someday, when American people know more about Buddha, maybe many become monk . . . Because Buddhism so kindness! So freedom! So special! Always say the truth. It's just natural. Everyone needs Buddha mind."

"You never know what Tsung Tsai is going to do," says Crane, "But I always find it wonderful. There's such a purity of purpose and purity of being. I've never met his like. I don't know if there *is* his like."

The Spreading of the Bodhi Tree

The passage to the Western world having been opened by the first pioneers, the Beats, and the Zen boomers, an ever-increasing array of Buddhist teachers began to arrive on America's shores. They're still coming, driven by the staleness of traditional forms, the openness of the American mind, political chaos—or simply, the desire to help all sentient beings by spreading the dharma. The clash of cultures, the difficulties of language, the mixing of Eastern ways of life with a high-velocity technological society, has not always been easy. But then, it hasn't always been difficult, either.

In the forty-odd years that have passed since the great migration of Zen teachers from Asia began in earnest, the American family tree of Zen Buddhism has developed so many branches, and spread them so widely, that it becomes impossible to trace them all in detail. As it is dangerously easy, in any case, to commit the Zen sin of "adding legs to a snake" by offering unnecessary explanations, we'll depart from commentary at this point and trust that the following stories, ranging in time from the 1960s to the present, and covering a variety of Zen lineages, will communicate in and of themselves the essence of each teacher's dharma.

Hitting Bottom (56)

When Clark Strand, the author of *Seeds from a Birch Tree*, was a monk studying with Eido Shimano Roshi, a dharma heir to Soen Nakagawa, he reached, after a number of years of practice, a point he calls the "lowest moment of my Zen career."

"My first marriage had fallen apart when I became a monk," says Strand, "and then I'd gotten involved with another woman, and that was falling apart too, and I didn't feel that I had any understanding of Zen at all." There was a very large retreat coming up, with more than ninety people scheduled to attend, and Eido Roshi had put him in charge of it.

"For the next week," says Clark, "I was going to have to completely give myself over to managing this event—and my heart was broken, and my spirit felt broken, and there was just nothing left. I remember I way-laid Eido Roshi right as the retreat was beginning. There were close to a hundred people in the zendo, waiting for us to come in. And I went and sat down with him in the meeting hall, crying, and I said, 'It's over, there's nothing left. Everything that I've cared about and loved, my whole life, has all come to nothing. I'm at the bottom.'"

At that, Strand says, Eido Roshi leaned across the table, put his hand out, and said, "Congratulations."

"It was an amazing moment," says Strand. "Part of me wanted to fly across the table and slug him. But another part knew that what he was saying was true. I'd been talking about emptiness and nothingness and renunciation all this time, and I hadn't understood anything. At that moment I understood, and I felt filled up. When you reach the maximum point of frustration, or desolation, and the authentic person steps forward, at those moments there is a real transmission that occurs. If he hadn't pointed like that I would've just stayed in despair. But by the time I walked down the hall behind him and entered the zendo, my tears had dried and I was clear. It was turned out to be a wonderful seven days—one of the best retreats I've ever sat."

Making Firewood (57)

The Ch'an (Chinese Zen) monk Deh Chun lived in rural Tennessee in the 1960s and 1970s, where he attracted a small but devoted group of students associated with a nearby university. When Deh Chun first came to Tennessee, there was a huge dead oak in the yard beside his cabin. One day one of his neighbors happened by and said, "You'd better cut that thing down, or one of these days it's going to fall on your roof."

"Oh, thank you," said Deh Chun. The next time he went into town he bought a hatchet at a thrift store. He promptly set to work on the tree's enormous trunk, chopping away for some time every morning, and showing no signs of discouragement at his minimal progress. Neighbors, seeing him working day after day, showed up with chain saws and power saws, offering to cut it down for him.

"Thank you, no," said Deh Chun. "I do it my way."

This went on for months, with such regularity that if his neighbors didn't hear the steady chop chop chop of Deh Chun on his tree on any given morning, they'd come over to make sure he was all right. It became a phenomenon, a cause for conversation; and before too long, this strange old Chinese fellow who'd moved in from out of nowhere had become a member of the neighborhood.

On the day the tree finally fell, with a crash that shook all the houses on his street, one of Deh Chun's friends asked him, "So what will you do now?"

"Make firewood," answered Deh Chun.

He later said that this was the way he'd taught them meditation: you just chop away, a little bit every day, and one day an enormous tree falls.

What Next? (58)

One day one of Deh Chun's university students was driving past a Methodist church when he happened to see Deh Chun outside it, with brushes and a small easel, painting.

He pulled over to find the monk was not painting the church at all, but a traditional Chinese landscape with tremendous mountains, streams and waterfalls and, in a clearing in a forest, a tiny, smiling hermit sweeping his hut.

"This monk just have great enlightenment," Deh Chun said in explanation.

"So what happens next?" the student asked him.

"Keep sweeping."

Every Little Bit Counts (59)

After working all day in the rock garden at his Los Angeles Zendo, Joshu Sasaki and his students had managed to set three large rocks into position. Sasaki Roshi stepped back at last and examined the arrangement for a long moment. Finally he said, "Top rock, down one half inch." With that, he retired to his quarters.

The stone in question was mostly buried and must have weighed over 200 pounds. Hoping to avoid extra work, or perhaps to test his teacher's powers of observation, one of the students piled up a half inch of extra dirt around its base and left it at that.

An hour later the roshi returned. He'd no more than glanced at the arrangement when he said, "Still one half inch."

Close, but No Cigar (60)

A karate student doing a retreat with Joshu Sasaki Roshi, of the Cimmaron Zen Center in Los Angeles, had been struggling with a koan for some time, with no results. Finally during a private interview he became so frustrated that he let out a great shout and threw a karate punch directly at the teacher, stopping inches from Sasaki's face.

The roshi was unmoved. "Right answer," he said. "Wrong koan."

Berry Pie (61)

Taking on a monastic regimen has not always been easy for Westerners—especially in the late Sixties and early Seventies, when discipline was not often equated with freedom. American Ch'an monk Hung Ju (Timothy

Tetsu), who trained under Ch'an master Hsuan Hua of Gold Mountain Monastery, became known in the 1970s after undertaking a 1000-mile pilgrimage for peace along the northern Pacific coast, during which he made one full prostration, forehead to the ground, every three steps of the way. The trip, in which Hung Ju and his companion, Hung Yo, faced fatigue, challenging weather conditions, and reactions both warm and hostile—and once, the terrible error of using poison oak leaves as toilet paper—took some ten months to complete.

But Hung Ju wasn't always so disciplined. In his book, *Three Steps, One Bow*, he tells a story from the early days of his ordination, after he'd taken on the traditional Chinese monastic prohibition against eating anything after noon. One day, wrote Hung Ju, he couldn't resist sneaking out of the monastery and down to a local bakery, where he bought a load of pastries. He ate them all except for one berry pie, which he smuggled into the monastery under his coat. As he tells it:

"That day, during afternoon meditation, I began to get hungry again, and my thoughts turned to the pie. During the evening lecture, while the Master was speaking the Dharma, the pie was all I could think about. I decided I was going to eat it after the lecture, the hell with the rules!

"It was about 10:00 PM, and everyone had retired, when I very quietly slipped out of the third-floor bathroom window, carefully shut it behind me, and climbed up the fire escape to the roof. I opened up the pie and sunk my teeth into that luscious sugary crust, biting down into those succulent, juicy red berries. 'Christ!' I thought to myself, 'If this isn't Nirvana, what is?' But just at that very moment, I looked over at the fire escape to see that someone else was climbing up onto the roof! I stood there terror-struck, with a mouthful of pie. There was no place I could run! It was the Master. I stood there unmoving for a moment while my brains began hemorrhaging. Then I began walking around in a circle on the rooftop as if in deep contemplation. The Master, too, began to circle the roof as if in deep contemplation, but he was going in the opposite direction. We passed each other twice without looking at each other, but on the third lap, I looked up and saw him grinning like a Cheshire cat. He said four words: "How does it feel?"

"It was just too much . . . We both erupted in laughter at the ridiculousness of the thing, the whole endless universal thing. Then he left me to finish my pie."

"That's the berry pie story," wrote Hung Ju. "The Master takes great delight in it."

Throwing Away the Key (62)

A problem developed in the early days of Tassajara Monastery in California, during the tenure of Tatsugami Roshi, an imposing and stern Japanese master who Suzuki Roshi had invited to America to lead a three month practice period. Retreatants had taken to sneaking into the kitchen between meals and stealing loaves of the famous Tassajara bread made by resident cook Espe Ed Brown. After this had been going on for some time, causing a good deal of distress in the community and confusion about what might be the best solution, a group of staff members decided to bring the problem before the roshi.

Upon listening to the story, Tatsugami, who had been practice leader for many years at Eiheiji Monastery in Japan and had no doubt fielded many more difficult problems than this, responded shortly: "Put locks on the doors."

Several padlocks were purchased on the next trip into town and the bread was locked away, temporarily solving the problem. This solution, however, created more difficulty, for many felt that locking the cabinets created an atmosphere of apprehension and mistrust in the community. After the discussion had gone on for awhile someone finally took the key, unlocked all the locks, and threw them in the creek.

This event occasioned more controversy, and the matter was again brought before the roshi. After listening to the story in silence, Tatsugami looked at the staff members who had been most vocal about the problem.

"The locks are on your minds," he told them.

The True Reason (63)

The Korean Zen master Hyunoong Sunim was holding a discussion at San Francisco Zen Center. A student asked him the reason human beings persist in habits that cause them harm, sometimes long after they have ceased to be pleasurable.

"In Christianity," answered Hyunoong Sunim, "this is known as original sin. In Buddhism, we call it delusion." He looked around the room. "Why is there delusion?" He shrugged his shoulders and lifted both hands into the air. "No reason!"

At this he laughed heartily.

Jane Dobisc, who later became a Zen teacher under Korean Master Seung Sahn, went on a pilgrimage to the East as a young woman, searching for a Buddhist teacher. At one point, she spent weeks trekking through the Himalayas to get to a particularly remote monastery. Reaching it at last she knocked upon the door and asked if she could see the Lama.

"Oh, no," replied the nun who'd opened the door. "He's in New York."

When Dobisc returned home, she discovered that Master Seung Sahn had been operating a practice center in Rhode Island all along, no more than a ten-minute drive from her family's home.

chapter six

THE TURNING WHEEL

You yourself are time—your body, your mind, the objects around you.
Plunge into the river of time and swim, instead of standing on the banks
and noting the course of the currents.

—Philip Kapleau

My first glimpse of Roshi Philip Kapleau, the grand old man of American Zen, is like a dream—or better yet, a *makyo*, those delusive visions that sometimes afflict meditators during long periods of zazen. I'm standing by the reception desk in the front office of the Rochester Zen Center when the adjacent door, with its sign saying something like "Private Quarters, Please Knock Before Entering," swings open and, as though in a scene from *Waiting For Godot*, three figures burst through it. Leading the way is Roshi's attendant, a tall dark-haired youth; in the middle is an old man, wearing—am I imagining this?—some sort of greyish flannel union suit, or pajamas with suspenders; and taking up the rear is my friend Eiho, white hair flying, who seems to be clutching those suspenders, or a kind of harness arrangement, to help Roshi stay upright. Lurching determinedly forward, head lowered as though to batter away obstructions, the roshi barrels toward—where? the shower?—while Eiho shouts, like a crazed rodeo cowboy, "He's going! He's going! Look at him go!" The scene is so sudden and dreamlike that I can't catch all the details. All at once it is over, as quickly as it began, and there is no one else around to ask for an explanation, or to confirm that it, in fact, happened at all.

My drive with Eiho from Zen Mountain Monastery through the Catskill Mountains of upstate New York had been perfect, winding through air-brushed grey hillsides of late fall, slopes filled with empty trees, punctuated by stands of still-changing color. We watched the sky with its change-of-season cloud wisps fading to purple, then slate-grey, and finally dusky indigo as the evening rolled in—all of it having that larger-than-life sense one often feels at the end of sesshin. Cindy Eiho Green, my guide for this journey, is white-haired, fiftyish, with translucent skin like onion paper, and blue eyes you could dive into, like a clear, deep lake—why is it, I find myself wondering, that so many long-time practitioners have these exceptionally deep, clear eyes? A long-time student of Roshi Kapleau, Eiho now studies with John Daido Loori, and is a full-time resident at Zen Mountain Monastery.

Our destination felt to me like a place of pilgrimage. The Rochester Zen Center, in many ways the home temple of American Zen, was the first major practice center established by an American. Ex-businessman Philip Kapleau, following his return from his thirteen years of training in Japanese monasteries in 1966, chose this unlikely industrial city at the edge of the Great Lakes in western New York after making an extensive tour of America in search of the ideal location to start a Zen center. Like Dainin Katagiri, Kapleau has said that he hoped the famously inclement weather would push his students to look inward.

Known for many years as the "boot camp" of American Zen, the Rochester Zen Center was famous for the discipline and intensity of its training, its emphasis on provoking *kensho,* or enlightenment experience, and its use of the *keisaku* or "Zen stick" to spur students onto harder practice. Kapleau's *Three Pillars of Zen* had been an important influence in my early years of training, and still stands as one of the classics of American Buddhist literature.

We'd arrived too late, after our five-and-a-half-hour drive, to visit Roshi Kapleau last night, or to get much of a sense of our surroundings. Now, in the daylight, I can see how lovely the center is, made up of several adjacent National Historic Register houses on a secluded residential street. Late October leaves drop in reds and browns along the brick paths, wooden walkways, and immaculate gardens of the interior courtyard, at the center of which sits a large stone Buddha with no face—just a perfectly blank, beginner's mind expanse of emptiness. This, explains one of the students working around the place, is meant to represent the Zen of America, whose features have yet to develop.

After zazen and breakfast, I help two young residents with bits and pieces of work—putting away picnic tables for the winter, stacking them one atop another in a narrow alcove between two walls. Our labor is relaxed, unhurried. We move several wheelbarrows, pile the tables in a corner, cover them with a blue plastic tarp, then move the wheelbarrows back into position. Then we're off to the woodshop, thoroughly modern and well-equipped, with an expensive-looking table saw at the center. I'd already noticed the immaculate woodwork everywhere about the place—each railing, each of the altars set here and there, the tables, the floors, all demonstrating close and careful attention to detail.

The workshop, too, is neat as an acupuncture lancet—but when the crew leader, an earnest, capable fellow in his twenties, whom I'll call Evan, hands out the tools for our next round of work, he gives the new arrival, wild-haired Mike, a leaf vacuum whose nozzle, despite liberal application of duct tape, keeps falling off. I'm relieved to find that not *everything* about this place is perfect.

I'm assigned to pull wilting chrysanthemums out of ceramic pots and trundle them off in a wheelbarrow to the compost heap: the dried blooms stiff in my hands, cold fall air crunching against skin, bright cool sun and wheelbarrow bouncing and wobbling on cobbled paths, all worthy perhaps, of twisting the old William Carlos Williams poem into a haiku:

Dried up husks of mums
crumbling in old wheelbarrow
—on which I depend

Later, Evan takes Mike and me up to the Buddha Hall, dominated by several life-sized bronze bodhisattva figures that appear to be ancient and Chinese. It's said that Roshi Kapleau found them being used as ornaments in a bar on one of his many trips to Mexico, and persuaded the owner to part with them. Stories like this abound; Katagiri Roshi once found a 900-year-old temple bell being used as a planter for a tree, and Kobun Chino found a similar artifact being used as an umbrella stand—both items, in these cases, having been restored to their proper uses. Still, there's something fitting about these grand figures standing for so many years in a bar—after all, isn't that the business of bodhisattvas, to penetrate *all* worlds in order to liberate all beings?

As we stand there, I mention to Evan and Mike how moving it is for me to be at the Rochester Zen Center—like arriving at the most important destination in a long, long pilgrimage.

"Why?" asks Mike innocently, and I reply, "Well, this is where it all really started, isn't it? Here and the San Francisco Zen Center . . ." and I suddenly realize, seeing his young, wide-open gaze, that he doesn't fully understand the significance of this place—that Roshi Kapleau, perhaps, is just a distant figure he's glimpsed from time to time, being pushed around in a wheelchair or helped down the stairs by his attendant, never truly grasping the importance of what this old man has done.

But now it's time to meet the roshi. He receives us in his quarters, feet propped on the pop-up footing of a reclining chair. He's dressed more conventionally than when I glimpsed him earlier, in khaki trousers and greenish canvas sneakers—real sneakers, the kind my Grandpa used to wear, with thick white rubber soles—though these still bear, incongruously, the curved white Nike teardrop. Set all about the place are Buddha and Bodhisattva figures and calligraphy—I'd heard the roshi had an extensive collection from his many years of travel. Still I can't help but wonder if any of these teachers ever tire of Asian imagery, and whether American roshis in centuries to come might substitute a more Western form of decoration—perhaps commemorative dishes with the faces of the ancestors on them instead?

I know Roshi's Parkinson's Disease is advanced, but I'm surprised to find, as I lean across to attach a lapel mike to his shirt, that my hands are more unsteady than his. "My voice is not so strong," he says simply, in a hoarse whisper that later, when I listen to the tape, will remind me of Marlon Brando's in *The Godfather*. As I'm stringing the wire from his lapel he says, "I saw you this morning through my window . . .working with the wheelbarrow."

He chuckles and I nod, not knowing how to respond. Eiho is present, and Rafe Martin, two of Roshi's close old students, but I can't help but wonder exactly what it is *I* am doing in their company. It feels so painfully intimate, sitting in this room with the three of them, like being with someone who's dying—it *is* being with someone who's dying, I realize—though at age eighty-eight Roshi Kapleau is displaying no need to hurry. Then too, there's the sense in him of "I'm not going to let mortality ruin my day or yours, so let's get on with it."

Rafe sits centered and silent as I test the recorder. Eiho, who with her white cloud of hair and those blue clear eyes looks like a cloud herself, has that professional cheeriness of the career nurse, and the comfortable presence of having known Roshi for a long, long time.

The going is slow at first, as Roshi Kapleau gets warmed up, meandering through his mind, walking back in time. Rafe, who is a professional storyteller and uniquely suited for this task, helps fill in Roshi's words when he can't remember all the details:

"So there I was in the zendo," says Roshi, "with Phillips and— who was that, Rafe?"

Rafe puts in, "The Abbot was Soen Nakagawa, wasn't it, Roshi? Soen Nakagawa pulled you and Phillips aside and asked—"

"He asked, 'what did Christ say when he was on the cross—'"

"And you said, 'My God, why hast thou forsaken me—'"

"And he said, 'No!'"

"And then he asked Phillips . . . ."

"Or did he ask Phillips first?"

They're like a symbiotic organism, these two men, student and teacher, who have practiced so long together, sharing the same mind.

After the story, Rafe asks him, "Didn't you used to travel with Soen Nakagawa?"

"With Nakagawa Roshi, yes—" Kapleau brightens at the memory. "We had a very wonderful relationship. He was three or four years older than I was, and he would take me to visit his friends—he had so many friends in every aspect of life. We used to call ourselves "the two hobos." He sighs. "I had such good friends in Japan."

Rafe and Roshi Kapleau had met a few days ago to decide which stories were the best ones to tell, so there's really very little I have to do. Again I have that feeling of unbearable intimacy, of sitting in on a conversation that's too private for me to listen to.

Now Rafe prompts, "Wasn't there a story to your meeting with Harada Roshi [Yasutani Roshi's teacher], when you first came to Japan?"

"I came for sesshin with Bernard Phillips," nods Roshi Kapleau, with his hoarse whisper, "and we were going to be introduced to Harada Roshi, so we had to go into the village to buy him a present. We bought the cheapest candy you could get anywhere. Usually it's a Japanese custom that you never open a present in front of a person. There's a very good reason for it, which is that somebody who can't afford good presents might be embarrassed. But this time he opened it. It was awful. I remember him taking a piece out to taste it. It was the worst imaginable candy you could get! You know the Zen saying, 'You have to eat it'?"

Rafe nods. "He saw right through you."

"Yeah." Kapleau pauses, as though reliving the scene. "I was still struggling with half lotus position. He was almost ninety, but he could bend down and touch his feet, do all kinds of postures I wouldn't dream of doing. He'd do these exercises every day with his attendant . . . I think he died at the age of ninety-two."

As our agreed-upon hour together winds on, the figures parade before us: Soen Nakagawa, Harada Roshi, Hakuun Yasutani—alive again, talking, walking, teaching. For a moment I'm overwhelmed at the privilege of simply being present. For a moment, I feel unworthy. Finally, forgetting myself, I'm swept into simply listening. And all at once, it becomes clear what it is I'm doing here: despite his condition, despite his age, this man still wishes to speak a word of Zen, as long as he has a bit of breath left to speak it. When I tell my own teacher, Daido Roshi, about this later, it brings tears to his eyes.

But now it's afternoon, and Roshi Kapleau is growing tired, his voice failing at the beginnings and ends of his sentences, like the far-away fall-off at the end of Zen chants—and through the window it's Rochester, with its tree-lined streets, leaves falling everywhere in a catastrophe of yellows and reds. Roshi, too, is a falling leaf, suspended in mid-drop, turning in the dharma air, going up in fire, in red and yellow patches, like we all are—suspended to rest for a moment in his Lay-Z Boy armchair in his front room, with Kuan Yin in her alcove above his head—voice whispering like wind in the branches, falling, failing, until it becomes nothing but sound itself, till the branches have rubbed out the meaning . . .

A Case of Unmistakable Identity (64)

A visitor for a workshop at the Rochester Zen Center arrived a day early. He assumed the older man he saw about the place was the janitor, only to find out the next day when the workshop began that he was the Roshi, Philip Kapleau.

When Kapleau heard this, he said it was the highest compliment he could have received.

Neither Hard nor Easy (65)

A student once asked Roshi Philip Kapleau whether the koan "Mu" was hard or easy to solve.

"Both," replied Kapleau.

"What do you mean?" asked the questioner.

"Easy," said Kapleau, "because once you resolve it, you realize the 'answer' was there all along. Hard because it takes longest to see what is closest to you."

What Does Zen Say? (66)
A person interested in Zen addressed Philip Kapleau, quoting the "Agnostic's Prayer": "Dear God—if there is a God—save my soul—if I have a soul." He then asked: "What does Zen say about God?"

·Kapleau remained silent.

A period of transition was about to commence. Although the process would take several decades, and would involve many difficulties, its intended outcome was clear: the ancient practices of Zen and other forms of Buddhism would take root in American soil. But how much would the outcome resemble Zen as practiced in its home countries of China, Japan, Korea, and Vietnam? Would the result be Zen at all?

When the historical Buddha, Shakyamuni, seated before a large assembly of practitioners gathered on Vulture Peak to hear him speak, held up a flower instead, only Mahakashyapa smiled in understanding. Thus, the Zen tradition has it, was the true dharma eye transmitted from the Buddha to Mahakashyapa, and passed down in an unbroken continuity of awakened minds to those practicing today. In truth, no one is exactly sure that it happened this way. There are known gaps in the ancient records, and many historians suggest that even Bodhidharma may be a composite figure, made up of several different monks who carried the teachings to China. Still, whether one accepts the chain of transmission as literal or legendary, it *can* be established to have existed unbroken for many hundreds of years, and this alone is enough to account for why the Zen tradition has taken it so seriously.

And so, lineage and succession have always been key issues in Zen Buddhism. It has traditionally been the right, and the responsibility, of each master to sanction one or more successors, or dharma heirs, whose understanding has become ripened through years of practice, and who are, in the teacher's estimation, fully qualified to carry on the tradition. It should come then as no surprise that these should become important, and sometimes muddy, areas in the Zen of America—particularly when so many early practitioners emerged from the counterculture, with its distrust of form and authority. Some practitioners, and even teachers, have questioned the relevance of carrying on the transmission; but although these issues would later boil over into full-blown controversy, in the Sixties and Seventies the tradition of mind-to-mind transmission was mostly accepted as a given.

One thing was clear, at least to the Asian and early American teachers who carried Zen practice to this continent: unless the torch could be passed to the next generation, establishing a lineage of Western teachers and masters, the dharma would never truly take root here.

Even as the earliest American teachers—Philip Kapleau, Walter Nowick, Robert Aitken and Jiyu-Kennett—returned from Japan in the 1960s and 1970s to initiate the first Zen practice centers founded by Americans on American soil, the centers already established here by teachers such as Shunryu Suzuki, Maezumi Roshi, Seung Sahn, and others, were starting to produce mature, well-trained students. The dharma wheel was beginning to turn; and it was looking like it might just keep on rolling.

The following are stories of pivotal moments between teachers and their American students, as well as of the passing of the first Asian teachers—the new Bodhidharmas who brought this ancient practice to the New World.

This Side Up? (67)

Bernie Glassman, as first dharma heir to Maezumi Roshi, became in 1978 the first American to go through the formal *zuise* ceremony in the Soto sect of Zen, at Sojiji Temple in Japan. This traditional event marked his formal sanction as a Zen priest, while his dharma transmission from Maezumi Roshi in 1976 marked his formal sanction as a Zen teacher. In a recent conversation, he gave this account of the event:

"I went through zuise mainly to pay homage to Dogen and Keizan Zenji. You're escorted to these formal zuise quarters—it's all red carpets, and you wear red slippers and a red kesa [a formal monastic vestment]. You're essentially abbot elect. There's a book that tells you how to lead the services. The books are different in each monastery, on purpose. That's very important in Japan, that there be some consistency but that every place has its own air, its own style. So I'm looking at the book—of course it's all in Japanese— though now they're in English too, and maybe other languages. But I was the first to do it, so they had to call somebody to go over it with me. It was a complicated process. We spent about an hour, and then I was up all night, going over and over it in my head so it would be right. The cues for when I was supposed to do certain things were in Japanese and I had to remember them.

"I remember it was one of the hottest Augusts ever in Japan. I thought it easily had to be 100 degrees. During the ceremony I had this tremendous concentration, because I needed to remember the whole thing, and I was just sweating, standing in a pool of water—my red zagu (bowing mat) was all water. And there was Maezumi Roshi—he couldn't be with me in my quarters, but there he was in the back, watching.

"During the ceremony, you are led to meet the old abbot who's hand-ing the position over for the day. He gives you this very important document which essentially makes you the abbot. It's got calligraphy on the outside, and you're supposed to tuck it in the front of your robe, so it's visible during the entire ceremony.

"Then there's a whole formal thing done in a big greeting hall—all of the roshis are there. It's beautiful. Finally I finish, and I come out to Maezumi Roshi. And you know the first thing he says to me?

"'You put the document upside down!'"

Now We Can Eat Together (68)

In 1971, Suzuki Roshi fell ill, and became jaundiced. For a long time all tests were inconclusive. Fearing hepatitis, his doctors insisted on a strict quarantine of all of his food and eating utensils as a precaution against spreading the infection. Finally Suzuki checked into the hospital for more extensive testing.

Zen Center secretary Yvonne Rand remembers visiting his hospital room on the day his results came through. She found him sitting on the edge of the bed, legs dangling, before a tray filled with food.

"Roshi," she asked, "what did they tell you?"

Suzuki smiled broadly and mouthed the words, "I have cancer."

"Cancer?" repeated Rand, slowly sitting down beside him. "But Roshi—then why are you smiling?"

"Now we can eat together again." With that he picked up a forkful of food and put it in her mouth.

Now the Real Work Begins (69)

When Zen teacher Sunya Kjolhede was a young Zen student at the Rochester Zen Center, she was working on the koan "Mu." During one sesshin, she'd been concentrating fiercely on the koan for seven days and nights when she heard the three bells announcing the end of the final dokusan of the retreat.

"I was downstairs in the zendo," says Kjolhede, "not thinking about beginnings or endings or anything else, just completely gripped by MU. Then that last bell rang out, and it was like everything sort of exploded. Suddenly it was all so clear! I found myself leaping up the stairs to the dokusan room. Before, I'd always been pretty overwhelmed by Roshi and the whole authority thing—now I felt like a lion. Roshi was just coming out of the dokusan room. Laughing, I threw out both my arms and pushed him back in. I can still see the expression on his face so clearly—how he checked me out, his bright eyes twinkling. We sat down on the dokusan mats across from each other and he asked me all sorts of questions. I thought the whole thing was hilarious, but I apparently answered them well enough for him to pass me on the koan."

After the sesshin, Kjolhede reports, "Everyone was standing around and talking outside the zendo and Roshi kind of sidled over to me and said in a low voice, '*Now* the real work begins.'"

Says Kjolhede: "At the time I thought he was making some kind of weird joke. Little did I realize then how true his words were."

Mountain Seat (70)

By the time Suzuki Roshi was diagnosed with gall bladder cancer in 1971, he'd already initiated the process of passing the dharma transmission to his long-time student, Richard Baker, thereby marking him as his sole American dharma heir, and one of the first Westerners to formally become a Zen teacher. This account of the Mountain Seat Ceremony, performed less than two weeks before Suzuki Roshi's death, and marking Baker's succession as Abbot of San Francisco Zen Center, was written by a San Francisco Zen Center student, Dennis Lahey, who witnessed the event. It originally appeared in *Wind Bell*, the Zen Center magazine.

. . . *When [Suzuki], at the head of the procession, entered the Hall, I was shocked to see him as frail and shrunken as the man who appeared, a ghost of the person whose immense vigor and spiritual strength had guided the center through the first uncertain years of its existence. He entered, practically being carried by his son, but holding his staff firmly, and thumping it on the matting as he approached the Mountain Seat . . . Richard Baker ascended the steps of the platform and stood, several feet above the onlookers, offering incense to the Buddhas and Bodhisattvas and the Patriarchs, to the benefactors of the temple, and, finally, to his own beloved teacher, Suzuki Roshi. He said:*

> *"This piece of incense*
> *Which I have had for a long time*
> *I offer with no-hand*
> *To my Master, to my friend, Suzuki Shunryu-daiosho*
> *The founder of these temples.*
> *There is no measure of what you have done.*
> *Walking with you in the Buddha's gentle rain*
> *Our robes are soaked through*
> *But on the lotus leaves*
> *Not a drop remains."*

Then Katagiri Roshi, acting for Suzuki Roshi, recited the brief authentication verse with a full-bodied shout, in true Zen fashion. For his sermon, Baker Roshi stated simply, "There is nothing to be said."

This was perfectly true. Then followed the so-called Dharma questions, when the other priests seek to test the new Abbot's understanding. The following dialogue ensued between Baker Roshi and the priest from the Mill Valley Zendo:

Bill Kwong: "Chief Priest!"

Baker Roshi: "Is it host or guest?"

Bill Kwong (shouts): "Iiiie!"

Baker Roshi: "Show me your True Nature without shouting!"

Bill then simply bowed, and returned to his seat.

Following congratulatory telegrams and such, the ceremony was concluded. Suzuki Roshi was helped to his feet and moved to the front of the altar to make his bow. But when he turned to face the people, there was on his face an expression at once fierce and sad. His breath puffed mightily in his nostrils, and he looked as if he strove vigorously to speak, to say something, perhaps to exhort the disciples to be strong in their practice, or to follow Richard Baker with faith; no one can say. He faced the congregation directly as if to speak, and instead rolled his staff between his hands sounding [its brass rings] twice, once looking to the left and once to the right side of the hall.

It was as though some physical shock had passed through the hall; there was a collective intake of breath, and suddenly, everywhere people were weeping openly. All those who had been close to the Roshi now realized fully what it would mean to lose him, and were overcome with a thoroughly human sorrow. As their Master falteringly walked from the hall, still marking each step with his staff, everyone put their hands palm to palm before their faces in the gesture known as gassho, and bowed deeply.

Flown the Coop? (71)

At a certain point in his training, Clark Strand was appointed without prior notice by his teacher, Eido Shimano, to be in charge of his New York City Zendo, promoting him over a number of other students who had more seniority. Eido Roshi proceeded to make various public references to this action—"Just enough," says Strand, "to get everybody stirred up and mad as hornets." Then the roshi promptly announced that after more than twenty years of residency in the U.S., he was going back to Japan for an entire year. Shortly thereafter, Strand accompanied his teacher to the airport and put him on the plane.

"I'd never given a public Zen talk as a teacher," says Strand, "or served in a position of authority. He'd hardly said a word to me on the way to the airport. I felt abandoned and forsaken. That very night I had to conduct a retreat for forty or fifty people. I had no instructions, hadn't been told whether I was to teach or not to teach, nothing. All of the students were seated in the zendo on the first floor, waiting for me. Probably a lot of them felt as abandoned as I did."

Panicked at having to face the group on his own, Strand stalled as long as he could on the upper floor of the building. Finally, he had no choice but to begin the retreat.

"I'd started to walk down," says Strand, "when I noticed the light on in Eido Roshi's office. This was odd, because he always made sure everything was taken care of perfectly. On his desk there was a book that had been left open. I thought, this doesn't make any sense. What's going on? I reached to turn out the light, and noticed the book was a koan collection, opened to 'Hakujo and the Wild Duck.' I sat down and read the koan. In it Matsu and Hakujo are walking. Hakujo points to a wild duck and says, 'What's that?'"

Matsu responds, 'It's a wild duck.'" Hakujo waits a second and asks, "Where did it go?"

Matsu says, "It flew away."

Then Hakujo reaches out and grabs Matsu's nose and twists it. "See," he says, "it didn't fly away at all!"

"I just sat there and laughed," says Strand, "Laughed at this wonderful teaching he left, knowing that I would see it. And so I went down and gave the talk, and that was the first Zen talk I ever gave. After that, it was easy."

Only Breath, Breathing (72)

Zen teacher Yvonne Rand, long-time San Francisco Zen Center secretary and one of Suzuki Roshi's primary caretakers in the last months of his life, gives the following account of his last days:

During the months before Suzuki Roshi died, his wife and I alternated taking care of him. At the time, each day just seemed like an ordinary day, and taking care of him was very straightforward and simple. There was a kind of presence and thoroughness in the way he was when he was dying, an extraordinary teaching of the inseparability of how one lives and how one dies. It was only afterwards, when I look back on those months that I realized that this was really extraordinary. But it was extraordinary ordinariness.

His doctor kept worrying about how much pain he must be in, as he had metastasized gall bladder cancer, which is supposed to be very painful. Suzuki Roshi always said "I'm fine." He did finally one day take some pain medication so his doctor would feel better. But he didn't like what it did to his mind.

Early on the morning of his final day, around 3 a.m., he told his wife he wanted to take a bath. After the bath he got back into bed and told his wife he wanted to see Richard Baker. [According to Baker's own account, upon his arrival he greeted his dying teacher by asking Suzuki Roshi, "Where shall we meet?"]

Suzuki Roshi responded by drawing a big sumi-e circle [the enso, or Zen circle, symbolizing wholeness, or completeness] in the air with his finger. A seven day sesshin was scheduled to begin that morning. Suzuki Roshi died just as the bell to open the retreat was sounding.

Everyone came, one by one through that first morning of sesshin, to do their last "dokusan" with him. Later I went with Richard Baker and Suzuki Roshi's son to the mortuary. The mortuary people let us prepare his body and put him in his robes and put his body in the coffin. They gave us a chapel room where someone could sit in meditation with him every day for a week. There was a sort of stage with sliding stained glass windows behind it. At the end of the week, when the time came to cremate the body, no one would leave. We just kept staying.

Finally the mortuary people, realizing no one was going anywhere, slid open the stained glass doors. The group stepped back there and lifted his coffin into the crematorium oven. Mrs. Suzuki pushed the button and started the fire, then we all went out and sat down until the cremation was over. The mortuary people didn't quite know what to make of it.

I think for those of us who were taking care of him, there wasn't this kind of sharp, "he's gone." What I learned from being in that situation was that there's actually a continuum of dying: death, sitting with the body, watching it change and then cremation, and then taking care of the ashes. So there was this very expanded process called "dying." And Suzuki Roshi really opened that *experience, so that I saw what was possible. His passing was just a continuation of his life. Toward the end he'd been so hardly there—he was like a wisp. And in the end there was only breath, breathing.*

Dainin Katagiri visited Suzuki Roshi just before he died. As Katagiri stood by the bedside, Suzuki looked up and said, "I don't want to die."

Katagiri bowed and said, "Thank you for your great effort."

Shortly before his death, Suzuki Roshi told Stan White: "Don't grieve for me. I know who I am. I know where I'm going. Don't worry about a thing."

Tea for Four (73)

John Daido Loori had been invited to the Naropa Institute to give a summer course in Mindful Photography, and ended up staying in an apartment next to Maezumi Roshi, who was also participating in the summer program. One night, there was a gathering at Maezumi's with a number of his students and other participants. At the time, Loori was a student of Soen Nakagawa Roshi, who was no longer coming to the U.S. very often to teach. Maezumi took to him for some reason, insisting that he stay beside him all evening, and continuing to ask him ambiguous questions which Loori had no idea how to answer.

"Daido," Maezumi would say, bending uncomfortably close to his face. "Ask me!"

"Ask you what, Roshi?" Loori would answer.

Maezumi would be silent for a while, then: "Daido, Tell me!"

"Tell you what, Roshi?"

This exchange went on for hours, until the small hours of the morning, as the gathering died down and the crowd dwindled away. Finally, Loori managed to pry himself loose from Maezumi and go back to his apartment to get some rest. Since it was so late, he stretched out on the couch in his living room, not wanting to wake his wife, who'd gone to bed long before. He'd just managed to relax himself enough to nod off when a knock came at the door. Loori rose to open it and found Maezumi Roshi standing there, immaculate and wide awake, dressed in formal robes with his head freshly shaven.

"Daido," said Maezumi. "Come with me."

Loori obeyed. Maezumi led him back to the apartment next door, which had been restored to perfect order. The round table in the dining area was now set for a formal Japanese tea ceremony. Oddly, though there were only two of them there, it had four place settings.

"Come," said Maezumi, gesturing toward the table. "We will have tea." He pointed to the first place, saying: "Soen Roshi," who was Loori's teacher. He indicated the second setting, saying: "Yasutani Roshi"—Maezumi's own teacher, recently deceased. He pointed to the third, saying: "Daido." The last was for himself. Maezumi then proceeded to perform a formal tea ceremony, serving all four places beginning with Soen Roshi, though only the two of them were present. As Loori sipped his tea he felt so moved that tears began to fall from his eyes.

When he looked up at Maezumi, he saw that he was crying too.

Maezumi Roshi's last dharma words, written on the evening before his death in 1995:

The Dharma of Thusness has been intimately conveyed from Buddhas and Ancestors.
It has been transmitted, generation after generation, down to me.
To complete or not to complete is of no consequence.
Enlightenment above enlightenment
Delusion within delusion
Is also of no consequence.
Manifest Genjo Koan
Play freely in inward and outward fulfilling samadhi
Maintain and nourish the one Buddha Mind Seal.
Life after life, rebirth after rebirth, practice diligently.
Do not regress.
Do not let the wisdom seed of the Buddhas and ancestors be discontinued
Thus I deeply implore you

The year 1995 in the Month of Azaleas, Los Angeles,
Abbot of Dairyuzan Busshin-ji,
Humbly,
Koan Taizan

part three

TRANSMISSION COMPLETE

Zen teacher Danan Henry reports a remark made by a visiting Japanese Zen priest during a discussion about the many challenges involved in transplanting Buddhism to the West.

"Yes," agreed the visitor. "The first hundred years are always the hardest."

HOW LONG IS A KALPA?

Walter Nowick used to tell his students: "Lao-tzu once said 'Every man is a good man.' However," he would add, "that's not the part that concerns us."

Stephen and I mount the hill to where Walter Nowick, with that peculiarly vigorous walk certain older men possess, is shuttling purposefully between a wheelbarrow and an arrangement of large stone blocks. I'd thought when Stephen pointed the place out from the road yesterday that the blocks were simply building materials left over from the fire that consumed Walter's house some ten years ago—and so they are. But as we crest the hill it becomes apparent the stones are not just lying where they fell, but have been arranged into a sort of mandala shape, with five enormous stone lintels, propped on supporting blocks, pointing out like fingers over the valley below.

Walter, wearing a white baseball cap and the kind of wraparound sunglasses one expects to see on a brightly-clad cyclist, is now kneeling, spading moss from the wheelbarrow into position around the stones. He rises to meet us. "Like my Stonehenge?" he asks, with a broad gesture toward the arrangement. His smile is brilliant—and his greeting reminds me eerily of a scene from my own novel, *The Hope Valley Hubcap King*, in which the hero finally meets the eccentric sage he's spent the whole book seeking, and finds the old fellow arranging a sculpture upon the ground.

"Walter," says Stephen as he embraces his old teacher, "Did you move these stones yourself? Weren't they all stacked up behind the barn the last time I was here?"

Walter shrugs. "I just tipped 'em into the wheelbarrow and from there on it was easy. I had Alan help me with the long ones, but the rest I did myself."

We look appreciatively at the arrangement. The blocks must weigh 150 pounds each.

"This is Sean," Stephen says.

Walter shakes my hand, then gestures to a tree stump and sits himself on another across from me. "Have a seat. Now, what's all this book business you want to talk to me about?" He peers at me from behind his sunglasses as I settle into place. "As you may have heard, I'm not very big on books."

We're off and running. Stephen had warned me that Walter was likely to be "squirrely"—his aversion to curiosity seekers, the press, and the like, is legendary. Although a world-class pianist, he's refused to record, tour, or perform in anything resembling the conventional manner. It's entirely possible, despite the fact that Stephen was a close student of his, that he may refuse to speak to me at all—as, rumor has it, he turned away Alan Watts once when the philosopher came to see him. Besides, as far as Zen goes, Walter is officially retired.

Walter smiles again, widely, and I see his teeth, small stone-like rectangles. "Well," I begin, "I'm compiling a collection of contemporary American Zen stories, and since I know you were one of the first Westerners to formally study Zen—"

"Ahhh, the first, the second, the one-half—what does that matter? But here, the sun's in your eyes—let's switch seats." With this he rises to his feet.

His combination of evasiveness and concern confuses me. "But then the sun will be in yours."

"That's why I've got these," Walter taps his wraparound shades as he herds me over to the opposite stump and we both sit back down. "So tell me," he continues, not missing a beat, "this is *your* book, isn't it? What does that have to do with me? How can *I* help with *your* book?"

"Well, Stephen and I practice together at Zen Mountain Monastery, and he's been telling me about his years of training with you—" At this point a car pulls into the driveway and Walter springs to his feet to investigate. He's no more than halfway there however, when the car backs up and drives off again. Walter takes a turnabout too, and now he's back and we're dancing the dance again.

"So what I'd like," I start over, "is to maybe hear a bit about your early experiences—"

By this time Walter's wearing a permanent half-smile as he jousts and banters at me from behind his shades. "I'm busy. I've got projects. Practicing. And what good is *reading* about Zen anyway?"

"But what if a book can lead people to practice?"

At this point a propane truck pulls up and Walter's off once more.

Stephen shakes his head and smiles at me. "You've got a tiger by the tail. He could go on for hours like this, or decide to give in and talk—or just cut the whole thing off." He shrugs his shoulders; I shrug back. I'm feeling strangely relaxed—through some internal process I don't entirely understand I've come to the conclusion that I might as well enjoy the experience, whatever happens. Even a refusal from Walter would be colorful.

But the interaction with the propane man must have brought him to some decision, because this time Walter just walks up and says, "Well, as long as you're here, maybe you'd like to see the Buddha Hall?"

Next thing I know, we're trooping down the slope, Walter between us, in the direction of a small wooden building. All at once, Walter turns and takes me by the elbow, practically lifting me into the air with the vigor of the action. He looks straight into my eyes—he's got his glasses lifted now, and he's got the palest, clearest blue eyes I've ever seen, like there's nothing in them but sky—and he says something like, "Well, so what do you think about all this then, Sean? Eh?" And again I see those small perfect teeth in that broader-than-life smile. With his white hair spilling from beneath that baseball cap he might have been a tow-headed ten-year-old, hurrying me along to his clubhouse to show me his baseball cards.

Then we're inside—"Watch your head," as I step through the low door, and "watch your feet," as Stephen steps through. "Well," announces Walter, "this is it—the Buddha Hall." Built, like his "Stonehenge," of salvaged remnants of his house, the roof is of smoke-stained boards shading darkly to charcoal at the edges. The far side of the building is unfinished, a blend of glass and Plexiglas panels with a blue plastic tarp tied across the gable. The walls are lined with ancient-looking Chinese and Japanese texts.

"Boy, Walter," I say, "For someone who doesn't like books, you've sure got a lot of them." Walter just smiles; I'm beginning to realize he's a bit hard of hearing from all those years spent operating the saw mill he and his students started at the farm.

Having invited us to sit on cushions on the tatami matting, he steps to the altar, where he assembles a small shrine, placing— who? Perhaps it's Kannon, Bodhisattva of Compassion—back upon his/her lotus seat. "It's original thirteenth century, given to me by my teacher before I left Japan," explains Walter. "I don't like to leave it up when there's no one here. I'm afraid it'll fall over. Don't know what I'll do with it one of these days—have to send it back, I suppose, since there's no one I want to leave it to. Wouldn't seem right for it to just end up in a museum." His words seem more than a bit poignant, given the fact that he's finished his career as a Zen teacher without leaving a dharma heir.

But now Walter's pulling down texts from the shelves, and he's rapidly building up a head of steam. He's explaining the differences between ancient Chinese and Japanese transliteration systems, pointing out ideograms and telling us how he had to learn both in order to study the classic koan collections, which in the 1950s were not yet available in English. Before I know it, he's moved to the Sanskrit roots of Indo-European languages, pausing every once in awhile to say with a sly smile, "But I don't suppose any of this is of any use to your book, is it?" before plunging back in. I don't care about usefulness at this point, I'm simply consumed by this spectacle of a man.

I remember reading somewhere an observation psychoanalyst Erich Fromm made about D.T. Suzuki. Some people, said Fromm, manage to maintain a childlike sense of life's wonder— but only at the expense of cutting off awareness of suffering, and thereby living in a world of illusion. There are some few however, who manage to retain their sense of joy and openness, without closing themselves off from any of life's harsh realities. Suzuki, according to Fromm, was of this type—and Walter strikes me this way as well: both eyes wide open, one seeing the light and the other looking into the darkness, yet somehow sustaining an unceasing enthusiasm for the wondrous absurdity of it all.

But Walter is on a roll, and the conversation is going by so fast I'll never be able to remember a fraction of it. So once our rapport seems well established, I venture, "Excuse me, Walter, but I wonder if you'd mind if I used a tape recorder? It's only a small one, very unobtrusive."

There's a moment of silence, during which he examines at me curiously. Then it's, "Naahh, what do you want to do that for?"

"Well—" I begin, "I'll never be able to remember all this . . ."

"So what do you want to remember all *this* for?"

"You see, my mind—"

"Ahh, there's nothing wrong with your mind!"

So I let the matter drop, and now I'm just *here*, not trying to remember, while the light slants bluish through the tarp and the entire history of the East, it seems, unrolls before us. At last, after an hour or more, Walter asks abruptly, "Are you cold?"

To which Stephen, who after living in Walter's community for fourteen years has probably experienced enough New England winters to last several lifetimes, says "yes," and we move up to the barn, where there is a pellet stove, to continue our conversation.

Stephen found Walter by chance, while on his way to Canada in 1972 with his wife-to-be in search of a spiritual community. At a crossroads along the way, they ran into some acquaintances who directed them here, and the Canada trip was abandoned. At that point, Walter had been teaching for only five years or so, having returned from Japan in the 1960s, bearing one-third of Goto Zuigan's ashes. His teacher had instructed Walter to return to America after his death, but told him to wait five years before teaching Zen. Partly, perhaps, to make sure Walter *did* return, his brother bought him 500 acres of farm and woodland on the coast of Maine to do with as he pleased. It turned out to be the perfect setting for one of the first Zen communities begun by an American teacher.

Walter first returned to teaching music, his primary means of support during his time in Japan. After the five years were up, he faced the daunting task of trying to invent an authentic form of practice that would work on American soil, without having any prior models from which to depart. Although a sanctioned holder of his teacher's Rinzai Zen lineage, Walter always eschewed the use of titles or ranks. He told me during our conversation that his own teacher rarely even used the word "Zen." Walter did maintain many of the aspects of traditional practice, however—including the custom of rejecting aspiring seekers in order to test their determination.

When Stephen and his wife-to-be showed up to inquire about entering training, they were greeted with the words, "Go away, he doesn't want to see you!" from a visiting Japanese monk. They left, and returned, and left again, not knowing how long this process might go on. Rumor has it that one student drove the nearly ten hours from New York City eight times and was refused on every occasion, only to be accepted as a student on his ninth attempt.

The last time the couple returned, they glimpsed Nowick himself, driving a tractor some distance from the house, and they set off across the intervening fields to approach him directly.

"No! No!" Walter began to shout, standing up in the tractor seat and waving his arms as he saw them approaching. "Go away! I don't need any more students!" But when at last they reached him, Walter climbed down from his seat saying, "So what do you all want from me, anyway?" When they explained that they wanted to become students of Zen, he said something like, "Well, I suppose I'm going to have to take you on then, aren't I?" and embraced them both.

It was Walter's custom during that period to deed an acre of land to each family that joined the community so they could build a house. Single people stayed in small cabins on the grounds. Many of the residents not only lived and practiced there, but worked alongside Walter every day, six days a week, except when a retreat was on. Ignoring the fact that many a sawyer ends up missing a finger or two, Walter set up a working sawmill on the property, and operated the saw himself day after day, never seeming to worry that the activity might not be entirely compatible with his other calling as a pianist—or perhaps trusting in the close awareness developed through Zen training to protect him.

Several years after moving onto the place, Stephen asked Walter if he could begin working at the mill, only to receive the same treatment he'd received when he'd asked to become a student. "No," answered Walter each time he asked. Finally Stephen mustered the boldness—no doubt the point of the exercise—to just show up one spring day, when the mill was starting up for the season.

"What are *you* doing here?" Walter asked him.

"I came to work," said Stephen.

"Hmm," said Walter, looking around at the other students. "Well, I guess as long as he's here, we can let him sweep up, can't we?" With that he handed Stephen a broom—and Stephen found his occupation for the next eight years.

Though such methods as these have given Nowick a reputation for sometimes being harsh—and apparently, he could be, if it was necessary for a student's practice—Stephen remembers his years of working with Walter as having been largely filled with warmth and laughter.

"He had a way of shaking you out of yourself," says Stephen. "If you showed up in a bad mood, or were down in the dumps about something, he'd tease and prod at you, point out the beauty of the sky or the day, till you had to laugh at yourself, and just get on with what needed to be done. Or he'd purposely get the truck or the tractor stuck in the mud, so that you had a project that needed focusing on—anything to bring you out of yourself."

Stephen had already shown me the zendo, set at the bottom of a slope in a traditionally Japanese setting, beside a pond with cattails. The interior reflected perfect craftsmanship—raised tans with rice stalk tatami mats and lots of exposed wood. The upright trunks of cedar trees served as support posts, the one marking the teacher's seat spiraled and twisted, as though struck by lightning. You could feel the years of intensive practice that had taken place here.

But now we're up at the barn, which currently serves as the performance space for the international opera troupe Walter put together after his retirement from teaching Zen, and for his own piano recitals. The acoustics of the place are said to be so ideal that it was used as the model for the famous Wolftrap performance "barn" in Virginia. Walter, trickster figure that he is, is spinning off on long tangents about culture and government and human nature. "Skullduggery. Nothing but skullduggery," he's fond of saying about corporations, big business, governments, and any other power structure he feels like taking on—and just when I think he'll never come back to Zen he turns with a smile and says, "but this isn't helping you with what *you* want to know, is it?"

"How was it," I ask, taking an opening, "to come as an American into the monastic atmosphere at Daitokuji, having to pay strict obedience to your teacher, no matter how difficult it became? Did you ever question what you were doing?"

Walter shrugs and smiles. "If you want to play the piano in a certain style," he says, "You find the person who teaches that style best, and do what they say. If you want to do something else, you do something else. But if you want to learn what *they* have to teach, you follow their directions." He's silent for a moment. "Besides, I had before me, every day in sanzen, this great shining man, Goto Zuigan. I never doubted he knew what he was doing."

We talk a little about his retirement from teaching, and his work with the opera company, which he established as a project to open cultural exchange between the United States and the Soviet Union at a time when cold war tensions were dangerously high. The group toured the Soviet Union, as well as other Eastern Bloc countries and Japan. Despite being made up largely of amateurs, some of whom were Zen students with no prior training in music, the group received standing ovations from Russian audiences who were accustomed to the best in Europe.

"I just couldn't feel comfortable any longer," said Walter, "with sitting here pursuing our own practice while out there tensions were building that could destroy the planet. In former times Zen could afford to be apolitical, even during times of conflict, because whatever the damage, it was going to be limited. But when you have war machines out there that can destroy everything—well, at a certain point, I just had to do something. What I knew how to do was music."

After three hours of non-stop, high energy interaction, I'm worn out, though Walter seems as fresh and bright as when we began. Finally, after we're interrupted by a phone call, Walter says, "Well, I've done plenty of talking at this point, don't you think—?" and I take this as a signal that he wants to draw the afternoon's dialogue to a close. We do, after all, have plans to meet him for dinner later that evening. As we walk back to the car, however, Stephen says this was just Walter's way of feeling *me* out, to see if I was finished. "He could have gone on that way for another couple of hours," Stephen says. "I haven't seen him this willing to talk in a long time. He was enjoying himself. He just wanted to let *us* off the hook."

Later, over dinner and drinks at the local Thai restaurant, Walter gets political again. "Everyone's got a point of view. How many points of view can you have? You can have 10,000 if you want. This one says I disagree with that one, that one says I disagree with the next, another says I disagree with both of you fellows. What does it add up to? Skullduggery!"

"Do you think Buddhism will really take root here in America?" I ask.

"Ahhh, most of these people, they're not really interested in Buddhism. They're interested in what they can *get*. Or they're interested in *talking* about Buddhism. Now Goto Zuigan, there was a man. Don't think that's me. Noooo . . ." Walter sips at his martini. "Do you know how long it will take to solve the problems of the human race?" he asks suddenly, leaning close, blue eyes boring into mine. "Many kalpas. Do you know how long a kalpa is?"

I shake my head.

"Imagine an angel flies down out of heaven every hundred years, and the sleeve of her kimono brushes the top of Mt. Fuji. As long as it takes to wear away the mountain. Or Manhattan— the whole city is filled with sesame seeds. Once every hundred years an ant takes one and carries it away. How long till they're all gone? That's a kalpa."

Eyes That See in the Dark (74)

Walter Nowick was giving a piano concert one evening. He was playing Beethoven's Piano Sonata #32, a composition legendary for its difficulty, when the power suddenly failed and the performance space was plunged into darkness. Without missing a note, Nowick played the sonata through to the end.

Later, he was asked how he'd managed to continue when he could no longer read his sheet music.

"If you can't play it in the darkness," replied Nowick, "—you can't play it in the light."

Don't Hurt the Bird (75)

An important aspect of practice in Walter Nowick's Zen community was the daily life of working on a farm. Despite the general belief to the contrary, many Zen Buddhists are not vegetarians, seeing the life of a cabbage to be as valuable as that of a chicken, and acknowledging the inevitability of taking life in order to live. But perhaps because the taking of life creates karma, Nowick always did the slaughtering of chickens himself.

One day as Nowick was at the chopping block, he noticed that one of the fowl being held by a student as it waited its turn was obviously distraught, maybe because the student was squeezing it too hard.

"Hey," Nowick admonished him, "Don't hurt the bird."

Light and Shadow (76)

Walter Nowick liked to tell his Zen students the tale of a New Year's Eve party where a knock came at the front door and the attendees opened it to admit their guest of honor: Fortune, dressed in all his finery. After all the celebration had died down however, someone heard a faint scratching sound coming from the back door. They opened it and a scrawny, filthy creature entered the room, bringing the festivities to a standstill.

"Who are you?" someone finally asked.

"Misfortune," croaked the creature, then pointed at the guest of honor. "Where he goes, I follow."

chapter seven

TAKING ROOT

When Zen teacher Mitra Bishop was traveling in Japan, a Japanese woman, on seeing her shaved head, approached her shyly and asked in English, "Are you Obasan (a Zen nun)?"
"Yes," replied Bishop.
"This is really funny," said the Japanese woman. "I'm a Jehovah's Witness."

Somehow, a remarkable thing has happened. Just as it occurred in ancient China, Korea, Vietnam, and Japan, the Zen teachings brought by Bodhidharma from India have, by some strange quirk of karma, taken root in twenty-first-century America. Estimates vary wildly, but it seems safe to say there are now over a million Buddhist practitioners in the U.S., a large number of whom are practicing Zen. The seeds brought by Sokei-an, Nyogen Senzaki, and D.T. Suzuki, and watered by Suzuki Roshi, Thich Nhat Hanh, Seung Sahn, and many others, are well on their way to growing into a great tree.

The transition has not always been easy. Questions of lineage and authentic transmission of the dharma have beset a number of teachers and centers, and controversy has sprung up in communities led by both Asian and American teachers, regarding issues of spiritual authority and ethical conduct. Though these growing pains have resulted in turmoil, they have also resulted in development. After all, traditional Zen Buddhism, being a monastic form, had little to say about worldly issues such as sexuality, relationships, and family, which are of tremendous importance in the West. But as it is quite a flexible form—being after all composed of emptiness—our American version of Zen seems to be expanding successfully to accommodate these new imperatives, and this period of rapid expansion and turmoil is settling down to a steady and reliable pattern of growth.

Social activism is just one of many issues that have risen to new prominence in Buddhism because of the influence of the West. Some changes, such as equal opportunity for women as practitioners and teachers, were part of Zen in America from the beginning, and are even beginning to exert an influence back in their countries of origin. Other factors, such as the intermingling of Zen practice with Christianity and psychology, and the dominance of lay practitioners, are still largely Western concerns. Some feel these developments will strengthen the practice; others fear that key aspects, such as the direct experience of realization, may be diluted or lost in the process. And what about the form—the "look" and feel of Zen ritual and costume; can it be Americanized without losing something essential? If it cannot, will Zen ever truly take hold here?

Right Action—Zen Practice and Social Activism

The mercy of the West has been social revolution; the mercy of the East has been individual insight into the basic self/void. We need both.
—Gary Snyder

"The whole notion of Engaged Buddhism," says Cynthia Jurs, a Zen teacher in the lineage of Thich Nhat Hanh, "is about practicing deeply with the awareness of the problems we face, and not avoiding them, but really looking deeply, and addressing things directly. How are we ever going to arrive at peace out there if we're not cultivating it within ourselves?"

"[Social action] arises from the sense that 'I include all others,'" explains Robert Aitken Roshi, one of the early American pioneers in the field. "It's an experience of inclusiveness, that *I* include the folks in Iraq that are being deprived. I don't see it as something that's 'improving' my realization. It's just that I'm oriented like that. And my Buddhism informs my social action."

"All people, whether perpetrators or victims, are in the same family, like it or not, and how you treat people is pivotal," says Hozan Alan Senauke, who at the time of this writing was director of the Buddhist Peace Fellowship, which was founded by Robert Aitken, Nelson Foster and others in 1978.

The bodhisattva path in Mahayana Buddhism, of which Zen is an outgrowth, has always insisted on the principle of liberating all sentient beings before oneself; but for most of the 1500 years or so of Zen's development, the majority of practitioners have been content to understand this teaching in spiritual rather than practical terms. With the rise of "engaged Buddhism" however, a movement that has come largely out of the collision of East and West, practitioners are increasingly feeling the need to bring these principles into the realm of social, environmental and political action.

Bernie Glassman, in his book, *Bearing Witness,* puts it this way:

If there's a gash in my left leg and blood is spurting out, my hands don't say, "Too bad, let the leg take care of itself, we're too busy to take care of it right now." If my stomach is hungry my right hand doesn't say, "I'm too busy to put food in the mouth." But that's what happens in life, in society. And it happens only because we have an illness called separation. If we don't see that the hands, legs, feet, head, and hair are all one body, we don't take care of them and we suffer. If we don't see the unity of life, we don't take care of life and we suffer.

True Intimacy (77)

A student once asked Philip Kapleau if the Bodhisattva of Compassion, Avalokitesvara, also known as Kannon, or Kuan Yin, actually existed.

"To meet (her) face to face," answered Kapleau, "All you have to do is perform a selfless deed."

Taking Care of Each Other (78)

An interviewer once asked Issan Dorsey about the relation between his work with the Maitri Hospice program and engaged Buddhism. Dorsey responded, "I don't understand this concept of 'engaged Buddhism.' If you fall down, I pick you up. If you cut your hand, I give you a Band-aid. This is not engaged Buddhism. This is how we take care of each other."

Right Action, then, means sweeping the garden. To quote my teacher, Oda Sesso: "In Zen there are only two things: you sit, and you sweep the garden." It doesn't matter how big the garden is.

—Gary Snyder

Lotus in the Fire: Freedom behind Bars

What happens in practice, and in bringing practice to people who are marginalized and suffering, is you realize that's you. That's certainly been my experience with men on death row. It requires such transparency, immediacy, and honesty. It's a world without consolation, but it's characterized by a lot of authenticity. The way I look at it is that I've matriculated in the best school in the world: the Penitentiary of New Mexico, and my teachers are the inmates and correctional officers who are there. I feel profoundly instructed by it.

—Joan Halifax

What is freedom? Is it dependent upon one's environment, on the conditions in which one finds oneself, or is it innate to the human condition and accessible anywhere? Questions such as these pose a more than theoretical dilemma to the growing population of Buddhist practitioners who maintain their practice behind bars.

The National Buddhist Prison Sangha had its origins in a letter sent to John Daido Loori of Zen Mountain Monastery in upstate New York from an inmate at the Green Haven maximum security correctional facility, requesting assistance in establishing a Zen practice group. Prison officials, having only the vague suspicion that Zen was associated with the martial arts, were reluctant to cooperate. The matter eventually went to court, with the outcome that Zen Buddhism was officially recognized as a legitimate religion to be practiced in the New York State prison system.

Fifteen years later, the Fire Lotus Sangha at Green Haven has become a large and vital group of committed practitioners. Zen Mountain Monastery has founded groups at several other prisons, and recently inaugurated the National Buddhist Prison Sangha, a nationwide network with the purpose of bringing together Buddhist inmates and volunteers. The program includes regular correspondence to guide inmates in their practice, donations and loans of books, audiotapes, and videotapes, and visits to area prisons for retreats, services, talks, and ceremonies. Geoffrey Shugen Arnold, Sensei, a Dharma successor to Daido Roshi, now directs the program. During a conversation I had with him at Zen Mountain Monastery about his many years of work with prison inmates, he told this story:

I remember a prisoner came in to see me in a private interview. He presented a koan he was working on, but he wasn't clear on it. Then he told me about a guy in the shop where he worked who had really been getting on his nerves—the tension just kept building and building. Finally something broke, and he couldn't take it any longer. He went running across the room, lunging for this other prisoner.

This student has an immaculate record. He's on an honors block. He's done a tremendous amount of work in the prison, trying to build the life that he'll have once he's paroled. But as he was running across the room, he consciously decided that he was going to throw all that away. He was so angry it seemed worth it to him.

At the last moment, before he actually collided with this other inmate, he thought, "What the hell am I doing? This is crazy." It was as though at that moment his mind of the dharma woke up, and he realized that he was in charge, he was responsible, and that what he was so upset about was really not that important. So instead, at the last second, he just sort of wrapped his arms around this other guy and hugged him—which completely freaked the other prisoner out, because it had been so obvious he was going to hurt him. But the fascinating thing was that what the student did was actually the correct response to that koan he'd tried to present—but in a real live situation. He showed me that he had actually realized that koan, by embodying it in a life situation.

Perhaps because the issue of personal freedom is so much more real to them than it is to the rest of us, many inmate practitioners take to the practice with an exceptional degree of dedication and sincerity. The taking of *jukai*, for instance—the formal commitment to uphold the moral and ethical Precepts of Buddhism—seems often to be a greater priority for them than for the average practitioner. Shugen Sensei explains:

Just a few weeks ago I went in to the prison, and there were two Sangha members who had just gotten into an argument the day before. The senior of the two, who had received the precepts, had really laid into this newer practitioner, and he felt badly about it.

I said, "Why didn't you apologize?" and he said, "Even though I know that's what I need to do, I'm afraid that if I do it right now I won't really be feeling that apology." He didn't want to just say the words. He wanted the other guy to feel that he was really sorry for what he'd done, but he was still too angry to do that. Still, he was well on his way to taking responsibility for it, so I was encouraging.

Then we went in to sit and I gave my talk, and I spoke about how you can never rest in your understanding, you can never just assume you've taken care of all the barriers, all the sticking places, and go to sleep. It's always possible to get lost in something, and to violate the precepts, to hurt somebody. At the very end—the guard was actually knocking at the door for us to leave—the student who'd told me about the argument said, "Wait a minute, I need to say something."

Now remember, in a prison environment a basic principle is not to show yourself as vulnerable. That's a cardinal tenet, because to do that is seen as showing weakness. So there's always a lot of posturing, presenting one's invulnerability. That's the game everybody plays.

So this student gets up and walks across the zendo, and kneels down in front of the inmate he'd had the argument with, and he takes off his rakusu [a vestment that is the mark of having taken the precepts], and says, "I ask your forgiveness. When you can forgive me, please give this back to me." And he puts the rakusu around the other guy's neck.

It really blew me away. To me, that's what it's all about. When it really counts, in a situation where in order to move forward you have to give something up that is very difficult to give up—that's the important thing. There have been many experiences like that, where I see that these guys understand much more about the dharma than they're aware they do.

Shugen Sensei comments on the heightened intensity of Zen practice in prison, where the triumphs, the moments of generosity, compassion and kindness are so vivid because they stand in such contrast to the environment:

In prison there's a tremendous emphasis on keeping things suppressed—to be vulnerable to one's feelings can mean opening yourself to a tremendous amount of misery and anguish.

There was an inmate who came to me one day and told me, "I've been in prisons a lot rougher than this one. I was in a prison where somebody got stabbed nearly every day." He said, "you get so used to it, that you just notice it, and go back to your conversation. You don't feel it, you just sort of pass over it."

But then he told me, "You know, I was in the yard the other day, and somebody got stabbed—and for the first time, it went right through me. In that moment I felt all the pain I carry, that this whole place carries." He said it in the most beautiful way, with innocence, like a child discovering something for the first time.

I looked at him and smiled, and said, "Welcome back."

For me, this was an incredible demonstration of how practice works. If you really engage it over time, you just naturally come back to your own humanity. It was one of those moments that make everything worthwhile.

Layman Pang meets the 21st Century— The Layperson's Revolution in America

"Your life is your practice," Zen teacher Maurine Stuart used to tell her students. "Your life is your koan. Once I went to New York to see Soen Roshi. 'How did you get here?' he asked.

"'I drove my car,' I said.

"'And how are you driving your life?' he asked.

"That's the question."

In the original Buddhist sangha, monks were not permitted to work, but were entirely dependent upon charity—the good will of the populace—for their daily sustenance. When Zen migrated to China, where the climate was more challenging, and the remoteness of many monasteries made relying upon the generosity of others impractical, monastics turned to raising their own food in order to survive. Ever since then, work—drawing water, carrying wood—has become inextricably associated with Zen practice.

In the West, neither charity nor self-sufficiency have proven, in the long run, to be a viable means for supporting Zen centers and practitioners. This condition is further complicated by the fact that the vast majority of Western practitioners are, for the first time in Buddhist history, laypeople rather than monks—a situation which raises not only the issue of work, but that of relationship and family practice.

Identity, or Responsibility? (79)

Zen teacher Steve Allen was driving Robert Aitken Roshi from Green Gulch Farm to a wedding Aitken was about to perform, when he remarked to Aitken that he'd recently attended a meeting at San Francisco Zen Center that had focused on what the identity of a priest ought to be.

"It seemed to me that was the wrong issue," Allen said to the roshi. "It seems the question ought to be not 'what is our identity' but 'what is our responsibility?'"

At that, Allen reports, Aitken, who had always remained a layperson, bellowed out: "Yes—that is the question! What *is* our responsibility?"

That, says Allen, ended the conversation.

Zen and Work

A student visiting with Thich Nhat Hanh asked after a meal if he might help out by doing the dishes.

"Go ahead," said Thich Nhat Hanh, "but if you wash the dishes you must know the way to wash them."

"Do you think I don't know how to wash dishes?" replied the student.

"There are two ways to wash the dishes," replied Thich Nhat Hanh. "The first is to wash the dishes in order to have clean dishes. The second is to wash the dishes in order to wash the dishes."

Zen teacher Les Kaye worked in various capacities for a large corporation throughout his many years of Zen training. In his book *Zen at Work,* he describes how he applied the insights gained from Zen practice to his anxiety about trying to make a sales pitch: "I learned something very interesting about fear: it arose only when I thought about the possible negative impact on *me*—Will I fail? Will I make a fool of myself?—rather than about the work and the potential positive effect on the company. As long as I kept my mind on what I was doing, I was OK. As experiences with work and with Zen multiplied, I began to recognize a variety of similarities between these two presumably different worlds of practice. Starting at the personal level, I saw that the being-in-the-world qualities emphasized in Zen were no different from the character traits that [my company] emphasized in its people: integrity, morality, a capacity for work, self-discipline, willingness to learn, attention to detail, responsibility, and perseverance."

"I remember," says Dairyu Michael Wenger, the Dean of Buddhist Studies for the San Francisco Zen Center, looking back several decades to the early years of his practice, "I was working at Greens [Zen Center's vegetarian restaurant], and it was a very chaotic situation. You'd really be pressed, getting up very early in the morning and working very hard. At the time I'd started to study the Lotus Sutra and I thought 'studying the Lotus Sutra—now *that's* what I really want to be doing.' But instead I was working very hard at the restaurant.

"I was wanting to see the Lotus Sutra as this idealistic, religious thing—but the Lotus Sutra is about what is happening right now. And at a certain point, because this is a very sneaky sutra, I realized the restaurant *was* the Lotus Sutra—and that was a very big turning point.

"Have you ever heard the teaching of the Five Perfections? They're the Perfect Time, the Perfect Place, the Perfect Teaching, the Perfect Teacher, and the Perfect Student. The Perfect Time always means right now, and the Perfect Place is right here. Where else is there—Tang dynasty China? The Perfect Teaching means that whatever you're dealing with is the thing you're dealing with—there's nothing else. The Perfect Teacher is whoever you're learning from. Even if they mess up, that's teaching. And then the hardest thing for people to realize is the Perfect Student. That we're not inadequate. We can meet the situation.

"You see, Zen training is about learning to be *anyone*. It's not about getting the ideal temperature or the ideal food or the ideal job or the ideal environment. Most of the time people just develop the things they're good at—but they're held back by what they're not good at. But if you have to hit a drum in a certain way, and you can't hit that drum, you learn a lot.

"Zen, in some sense, isn't about outcomes."

Sacred Vessels (80)

Brother David, a Viennese psychologist who came to the United States in the late Forties, became a Benedictine monk, and went on to practice Zen, was head dishwasher one summer at Tassajara Monastery. Afterward he sent the work foreman the following suggestions for future dishwashers:

We should listen to the sound of the water and the scrubbing, to the various sounds the dishes make when they hit each other. The sounds of our work tell us much about our practice ... Most people dislike dishwashing. Maybe they can learn to appreciate the touch of the wooden bowls, the pots and mugs and everything they handle, the weight of what we lift up and set down, the various smells and sounds. St. Benedict, the Patriarch of Western monks, says that in a monastery every pot and pan should be treated with the same reverence as the sacred vessels on the altar.

There has never been an Enlightened Person.
There are only enlightened activities.
—Bodhin Kjolhede

Family Practice

During a retreat with Thich Nhat Hanh one participant told the story of how his three-year-old son had begged his parents to be left alone with his newborn brother. The adults overheard from the next room as the child asked the infant: "Quick, tell me where you came from and tell me about God. I'm beginning to forget."

Although the Buddha provided guidance for laypeople—and some of his lay students were said to have realized themselves deeply—the traditional Buddhist teachings provided a minimal amount of direction in how to conduct oneself in relationship and family matters. The famous Layman Pang, who lived in Tang Dynasty China, and is perhaps the most common example set forth of an enlightened member of the laity, had unusual resources at his disposal, as his wife and young daughter were said to have both been enlightened as well. For most contemporary practitioners, however, the integration of family and practice remains an ongoing challenge as individuals develop new strategies to successfully balance these two apparently opposing realms.

Then again, maybe some of our family members are more enlightened than we think.

Perhaps the following story, related to me by a long-time practitioner and close student of Philip Kapleau, will serve to illustrate how family life and practice can serve to mutually inform and clarify one another:

I'd been studying Zen maybe eight years. I was a relatively advanced koan student, and one day my wife, who was also a practitioner, came to me and said: "You have a twelve-year-old son, and you're enjoying what you're doing very much, but if you keep doing what you're doing, you'll never know your son, and you'll have missed something that's irreparable." Then she walked out.

She said it in a tone which really allowed me to hear it. So I took a hard look at myself, and I realized that very little of what I had experienced in Zen was actually being manifested in my life. I understood it all intellectually, but it wasn't happening directly from my practice.

During my next sesshin, in my first dokusan with Roshi Kapleau I explained what was going on. He said, "You can work on this from one of two perspectives. You can continue to work on your next koan and see what happens. Or you can work on the koan Who? Who is the one who is unhappy with their life? Who is that?" There's no such formal koan—it's related to the koan "Who is it that hears?" which is in The Three Pillars of Zen. But Roshi Kapleau suggested using it as a koan—and without hesitation that's what I decided to do.

And working on that koan, something opened in a way that changed my life. When I came to dokusan at the end of that sesshin, he didn't test me, as a teacher normally would. I knew what I had seen, he knew I was satisfied, and so he was satisfied. What I appreciated so deeply was that Roshi Kapleau did not say: "Well, we could investigate your problem using zazen." What he did say was: "You can investigate who you are, and you can do it this way or you can do it that way." He didn't give me permission to roll around and analyze it.

When I came home everything was different. My life turned. From that day on my relationship with my son totally changed—in terms of time spent, responsiveness, a willingness to be interested in what he was interested in even if I wasn't. I started mountain biking with him—at that point in my life I really didn't want to be riding through the mountains of Colorado at 10,000 feet—it's very exhausting. But I did it and, of course, enjoyed it. Something shifted that was important. My son is now twenty-four, and we're as close as can be. I also gained an enormous amount of respect for my wife, for what she did and how she did it. But that's what it's really about—to open your eyes and look around you at the people you're living with day to day and see what you create in each moment.

Transformation (81)

A practitioner in the lineage of Thich Nhat Hanh tells of discovering a dead baby squirrel in her yard with her young son.

"Feeling sad, we watched our breathing for a moment. I was on my way out but my son told me that he would bury the squirrel. When I returned home I saw a stick with a piece of paper attached to it propped next to one of our rosebushes. I bent down to look at it and on the paper read in my son's careful printing:

> Here lays
> a small dead squerl
> ready to become
> a Rose

Performing Magic (82)

A group of children attending a special weekend retreat at Zen Mountain Monastery were listening to stories around a fire one evening. They had been told they might receive a visit by a legendary local figure, the "Wizard of Mt. Tremper." Sure enough, after some time a tall figure wrapped in a cowl materialized from the night and stepped into the firelight.

"I," he intoned in a deep and resonant voice, "am the Wizard of Mt. Tremper!"

Speculation continues regarding the resemblance of the hooded figure to the monastery's Abbot, John Daido Loori.

"Oh, Wizard," asked one of the children, "can you show us some magic?"

"Yes," said the mysterious magician. "Breathe in." The child did as instructed. "Now breathe out." The child did so.

"*That,*" announced the Wizard, "is magic."

A Turning of the Heart (83)

During a practice period at the remote Tassajara Monastery in California, Zoketsu Norman Fischer and his wife, who were the only students there with children, shared the care of their twin six-month-old sons, each taking a turn while the other was in the meditation hall. Although he loved taking care of his sons, Fischer sometimes found it painful, in his words, to be the "only human being for fifty miles around who wasn't in the zendo." As he tells it:

"I remember one day I had a powerful insight. I used to feed the children in a wheelbarrow because then they wouldn't run away, and plus they would make a huge mess, and all I had to do was hose it out. I remember feeding them one of these times, feeling very upset that I was missing the dharma talk, and seeing the roshi walk out of the zendo first, as he would do afterward—and I had this insight. I realized that if the dharma was really real, and it was as it is said in the sutras, then it must be that feeding my sons *was* the dharma talk. And if I *really* paid attention to what I was doing when I did that, I would get just as much benefit as I would from the talk.

"After that, I never complained. I can say to people, and really mean it, that whatever their lives are can be the Dharma. If they really view it that way, and do daily practice—that's the bottom line, they have to do the practice of zazen—then it really is possible to make whatever is in their lives into a teaching. After all, Zen is a religion. And religion is about the turning of the heart. So I think that people can find a way to practice significantly, and turn their lives around deeply, in whatever situation they're in."

A long time Zen practitioner was about to set off on a car trip with his five-year-old son to a lake in upstate New York.
"How long will it take us to get there, Daddy?" asked the boy.
"Oh, it's about three hours from here," said his father.
"Well, where is it one hour from?"
"Hmm," his father thought it over. "Albany, I guess."
"Well," suggested the boy, "Why don't we go from there?"

When West Meets East—Zen, God, and Christianity

A life-long Catholic reported at the end of a Zen retreat: "I have spent my whole life trying to be Christlike. Now I realize: just be Christ."

In his afterword to *Zen: Dawn in the West*, Philip Kapleau writes about how tired he had become of conventional religion and the "presumptuous statements" made by religious leaders such as "God is good," or "God is almighty."

"After having gained some Understanding," says Kapleau, "I knew that God is neither good nor almighty nor anything else. In fact, God isn't even God!"

There is some controversy over whether Zen in particular, and Buddhism in general, qualifies as a religion. What, after all, is one to make of a tradition that refuses to conceptualize absolute reality, or hypothesize the existence of a divine force, much less a divine being? The position remains ambiguous enough that the more liberal elements in Catholicism and other Western religions have often seen no contradiction in practicing Zen alongside a theistic brand of religion. It is increasingly common to hear of Catholic priests, Rabbis, and Sufis becoming Zen teachers. Contrary to the old adage, the twain are meeting, in ways the Buddha himself could never have foreseen.

How Original Can You Get? (84)

The Jesuit priest Father Robert Kennedy, who is also a Zen teacher, uses zazen to cultivate a state of deep silence in those present before performing mass. A Zen student who attended an interfaith retreat with him was heard to ask afterward:

"I have a much better feeling now for Christianity—but the one thing I still can't fathom is the doctrine of Original Sin. I mean, how can it be that the moment we come into the world we are already sinful?"

"Would it help you understand it better," replied Father Kennedy, "if we called it Original Suffering?"

Making Contact (85)

Former Oakland Mayor Jerry Brown, who spent time in a Jesuit seminary before entering politics, was a visitor at Tassajara Monastery and the San Francisco Zen Center before and during his first term as Governor of California, and later spent six months in Japan pursuing the study of Zen. There he did retreats with Father Lasalle, a Jesuit Priest who was also a Zen teacher and held six-day Zen retreats combined with Catholic Mass. Brown studied too with Yamada Roshi, the lay Zen teacher and hospital administrator who was also Robert Aitken's teacher. Brown reports:

"Father Lasalle said contemporary theology had gone astray from the experience of Christ, that there was a lot of talk about Christ, but it didn't really provide a method for making contact with Christ—and that's what he saw Zen practice as offering. In the Jesuit retreats there would be dokusan with Father Lasalle, eight to ten hours of meditation daily and meals in silence. It was a traditional Buddhist practice room, except in the middle there was a rock with a crucifix on it and on that rock Father Lasalle would say mass. It was unusual, because by being silent all day the Mass had a power that it lacks when you just stop in a church in the middle of your busy activity. Mass in the context of a sesshin is qualitatively different—the words actually come alive. The central act, where the priest says "this is my body" has a power to it. The separation, the dualism breaks down.

"During the retreats with Father LaSalle, when he held up the host saying 'this is my body' I had a very clear sense that he could say that. The body of Christ . . . his body . . . There was not a distinction. That was something that I certainly never experienced in a church up to that time. If there's a way to go to Mass I would say it'd be after meditating ten hours a day in silence."

Zen is simply the key that opens the door to our vast potential for goodness . . . . Opening the door means tuning in to what we are, how we think, what we say, and what we do with our bodies. We must be thorough; we must thoroughly be who we are in each moment throughout the day without expecting anything for it. Opening the door can be a difficult thing. But we must open the door in order to penetrate the thin layer of illusion that is blocking us from our unlimited, spontaneous, available goodness.

—Tenshin Reb Anderson

chapter eight

SETTLING IN: POINTS OF PRACTICE

We all carry this very deep territory, these very deep strengths, but without judiciously applied training that really puts you in touch with that power, you'll never know it.

—RAFE MARTIN

What are the essential elements of Zen practice? Which practices and doctrines are central, and which more peripheral? Which are free to change, or to be dispensed with entirely? What changes would alter the tradition so much it could no longer be called Zen?

In this section, we'll look at some of the elements traditionally associated with Zen practice, and examine how they are changing, or holding their own, in America.

Zazen

Whatever made people think Mind isn't rocks, fences, clouds, or houses? Meditation is the art of deliberately staying open so that myriad things can experience themselves.

—Gary Snyder

Zazen remains the heart of Zen practice, and the mark of the Zen school, which began as a return to basics during a period when Buddhism had deteriorated largely into empty ritualism, academic study, and philosophical debate. The emphasis on sitting meditation advocated by Zen Buddhism was a return to direct experience of the ground of being, to the realization the Buddha himself experienced and sought to pass on as the most essential element of his teachings. The gate, Shakyamuni always taught, was meditation. Robert Aitken Roshi, when asked what the core of Zen training was, answered unswervingly: "Zazen, certainly, is the most important thing. With all that it entails."

This "all that it entails" can include a variety of practices, from following the breath, to the clarification of koans, to the "just sitting" practice of shikantaza.

"What does zazen do?" muses one long-time practitioner. "It's a mystery. We can make assumptions about it, but they're just notions. If I had to describe it, I'd say it has to do with the space inside our minds. Minds make thoughts all the time, but there's space between them—silence—as well. I think practice enlarges the silence, so there's more room for reality. Reality is happening all the time—but *we're* not. So there's some space in there that gets bigger with the practice, more accepting of oneself, of others, of life in general. More spacious, in terms of having less need to rush in with noise all the time, to always need to have something going on. Then, as they say, there's room for the ten thousand things. Everything else can come in."

"This is the point," says Zen teacher Jakusho Bill Kwong. "— to fathom all the intricate layers of who we *think* we are until we become fully who we are."

Press "C" (86)

Zen teacher Barbara Rhodes likens the process of training the mind to using a pocket calculator.

"Between each thought there's a resting place. If you studied an electroencephalograph you'd see that the mind has resting places. In order for us to perceive something clearly it's important to return to our resting place—not to carry over an idea from the past or an idea about the future.

"It's somewhat like a calculator. You put in one plus two and you get three. Then you put in two plus two and you'll get seven—unless you've pushed "C" for "Clear" between the two calculations. So it's very important to push "C" or you're going to carry over the last calculation into the present one. So let go of any ideas, just push "C"! The point is to return to your center and listen, trust, have faith, have courage. Push "C"!"

[It can be painful to get] in touch with . . . afflictions in ourselves that we've managed to keep in the shadows, that we've defended ourselves against for so long. But we have to go through them to see what is beyond. Zazen scours the mind, stripping away the thought-residue that obscures the self.
—Bodhin Kjolhede

Form and Ritual

In Zen practice we use incense a great deal. We light incense at the start of zazen, and we offer incense during ceremonies. Our lives should be like the incense sticks we offer: both straight and bright. To offer incense is to offer our lives—to stand upright, to give light, to purify, and to encourage. In addition, this offering means to have no regrets as our lives get shorter. We just do our best to burn as cleanly as we can.
—Les Kaye

Is form and ritual necessary for the practice of Zen? What forms will develop as Zen becomes less exotic, more truly American?

When Philip Kapleau was first training in Japan, he reports, he experienced great difficulty in making himself perform the requisite prostrations at the beginning of dokusan, or private interview with his teacher. Why, he wondered, should he bow down before another human being? What did this have to do with Zen?

Finally, his teacher, who had been observing Kapleau's awkwardness with bemused interest, explained, "Kapleau-san, when you make prostrations in dokusan you are not bowing down before me, but before your own Buddha-nature."

"Aha," thought Kapleau, "So I'm not bowing down to him. I'm bowing down to my*self*. That's different."

Thereafter, says Kapleau, bowing came more easily—though it did take some years for his reluctance to vanish entirely.

Gesture Reciprocated (87)

When Zoketsu Norman Fischer, who later became Abbot of the San Francisco Zen Center, first came to the Berkeley Zen Center, having heard about Zen through the writings of D.T. Suzuki and others, he was confused by certain ritual aspects of the practice—specifically, bowing.

He went to the resident priest, Sojun Mel Weitsman, for clarification. "I thought this was Zen," he said. "Who are you bowing to?"

Weitsman beckoned him close to the figure on the altar, which was actually not a Buddha, but a very small Kannon bodhisattva figure, no more than a few inches tall, hands palm to palm in prayer position.

"You see," said Weitsman, "When you bow to this Buddha, it is also bowing to you."

Says Fischer, "After that I never gave it another thought. I've been bowing ever since."

Enlightenment and Delusion

When his students asked Shunryu Suzuki, "What is enlightenment?" Suzuki Roshi was known to reply: "What do you want to get enlightened for? You may not like it."

"Enlightenment?" said Robert Aitken during a phone conversation he and I conducted between his home on the Big Island of Hawaii and mine in northern New Mexico. "You won't hear that word much in the Diamond Sangha. And you won't hear the word kensho or satori, or anything like that, either. The words themselves hold out such unreal kinds of expectations of 'be-all and end-all' experiences that we just don't use them any more. But that doesn't mean that folks aren't experiencing realization, because they are. In all of the writings of the great past masters, it's very clear that there is no end to understanding. It goes on and on, becoming clearer and clearer and clearer."

"The way people are talking about these things seems to be becoming much more subtle and refined," I said.

"Or realistic," replied Aitken, with a laugh.

"I think big experiences are very important," says Dairyu Michael Wenger, Dean of Buddhist Studies at the San Francisco Zen Center, "and I don't think they can be codified. I think it's as mysterious as anything else. Some people have big experiences, and they're never integrated . . . other people have a little experience, and it completely covers their whole life. The big experiences that I had, early on in my practice, I couldn't manifest. Now I don't recognize that I have such big experiences, but things seem to move. I think the point is to recognize the experiences you have, and let go of them . . . not to feel afraid to talk about them, but also, to not feel compelled to talk about them."

Satori, or kensho—to the Zen boomers of the Fifties and the hippies of the Sixties, it was the ultimate holy grail. But in the Zen world, talking about enlightenment experiences is a bit like discussing your sex life. It can be done, under the right circumstances, but it has to be for the right reasons—and it's not for general public consumption.

Why? The danger is that we may cling to such an experience, and create a new self to replace the one we've "forgotten"—a new, "enlightened" self perhaps, who goes around dispensing wisdom or—God forbid—spouting falsely Zennish aphorisms. The ancient masters pointed to this as one of the easiest places to get stuck in practice; and they regarded this type of "stinky," self-conscious Zen as a great embarrassment. A true Zen teacher is supposed to manifest the greatest ordinariness. When you've reached the top of the mountain, says the Zen tradition, it's time to come down the other side, return to the world, and help others.

There are other issues, particularly in the West, where for the first time all the major forms of Buddhism are coming together, each having its own slant on the matter. Is it appropriate to actively seek enlightenment, to let it arise naturally, or to disregard the matter entirely? Does true understanding require one to have experienced realization for oneself, or is it more important how whatever understanding we do have is manifested? Why is it that those who have had major experiences of awakening still sometimes behave irresponsibly?

These questions are still working themselves out in the West. The following are some of the many voices who are currently contributing, or have contributed, to the ongoing dialogue.

The enlightened man neither opposes nor evades what lies before him. Everything depends upon the occasion and the timing. When he needs to act he acts. When one's action is decisive and one responds with nothing left over, it is as though he hasn't acted at all.

—Philip Kapleau

The definition of an enlightened person is one who always has everything they need. At every moment what they need is there; they're not seeking anything. If you really are seriously practicing to be free and to simultaneously realize enlightenment, you never seek out of the immediate situation, no matter how bad it is. You transform the immediate situation into what you need.

—Richard Baker

How do you establish a real foundation that can lead to enlightenment? Very simply, you must start from the beginning and go through a process of training and practice. After a long while this may culminate in what can be called "gradual enlightenment." When you finally reach that point, however, that single dramatic event can be considered "sudden enlightenment." It's like going on a trip; you have to take the first step before you can reach your goal. But after many steps, suddenly you are there.

—Master Sheng Yen

If a candle is brought into an absolutely dark room, the darkness disappears, and there is light. But if ten or a hundred or a thousand candles are added, the room will become brighter and brighter. Yet the decisive change was brought about by the first candle which penetrated the darkness.

—D.T. Suzuki

The moment of awakening may be marked by an outburst of laugher. But this is not the laughter of one who suddenly acquires a great fortune. Neither is it the laughter of one who was won a great victory. It is, rather, the laughter of one who after having painfully searched for something a very long time finds in one morning in the pocket of his coat.

—Thich Nhat Hanh

Enlightenment is not anything a person with an inquiring mind is looking for, any more than the pursuit of happiness could be a life goal. What you come to is a working principle that enables you, without thinking, to deal with everything at once.

—Mary Farkas

As for realization, once you think you have attained something, you will be down ten thousand feet below, and you will have to start from the bottom again.

—Nyogen Senzaki

Expressing Enlightenment (88)

Les Kaye, frustrated by the emphasis of his Soto Zen teachers on form, and their lack of emphasis on enlightenment experiences, once complained to Katagiri Roshi: "You never speak about enlightenment!"

"Oh?" Katagiri raised his eyebrows. "Don't you think so?"

Years later, says Kaye, he realized that "[Katagiri and] Suzuki Roshi did not encourage us to try and attain enlightenment; rather, [they] encouraged us to *express* enlightenment."

Hitting the 900-Year-Old Bell (89)

Zen priest Jean Leyshon lives in New Mexico, although she trained primarily with Katagiri Roshi in Minnesota. One summer Sasaki Roshi led a sesshin in New Mexico and Leyshon attended. The roshi, knowing she was a Soto Zen practitioner and student of Katagiri's, gave her the koan "How do you manifest Shikantaza when you see a flower?" Leyshon worked very hard on the koan all week without passing it, then returned to her home in Silver City. She was resting the afternoon after she returned, listening to the loud buzz of the many cicadas in the trees; growing louder, then softer, then louder again.

"Then all of a sudden," says Leyshon, "all the cicadas stopped at once. It was like that famous story of the bottom falling out of the bucket. It was exactly that. I felt like I was ripped apart. As if I'd died. After that some of the things Katagiri had said in his lectures—well, it wasn't anything I could have known before, but now I realized he was talking about something real. I never went back to Sasaki to see if this was passing the koan, but I understood I'd had some sort of experience. I didn't know if it was big or little, but then I thought to myself, everything I've been taught says that whatever kind of experience you have, let go of it. Still, no matter how much I knew that, I was still carrying it. There was something in my body and mind that just couldn't let go."

The following year, Leyshon went to Minnesota to spend another summer practice period with Katagiri. She served as *jisha*, the roshi's attendant. There was another roshi visiting, and the two were trying to translate a chant for a *shuso* [head trainee] ceremony from the Japanese. Katagiri gave Leyshon a line of the chant and asked her to help with it.

"To help you translate it," said Leyshon, "I'd have to understand it."

Katagiri grabbed her arm and looked at her. "Please understand it," he said.

Leyshon examined the partial translation he was working with, then spoke to a friend who understood Japanese about some of the characters.

"And then I got part of it," says Leyshon. "It wasn't any kind of a literal translation, but it was my understanding. In the zendo, there was a 900-year-old temple bell from Japan that Katagiri had found somewhere in the States—people were growing a tree in it, and when he explained what it was, they gave it to him. So the first line became 'Hitting the 900 year old bell.'

"I had to leave the practice period a day or two early, and the day I was going everybody was in the zendo. I was getting ready to leave when I realized the second part of the line. So the entire thing became:

Hitting the 900 year old bell
Whole world together goes in emptiness

"I wrote it out and left it on Katagiri's desk and put his glasses on it so I knew he'd see it. I remember coming down the steps of his trailer, and my whole body was shaking.

"I remember I was driving in the car and we stopped right at sunrise. And I had this feeling he'd read it. And the whole thing, that whole experience I'd had the year before, suddenly fell away. There was something in me that just wouldn't let go until I'd expressed it."

Not Knowing

I must confess that I don't have the faintest idea what my purpose is or what's going on, and I never have. I became comfortable with that mystery a long time ago—that I would never know how any of these things fit together in any explicit way.

—Gary Snyder

In Zen, once you've pinned something down and defined it, you've killed it. Zen stresses meeting each situation and each moment in a state of openness—what Suzuki Roshi called "Beginner's Mind"—without being burdened by preconceptions based on what has happened before, or anxieties about what is to come. This does not mean disregarding useful and necessary knowledge. It means greeting each situation from a condition of emptiness and readiness, in the awareness that we do not know what the outcome will be.

Buddhism, alone among world religions—and especially Zen Buddhism—is perhaps unique in its encouragement of the state of doubt. This is not just any doubt, but Great Doubt—the doubt of having a great question, as the Buddha did when he left the palace where he'd spent his youth and, glimpsing an old person, a sick person, and a corpse, realized his understanding of existence was incomplete. Or as Eihei Dogen, the founder of the Soto sect in Japan, did when he saw the smoke rising from the incense stick beside his dead mother's body and realized he must dedicate his life to the pursuit of realization. Why such emphasis upon a condition that is often regarded as negative? Because it leads to a state of questioning and searching that is generally, though not always, a prerequisite to awakening. In other words, the search does not begin until one knows that one does not know. Finally, even the experience of realization must be let go—for if one regards one's understanding as complete, there is no room for further growth. As Suzuki Roshi put it: "In the beginner's mind there are many possibilities; in the expert's there are few."

"The practice is so simple, really," said Bernie Glassman as we talked on the lawn outside the offices of his Buddhist Peacemaker Order near Santa Barbara, California. "Whatever it ends up you think you've got—let go of it. I worked on 'the essence of unknowing' as a koan three times with three different teachers. Each time I had to let go of what I'd grabbed onto the previous time and come up with a new answer. Where I'd get caught was if I was coming from a place of 'knowing.' It's very difficult to let it all arise and not let your sense of what it should be or what it may mean get in the way—just to let it all arise without 'understanding' how it's supposed to be."

Sometimes It's Better Not to Know (90)

Once when Zen monk Ryushin was traveling as attendant to John Daido Loori, they stepped out of a motel room in the pre-dawn hour to see, overhead in the still darkened sky, a most unusual phenomenon. A bright light sprang into existence and, with a great whooshing sound, expanded to an enormous ball of color, before contracting and fading, then springing out again. They watched in wonder as the process repeated itself several times, but remained entirely baffled as to what might be causing it. Then all at once Rysuhin exclaimed, "I know what it is! It's a hot air balloon. The flame is coming from its heating mechanism."

Loori looked at Ryushin. "You just killed it," he said.

Nothing but the Truth (91)

Zen teacher Jitsudo Ancheta likes to tell the story of a Native American medicine man who was called before a court and asked to swear to "tell the whole truth, and nothing but the truth."

"I can't do that," replied the medicine man.

"What do you mean you can't do it?" demanded the judge.

"I don't know the whole truth," he answered.

Zen mind is one of those enigmatic phrases used by Zen teachers to make you notice yourself, to go beyond the words and wonder what your own mind and being are. This is the purpose of all Zen teaching—to make you wonder, and to answer that wondering with the deepest expression of your own nature.

—Richard Baker

The Absolute

When we see into the emptiness or illusory nature of things, of life and death, of sickness and health, of youth and old age, then we're master of all things. We are free to be healthy, we're free to be sick, we're free to grow old.

—Geoffrey Shugen Arnold

In Zen, the absolute basis of reality, like the self, is often described as empty. But this does not mean blankness. In fact, it does not mean anything you can put your finger on at all. A student of Ch'an Master Sheng-yen described the experience of emptiness this way: "Given the Truth that nothing exists, we are presented with an endlessly varied universe, whose existence is impossible, yet whose appearance is vividly undeniable . . . Like a child, one can only laugh in sheer delight."

As the Heart Sutra, the essential text of Zen, so famously puts it: "Form is no other than emptiness, emptiness no other than form; form is exactly emptiness, emptiness exactly form."

The point is, as Philip Whalen tells us, that this emptiness is full of everything.

Full of Everything (92)

Zen teacher Philip Whalen, in speaking of the absolute basis of reality, put it this way: "There's a great misunderstanding about what emptiness is, the idea that emptiness is something that happens under a bell-jar when you exhaust all the air out of it. That's not quite where it's at as far as I understand it. The emptiness is the thing we're full of, and everything that you're seeing here is empty. Literally the word is *shunya*, something that's swollen up—it's not, as is often translated, void. It's packed, it's full of *everything.*"

Absolutely Not (93)

When asked about the Absolute basis of reality, Rev. Taizan Akiyama of the Milwaukee Zen center likes to reply: "There *is* no Absolute."

Self and No-Self

Some people think that . . . Buddhist practices dissolve the "self." Others say that before we can dissolve the "self" we have to have a healthy "self." I don't think that is so. You cannot dissolve something that is not there. This is a false problem that has become a problem itself. What has to be dissolved are our wrong views concerning the self.

—Thich Nhat Hanh

Self? At the bottom, says Zen, it's not there. We're a collection of aggregates, a grouping of characteristics—a story assembled by our minds, made up of bits and pieces of the half-remembered past and the imagined future. Take a look for yourself. Underneath it all, if you search long and hard enough, you eventually find . . . nothing. Give it a try.

Of course, that's not to say we don't have to take care of our lives.

"Forgetting the self is a peak experience," says Robert Aitken. "The Buddha Shakyamuni had a self, an ego. He knew very well who he was, what he had to do. And that's ego. It's self-image. Without ego you can't practice. You've got to have a good stout ego. But the point is, the experience of forgetting the self, and finding true intimacy with other, is a momentary experience. It's a gate that opens. You walk through that gate, and you can find in ordinary life a far deeper intimacy with all beings."

As John Daido Loori puts it: "Life and death are nothing but movement. It's like a flame that burns in the night, moment to moment . . . it's not the same flame in every moment, nor is it another. We're born and we die, moment to moment to moment—that is the Buddhist perspective. Underlying everything is impermanence, constant change, a constant state of becoming. Who you were yesterday, the day before, a year ago, five years ago, is not who you are now—not physically, not mentally, not intellectually. There is not an atom or molecule in your body right now that is the same as it was five years ago. We are in dynamic equilibrium with the universe. The universe passes through us. So what do you call the self?"

The self is not to be despised. It is your vehicle to selflessness.
—Ch'an Master Sheng-yen

Mindfulness

Seeing our moment-to-moment automatic conditioned reactions is crucial. Without that we will just continue the mess we are creating in our world . . . . Simple awareness of what's arising makes it possible to let go . . . . Awareness this moment reveals what needs to be done or left alone.
—Toni Packer

The practice of Zen is not limited to seated meditation.

"Wherever you are," writes Bernie Glassman, "You are in the zendo. We think the zendo is that special place . . . and we are going to try to do something special there, try to be concentrated or quiet, and when we leave we can start screaming again. We don't see the whole world as a zendo. Of course, we need a 'special place' and 'special training periods.' But really, every day is a special day, every place is a special place, *as it is*."

"One day when I was walking down a canyon path," remembers Joan Halifax, "I realized I was making a literal impression upon the Earth. I stopped and turned around to look at my footprints and they were even and smooth, a kind of script in the dust. That was on Thursday. On Friday, I hurried to the office on the central part of the land and halfway there I caught myself, stopped and turned around to look at my tracks. There was a different message on the Earth. It was then that I saw how completely each step that we take is a message of alienation or awareness to Earth."

The practice of mindfulness, or close moment-to-moment attention to what is directly in front of us in the present moment, is common to all branches of Buddhism, although the emphasis placed upon it as a practice varies from one to the next. In most schools of Zen, the emphasis is placed not so much on observing one's activity, but *becoming* it—being so present to one's experience that all sense of separation is lost.

As Gary Snyder puts it: "A simple message of (Zen) teaching is that much of the pain, suffering, and confusion you encounter in your own life is simply caused by not paying attention to what you have closest to you from the beginning and then using it well: body, speech, and mind."

Ask Not for Whom the Bell Tolls ... (94)

In the tradition of Thich Nhat Hanh, a bell is used as a signal for mindfulness. At any point during the day, upon hearing the sound of the bell, the community is reminded to put down what they are doing, take three breaths, and return to their activity with mindful awareness.

Early on in her practice, Zen teacher Cynthia Jurs was undertaking a solitary retreat at the Lama Foundation in northern New Mexico. She was several days into the retreat when she woke up one morning feeling a bit out of sorts. She went outside to relieve herself, and on stepping through the low doorway of the retreat hut, banged her head on a bell that was hanging from the eaves. Grumbling to herself at whoever had left it in such an inconvenient location, she finished her business, returned to the hut to get her toothbrush, and stepped back outside to brush her teeth, only to hit her head on the bell once more.

Mood worsening by the minute, Jurs went back inside to fix breakfast. Afterward, she stepped outside and struck her head on the bell a third time. This time, says Jurs, she finally said to herself: "OK Cynthia, what is going on? I think you'd better stop, breathe, and return to the present moment!"

Drawing inspiration from the story of the Buddha, she decided she was going to sit down and not get up again until she'd had some sort of insight.

Making a spot outside, she sat and meditated for several hours. While sitting there she had, she says, "the biggest breakthrough I'd ever had in my practice—one that brought a tremendous amount of clarity around the real purpose of my life."

Partly as an outgrowth of this experience, Jurs was inspired to do many more years of training, eventually becoming a teacher in the lineage of Thich Nhat Hanh. "But it took hitting my head on that bell three times to stop me," she says, "To stop me to where I could really penetrate down through the depths of my own patterns, and see clearly where I was going."

Suffering

No matter how far out on the sea of suffering we've sailed, all that is required is to turn toward awakening. It's never too late, but it takes that turning, and no one can do that for us.

—Bonnie Myotai Treace

The First Noble Truth of Buddhism—Life is Suffering—is a doctrine that has caused innumerable Western practitioners a good deal of bafflement, dismay, and, well—suffering. At least until it becomes apparent that the point the Buddha was trying to make is not "life's a drag and then you die," but rather, the doctrine he articulated in the Third Noble Truth: that there is a path *out* of suffering.

In other words, as Paul Reps put it in a talk at the San Francisco Zen Center: "What the Buddha actually came for was to liberate us from suffering—certainly not to burden us down with more of it."

Nevertheless, it is a key point of practice to be willing to look unflinchingly at our pain, to learn to accept it and to work with it. Life inevitably involves pain; but what we discover, in the process of Zen training, is that much of our *suffering* is actually caused by trying to avoid this pain—by not accepting our circumstances, and reaching for outside sources of gratification to distract ourselves.

This is the suffering, says Buddhism, that we can do something about.

"If you could change one thing in your life," writes Zen student Maureen Jisho Ford, "get rid of one person or alter one situation what would it be? That is your practice. If I could take it away from you, I would not do so, because . . . I would be robbing you of the opportunity to grow and to learn. It is only when life grabs you by the back of your neck and flings you to your knees that you cry out, "Why, why, why?" That "Why?" is the beginning of the spiritual journey."

Just as It Is (95)

Pat Enkyo O'Hara, who is now the resident teacher at the Village Zendo in New York City, was serving as caretaker of altars and offerings during a three-month training period at Zen Mountain Center in Idyllwild, California. During one very formal memorial ceremony, as she was carrying a tray of "elegant, lacquered wooden offering cups" between two buildings, one of the cups tumbled from the tray and landed amongst some rocks, resulting in a prominent chip in its highly polished surface.

"Devastated," she went to Maezumi Roshi and announced her intention to order a new one from Japan.

"Why?" asked Roshi. "With the chip it is more valuable. See? Just as it is."

Over the years, says O'Hara, "this has emerged as his great teaching for me . . . he was broken. I am broken. And when we can see that we are all chipped and broken, we begin to value our life as an expression of the teaching that we are truly perfect and complete, just as we are."

The Wish-Fulfilling Jewel (96)

A student once asked Zen teacher Steve Allen, "If you were given a wish-fulfilling jewel, what would you wish for?"

"To stop wishing," replied Allen.

Old Age and Death

Cancer—it stops you in your tracks. Where did you think you were going?
Sometimes it takes a really extreme circumstance—like facing our own mortal-
ity—before we're willing to look at, and really drop, our own stuff.
—Katharine Thanas

It is said that when the historical Buddha, Shakyamuni, left the palace in which he had been brought up and saw for the first time a sick person, an old person, and a corpse, his lack of understanding of why these things should exist propelled him toward a life of practice and, eventually, liberation. Ever since, contemplation of death has been a key element of Buddhist practice, often used to inspire the practitioner to a vigorous effort toward awakening. The original Buddhist robes were made from bits of cloth used to shroud the dead; and there are a number of traditional meditations, sometimes performed on burial or charnel grounds, which focus upon imagining the dissolution and decay of the physical body. It was traditional in China and Japan for a master to not only die well, but to leave a last poem as a teaching for his or her students.

It should perhaps come as no surprise then that Zen in America should carry on the traditional importance assigned to the deep consideration of mortality, and even extend it into realms such as contemplative work with the dying and the founding of hospice programs such as Issan Dorsey's Maitri Hospice for victims of AIDS.

After sitting all night with a dying friend, Zen teacher and death-and-dying activist Yvonne Rand remembers looking out of the window at dawn. "It had rained during the night," she recalls, "and in the early morning, there were these big, fat raindrops suspended from the bare branches of the tree, catching the first light. To this day I can completely see the light reflected in those drops of water, their beauty absolutely inseparable from the brevity of their existence. The same thing that was happening with the drops of water was happening right there in the room. They were completely of a piece."

I'm OK—How About You? (97)

A young Zen student was working on a construction project on a rocky hillside at Shasta Abbey. When Jiyu-Kennett Roshi, who was getting a bit older and experiencing some health problems, came to visit the site, he took her hand and helped her across a rocky patch of ground, remarking, "It must be difficult to not be as agile as you once were."

The roshi paused and looked at the student. "I'm doing all right with it," she responded. "How is it going to be for *you?*"

The student, who is now in his late forties, says he still thinks of the exchange at least once a week, as he copes with the changes of growing older himself.

Problem or Challenge? (98)

Maurine Stuart, who struggled with cancer for a number of years, was known for the clarity, presence, and vibrant quality of aliveness with which she faced her illness. The day after a final, unsuccessful surgery, when she'd been given only a short time to live, one of her students, Trudy Goodman, visited her in the hospital. She reports:

"I remember walking into her hospital room the day after her surgery. It was the only time during the whole period I'd ever seen her crying. But when she saw me come in she dabbed up the tears. Then she looked right at me, straight in the eyes, and all she said was: 'This is going to be really challenging.'"

Nowhere to Go (99)

Zen teacher Issan Dorsey, who established the Maitri Hospice in San Francisco, was on his deathbed when one of his closest friends, Shunko Jamvold, came to visit him.

"I'm going to miss you," said Shunko.

"I'm going to miss you, too," responded Issan. He was silent for a moment. Then he asked, "Are you going somewhere?"

Trading Places (100)

Richard Baker used to say to his Zen students: "If you're with someone who's dying, and you're not willing to trade places with them at that very moment, then you're not really practicing."

When Issan Dorsey was dying of AIDS, Baker came to visit him, saying, "I wish I could trade places with you right now."

"Don't worry," responded Dorsey. "You'll get your chance."

Universal Sound (101)

Su Bong Soen Sa, the Hawaiian American dharma successor to Seung Sahn, died early, at age fifty-two, having suffered a damaged heart from an earlier attack. He was giving a formal interview at the time in his full robes to a young girl who, at age fourteen, was already a serious koan student. Su Bong Soen Sa had just asked her the koan: "What is Universal Sound?"

The student hit the floor with her hand.

Sitting there in his robes, Su Bong Soen Sa said, "Correct"—and died.

What Is Zen?

As flying is the essential thing for a bird to be a bird, to study the self is the essential thing for us human beings to be human. A human being is a living being that needs to study the self to become the self.
—Rev. Shohaku Okumura

Traditional Zen stories are filled with masters who live beneath bridges, indistinguishable from the beggars, or old women selling tea by the side of the road, whose wisdom surpasses that of the supposedly wise abbot or sutra master. When the enlightened sage comes down from the mountain, having seen the ground of being, he or she is supposed to appear ordinary, indistinguishable from anyone else. The truly enlightened person *may*, in the traditional Zen world, be the abbot of a monastery. Then again, they may be the old tramp by the side of the road.

What *is* Zen? There are hundreds of answers, contained in hundreds of koans. But, as the teachings of Zen frequently remind us, even the wisest of sages cannot say what it is.

How You Play the Game ... (102)

Once when Zen teacher Gerry Shishin Wick, who is a great baseball fan, was visiting Zen Mountain Monastery, a student volunteered to drive him to the Baseball Hall of Fame in hopes of gaining some Zen insight along the way. The Hall of Fame was some hours away and Wick, who'd been eagerly awaiting the trip, invited a friend along for the ride.

Many hours later, the driver staggered back into the monastery dining hall, having spent his only full day off from the rigorous training schedule visiting an attraction in which he had no interest. Another student eagerly asked him what he'd learned.

"Nothing," replied the driver. "All they talked about was baseball!"

Die Now (103)

Dosho Mike Port, on a visit to Japan, was having tea with Rinzai Zen master Harada Shodo Roshi, when he asked: "What is the essence of your teaching?"

"Die now!" cried Harada. With that he sprang to his feet and left the room.

"People want so much," says Jakusho Bill Kwong. "We want to be someone else. 'I want to be stronger'. 'I want to be more directed'. 'I want to be superwoman.' But it's not possible. You must accept your condition. But 'accept' is active. Who you are is active. Passive acceptance—that's the immobile, inanimate Zen. It's not the Zen I'm talking about. There's passion here. Spirit for the quest. This is important: the sincerity of our quest and how we go about it. It's a long path. Are you prepared? Do you want to walk on this path? Don't think about it too much. Just walk! C'mon, let's go! That's Zen."

—Jakusho Bill Kwong

chapter nine

THE FARTHER SHORE: NEW DIRECTIONS IN AMERICAN ZEN

Zen is not about nonmovement . . . Sitting is a centered, strong position in the midst of movement. When you get a top spinning just right, even though it's going very fast, it's so stable that it doesn't even look as if it's moving. If it's slightly off balance it wobbles. It has to be centered and moving very fast in order to be stable. That's what Zen is all about.

— BERNIE GLASSMAN

Bearing Witness: Bernie Glassman and the Buddhist Peacemaker Order

Bernie Glassman was wearing suspenders, red ones, that my wife Tania swears were ornamented with white daisies, though I don't remember this. We'd driven the six hours from San Francisco to Santa Barbara that morning for a one-o'clock meeting which I should have confirmed the day before, but didn't.

Glassman, the senior teacher of the White Plum lineage, founder of the Buddhist Peacemaker Order and first Dharma heir to Maezumi Roshi, lived at the time of this writing in the area locals call "The Mesa," at the top of a cliff that drops a hundred or more feet to the flawless blue Pacific below. His home was in an updated former hippie beach shack compound that, rumor has it, used to belong to the Beach Boys. Although the compound has since turned into a very pricey bit of real estate, it still has that funky surf haven feel, with lawns that sprawl to the edges of the cliffs, palms and agaves, and a sturdy white-painted stairway winding all the way down the cliffside to the beach below. In other words, it's about as close to the Pure Land as you're likely to get on the planet, especially on this late summer day with its unbroken expanse of blue sky spilling down to an equally unbroken expanse of water.

Glassman, who I know from my graduate student years at the Naropa Institute, had e-mailed me the gate code in advance, so that when Tania and I roll up in our rented Geo Metro at 1:00 p.m. on the dot and punch in the numbers, the gate rolls open as though by magic—but there is no answer to my knock at the bungalow that is supposed to be his. We circumnavigate the yard and peer in the back door, which is standing open; Japanese calligraphy adorning the walls tells us that this must be the place. "Bernie?" I call, through the open door. "Roshi?"—for between his stature in the Zen community and his own disarming informality I've never known what to call him, and I've always figured the best approach was to hedge my bets. His Buddhist ordination name, Tetsugen, seems to have fallen out of usage almost entirely.

There is no answer. We sit down to wait, enjoying the sight of pelicans flapping by. But Zen masters are not known, generally speaking, for being late to appointments, and by the time fifteen minutes have passed I'm sure there's been a foul-up. Whatever reservoir of Zen calm I might have left after several weeks of shuttling through the Bay Area's endless traffic jams in search of Zen teachers is in danger of draining away, since we've left this quite important interview for last, and tomorrow we must drive back to San Francisco to catch our plane.

Leaving Tania sitting on Bernie's deck in case he shows up, I jump in the Metro and jet off in search of the nearest pay phone. The number I have for his Buddhist Peacemaker Order yields only an answering machine—though it does give several other numbers to try, which I attempt one after the other until all my change has run out, succeeding only in connecting to an-ever expanding Indra's Net of phone machines, each linked to and perfectly reflecting all the rest.

It is now 1:30. I jerk open the door of the Metro and rummage under the seats for lost coins, coming up in the process with a quarter and two nickels—never underestimate the value of disorder!—along with an almost exhausted pre-paid phone card. Heading back to the booth, I use the card to phone information, which gives me an entirely new number for the Buddhist Peacemaker Order, a scant instant before the card runs out and cuts me off. Down to my last thirty-five cents, I dial the new number. Remarkably, it is answered by a live human being, who shortly puts me onto Bernie—a miracle that convinces me I must have done something right in a prior lifetime. Sure, he remembers we had an appointment scheduled. Only problem is all his dates got deleted in conversion to a new computer system and he wasn't sure when it was—can we meet him at the Peacemaker Order's new offices, in the Villa Maria conference center in Montecito?

I jump into the Metro, swoop back to pick up Tania, and we leave Endless Summer behind for the sandstone-walled estates of Montecito, home of Hollywood escapees such as John Travolta, and all manner of other millionaires. I can't help but find it ironic, as we wind past one mansion after another, that Glassman Roshi, known for his pioneering work with the homeless, with AIDS victims, and for leading street retreats in the Bowery in New York, should have landed in this Lifestyles-of-the-Rich-and-Famous setting at the foot of the Santa Ynez Mountains. But then again, hasn't Bernie always taught that we should cultivate a mind that excludes nothing? And given that he is perennially in need of funding for his next visionary project, it's entirely possible this might be the perfect setting to attract it.

Bernie Roshi, as his friends sometimes call him, is nothing if not diverse. A summing-up of his Zen-related activities and projects over the last several decades creates a substantial list. Since receiving the dharma transmission and setting off on his own in the 1970s he has, among many other achievements:

- Established a funding base by founding a gourmet bakery in Yonkers, the New York community where he has vowed to end homelessness.
- Founded the Greystone Bakery job training program for inner city residents.
- Secured government funding for day care and housing programs for single mothers.
- Founded the House of One People, an ecumenical community worship center.
- Synthesized ancient wisdom with the "12-Step" approach in his "How to Raise an Ox" Zen training program.
- Organized numerous interfaith retreats between Jewish, Christian, and other denominations.
- Passed the dharma transmission to Rabbis, Sufis, and Catholic priests.
- Established an AIDS facility for the homeless.
- Led a series of seven-day "street retreats" in New York City's Bowery.
- Assumed leadership of the White Plum Lineage of American Zen teachers in the wake of Maezumi Roshi's death.
- Founded his ecumenical and interdenominational Buddhist Peacemaker Order.

As if all this was not an unusual enough path for a Buddhist teacher to take—perennially raising in the minds of his detractors the question, "But is it Zen?"—there are the Auschwitz retreats. Glassman's Buddhist Peacemaker Order is based on his conception of Bearing Witness—to suffering, to poverty, to warfare—as a means of healing. As an ecumenical organization including clergy members of all faiths, the Peacemaker Order has begun leading week-long Bearing Witness retreats at Auschwitz for one hundred or more people at a time. Participants have included both Holocaust survivors and the sons and daughters of former guards, soldiers, and S.S. officers.

"Bearing witness," says Rose Gordon, a student of Joan Halifax, "is an experience, not of merely 'checking a situation out,' as in remaining a tourist or spectator, but of *being* it—not shutting out of my awareness a whole lot of facets of this moment simply because I don't want to know about them." Commenting on a Peacemaker retreat she attended at Auschwitz, she says:

"It's such a potent situation. The group was very diverse. There were people whose fathers had been S.S. officers, and people whose parents had survived the camp. There was a German woman whose family maintains that the concentration camps were a lie, that the Holocaust didn't happen. This was her second year at Auschwitz. There was a man who was one of the few people to escape Auschwitz, and several men whose fathers had fought the German army and had been held in prisoner of war camps.

"We went out to Birkenau and did zazen. Each person had a list of names of those who had died there. We sat in a large circle on the railroad tracks at the selection site and during zazen people chanted the names of the dead. The voices came in unison from the four directions, in all manner of accents, rising and falling, like the wind in leaves, or the murmuring of a stream. During our time there we read the names of several thousand people who were on the death rolls. There was an all night vigil in the children's barracks, and a Catholic Mass led by a Polish priest in one of the prisoners' barracks.

"One morning the mist turned to rain and we moved to one of the barracks, laying our sitting cushions on the earth and stone. The light was dim, and a line of candles, an impromptu altar, formed along a covered stone trough that ran down the center of the barracks, providing us enough light to read our lists of names. A gypsy woman sang to us there. She was the only survivor of her small village of ninety-six people, the only one left alive to tend their graves. Her song needed no translation.

"It was very cold, and we'd go out of the gate in front of Birkenau, and gather around the soup kitchen wagon that came each day, feeding us hot soup in plastic bowls. It really helped me realize what a blessing it is to have a bowl of hot soup.

"Birkenau is famous for this bluish mist that descends—the German soldiers used to halt all movement in the camps when the mist was thick, because you couldn't see and they didn't want people to escape. We walked through that mist one night, using the railroad tracks as a guide, on the way to the vigil at the children's barracks. I couldn't see more than half a hand in front of me. We started to hear dogs bark out in the village, and the whistles of trains. These were sounds I'd heard in war movies; and in the context of Birkenau, they lost their innocence and became threatening. It was as if the 1940s were bleeding into the 1990s.

"But I was always totally aware that I had the strength of this circle of zazen to sustain me in bearing witness. I don't know how visitors can spend more than one day in the camps without this strength and support. Actually I can't imagine how anyone survived Auschwitz at all, given what we saw."

Poet Anne Waldman was director of the Jack Kerouac School of Disembodied Poetics writing program at the Naropa Institute (now Naropa University) in Boulder, Colorado for many years, a good portion of that time in conjunction with Allen Ginsberg. She and poet Andrew Schelling, who served for some years as the program's chair, remember participating in one of Glassman's first street retreats, held in the days leading up to Easter, 1993.

"On the retreat," said Andrew, during a conversation on a sunny fall day at a picnic table behind his Naropa office, "were Peter Matthiessen, myself, Anne Waldman, and Rick Fields, as well as three Naropa students who had never been in New York City before. Their introduction was to live on the street in one of the city's most devastated districts, the Bowery.

"The rules were that we had only the clothing we were wearing, one piece of ID in case we got picked up by the police, and two dollars a day as a kind of emergency fund for phone calls or coffee. After our orientation at St. John the Divine with four or five formerly homeless people who gave us an account of what it was like on the street, we walked down through Central Park to the U.N., where we were going to hear the theologian Hans Kung speak. It was comical for the thirteen of us, all pretty scraggly with our scruffy beards and beat up clothes, trying to get admission past the guard at the U.N. We did get inside, only to find that the talk had been over for more than an hour.

"We had been scheduled to sit our first period of zazen at a little park on the corner of Bowery and Houston, but we arrived to find there was no park. Bernie took out his map and we poked our way west on Houston to find a place for zazen. I was walking behind the group, having a conversation with Rick Fields, and we stopped to cross at a traffic light. Midway across at the median, we looked east, and about a block away, in the middle of eight lanes of roaring traffic, was Bernie trying to read his map. Trailing behind him were ten Zen students. Rick clutched my arm with a dramatic gesture and said, 'This is the trouble with religion: Zen master crosses street the wrong way, all the students follow.' Rick is quite close to Bernie, and he said it in a very fond and joking way, but it *was* lethal looking, these eleven ragged people straggling down the middle of the street.

"We finally found a park, and had our zazen session on the basketball court. We had to brush off a litter of crack vials and needles to sit on the asphalt. That was one of our few meditation sessions, because from then on we were on the street and the immediate lesson one gets is that survival out there is a full time job. You don't have the leisure to sit down and meditate, if you expect to find food and shelter or a few coins for coffee that day."

"The weather looked a little menacing," remembered Anne Waldman, "colder than we'd anticipated, and drizzling with rain. We had just two women, and had elected not to split up and stay in the shelters, which were said to be dangerous for women. So we all stuck together and constructed this cardboard condominium on Hester Street."

"An old homeless man kindly told us to go down to Chinatown," Andrew said, "where we would find good shelter by pulling cartons out of dumpsters. The stores receive large vases from China, packed in enormous cartons filled with insulation. So we gathered lots of cardboard and some carpet scraps and got very innovative. After our cardboard condo was built Anne and I drifted off to panhandle on Mulberry Street, to raise money for coffee. We asked for change for two hours and didn't get any. The first lesson of being on the street is nobody wants to deal with you as a human being. When people see you panhandling they cross the street or engage immediately in a very animated conversation with their companion in order to avoid you. We spent the night, very cold, and before dawn the garbage trucks began their crawl. We were terrified we might get mistaken for a big pile of refuse and flattened, and the police cruisers were flashing their lights at us, so we scattered out of there pretty early. We looked back just in time to see the garbagemen dismantle our condominium and chuck it all into their trucks.

"Our schedule quickly came down to this: get up early, get down to the Bowery Mission, get in line so we could have breakfast. When the doors opened we would be admitted for a two hour haranguing by the people who ran the Mission. They had a whole revivalist show going on before every meal was served to make sure we had our religion."

"I was sitting up front trying to sing the hymns," Anne recalled. "It was warm and sheltered and sort of invigorating after being out in the street, knowing you were going to get a meal afterwards. We had to sit through this church service for two hours with these rosy-cheeked Bible Belt kids who came in from Oklahoma to testify about finding Christ. They were on some kind of soup kitchen circuit. It was quite a large gathering. I remember people ditching their drugs and so on as they came in."

"People on the street were curious," said Andrew, "'who are you, and what are you doing?' Some were openly hostile, and a number of times we'd hear, 'Well, in five days when you guys are finished you get to go home and take a bath. I don't get to go home.' Most were just curious though, and interested.

"Bernie evinced the most unstinting delight and enthusiasm for every experience that came our way. Which I think is something that helped keep everybody there. Nobody had to stay, after all—there were people on the retreat who lived in New York, who could have simply caught a subway home. And there were plenty of times when it seemed like that might be a reasonable thing to do."

"Bernie was so elemental," said Anne, "like a rock, and he was so good on his feet. When it looked like we couldn't do something, he had another solution. I was very, very moved by his vision of empathy."

Andrew Schelling:
Spring Sesshin in the Bowery
April 1992

Thirteen of us trail through the Bowery behind Tetsugen Sensei. He's scouring the street map as though it were sutra. We might as well be lost down some Chinese gorge, rock walls soaring in mist. The soot-black tenements lean overhead, some sealed off with razor wire. They are today's hall of practice. Among them we locate the little park. Sensei's schedule says we're to sit zazen three times a day by the basketball court. But first to clear off a litter of crack phials and needles. "Sweep the garden"—adage of some buddha ancestor who set a good riddle? Or can we picture a future monasticism—half the year given to mountain retreat, raven and rattlesnake comrades, twisting along pine forest cliffsides—half the year inside cities, like Catholic Workers on 34th St. ladling soup? I mean just till we pull through this particular epoch.

> *Formal and*
> *desolate the crab*
> *apple blossoms*
> *"the Bodhisattva moves through all worlds"*

"What is he going to do next?" is a common refrain in the Zen world when the subject of Bernie Glassman comes up. When we finally do reach his offices in Montecito after an extensive search, I am surprised to find him not head-shaven as usual, but full-bearded with a small grey pony tail at the nape of his neck, and sporting the infamous red suspenders. In this most recent phase of his evolution he has, as it turns out, decided to disrobe. Not to leave the practice, he explains, only the priesthood. Just the latest unconventional move in a long history of unconventionality, certain to raise many eyebrows on his upcoming visit to Japan a few months hence. During our talk, I ask Glassman to look back over his thirty-plus years as a Zen teacher and activist, and particularly at the changes his activities have gone through over the years.

"It's all been important and it's all been right," he says. "I would never leave something that I was doing until I felt there were enough people doing it—but once I feel there are enough people to carry it along, I need to move on."

So, I ask him, what next?

"When I got involved in Zen," Glassman says, leaning forward with a sudden vitality, "and probably this is true for many people—a lot of my heroes were the unconventional people. Then, once you get into training, everybody becomes conventional. Well, I hope I always remain unconventional. I've trained in the conventional side of it, but I feel free—" He leans back and rummages through his pockets, and what he does next is something I never could have predicted in a million kalpas.

"For instance—I can put on my *nose*." Glassman suits actions to words by pulling from his pocket a rubber proboscis of the type preferred by clowns, and sticking it on over his own. "Trungpa Rinpoche once told me they had an extra position in Tibetan training monasteries—that of the jester. Well, I've always wanted to be a clown—a jester—and that's what I want to bring to this stuff now, because it's gotten too sanctimonious, and there's too much conventionality." He grins at me from behind his nose, reveling in my reaction.

"I've created an order of clowns. It's called the Order of Dis-Order. We have a Wizard of Od . . . We just had our first major installation of clowns. One of the rules is we have to have our nose with us all the time. At 'Change Your Mind' day, whenever anybody asked me a question I'd put my nose on before I would answer. I did a workshop with Ram Dass. I was there with my nose and he's got his wheelchair, so there were the two of us . . ." Glassman laughs. "I'd like to see at every center and every major event a clown who is free to say what they want.

"That's the feeling I'm after," he says, as the shadows across the mountains grow long and our conversation draws to a close. "Like the jester in the courts. For the Japanese to do that, that's a stretch, but for us . . . imagine Bush and Gore with noses on!" He grins widely at the thought. "Even if *you* don't have a nose, if you can imagine a nose on them, you're not going to be so uptight."

Living in the Now (104)

After a reading Bernie Glassman gave during a book tour, a woman in attendance stood up and asked him, "What does it take to live in the Now?"

Glassman answered, "Would anyone who is *not* living in the Now please stand up?"

Zen and the Art of Art: Natalie Goldberg's Wild Mind School of Writing Practice

Natalie Goldberg always shares with her writing students the three most important pieces of advice she received from her teacher, Katagiri Roshi:

> *Continue under all circumstances.*
> *Make positive effort for the good.*
> *Don't be tossed away.*

"All right, ten minutes, go!" says Natalie Goldberg, picking up her pen and diving into her five millionth empty page, one of her infamous fast-writing pens clutched between her fingers. Young for her years, dark-haired and intent, she chuckles occasionally to herself as she writes, bending over the page with all the earnestness of a child making her letters for the first time. But then, Natalie might say, if you're doing writing practice correctly, you *are* making your letters for the first time.

It's spitting rain in the twilight of a Minnesota fall, and we're in the zendo of the Clouds and Water Zen Center in Minneapolis/St. Paul, where Natalie is teaching her weekly writing practice class. She's come here for a year to deepen her practice with Dosho Mike Port, a dharma heir to her teacher, Dainin Katagiri, and to go through a new level of lay ordination in her lineage. We're onto our third or fourth writing of the afternoon, and I don't remember what this particular assignment is any more—but at this point, I'm writing about where we are. It's a former railroad warehouse, a grand old building, the zendo on the ground floor with its shoji screens, exposed water pipes and quadrant of white industrial pillars—the four pillars of Zen, I joked to Dosho when he showed me around this morning after zazen.

They've stripped and refinished the lovely wood floors that would cost a fortune today—thick and deep grained, they still bear an odd array of humps and gouges (during walking meditation, one has plenty of time to notice such things), as though some variety of heavy machinery was once dragged regularly across them. They also now bear an array of black sitting cushions—zabutons and zafus—in place of whatever railroad machinery once dwelt here. Tall rectangular windows peer out over the street, through which, between the scratching of pens, come the whine of engines climbing their gears upward in the city traffic.

Nat is sitting, scribbling away in front of the altar, with its candles and ikebana flower arrangement and two brass bodhisattva figures: Manjusri with sword upraised, enjoining us to keep our pens moving, and Kannon, with her countless arms reaching out to help all sentient beings—or perhaps, wield countless pens. As always, she'll do whatever is appropriate to the situation. This morning we chanted the Heart Sutra, and now the circling shadow of the ceiling fan blades against the pillar in front of me, alternately dark, then light, then dark again, seem to speak its echo: form—emptiness—form—emptiness.

The best feature of the place, though, is the dokusan room, where Dosho Sensei gave me advice this morning on my practice—and where, Natalie recently told me, she'd leapt at Dosho in response to a koan she'd been trying to answer and pinned him against the floor, glaring into his face (don't try this in your home), and he'd responded simply, "Pretty good." Converted from an old bank vault, it is set into the brick of the back wall, its gigantic steel door, with numbered dial still intact, standing permanently ajar—welded open at the hinges, lest it swing shut and trap some unsuspecting Zen student in dokusan hell forever.

"Make writing your practice," Katagiri Roshi had suggested to Natalie Goldberg, years before when she was a beginning Zen student at the Minneapolis Zen Center.

"Why?" she'd asked innocently.

"Because you like it," Katagiri told her.

Now, twenty-five years later, Natalie continues to exude unquenchable enthusiasm for the two practices around which her life is built: writing and Zen. She doesn't make much distinction between them. "I teach people to accept their minds," she says, "just like in zazen—it's all just studying mind. No good, no bad. In writing practice we use the same basic principle as in zazen— you make a commitment for a period of time, and you keep the practice going no matter what. In the case of writing practice, it's usually ten minutes. The basic rule is: keep your hand moving. No editing, no going back or crossing out, forget about spelling or punctuation. If something comes up that feels dangerous, go for it. That's where the juice is. By keeping your hand moving you don't leave any space for what we call monkey mind—the commentator, the internal critic, to come in and get in the way."

"Katagiri Roshi taught me to trust my own deep mind," she explains to me later, "to let it come forward—not to try to be Hemingway, or to be the best writer in the world. To let writing do writing. We're taught many structures from the outside in.

But I'm using writing as a tool to come from the inside out. This approach brings a shining self-confidence—you learn to just rest in your own mind with a belief in who you are, and with your feet on the ground."

That it works is pretty much a proven fact. Natalie's system of writing practice, as delineated in her best-selling book *Writing Down the Bones* and the sequel *Wild Mind,* has made her perhaps the most sought-after writing teacher in the country, and gave rise to a boom in books on writing and creativity that is still going on today. Natalie is also the author of *Long Quiet Highway*, a memoir of her years with Katagiri Roshi, one of the best personal accounts of Zen training available.

"When you're writing, where do your words come from?" Natalie addresses the room, now that we've set our pens down and are ready for a bit of guidance. "Out of nothingness," she answers herself. "When your words come out of nothingness, writing does writing. This is the ground of creation—a connection with your Wild Mind, which doesn't end where your skin stops. Wild Mind is not only you—it's the clouds, the wind, the glass you're drinking from, the person beside you—it's all life coming through the pen, or the paintbrush, or camera eye, or singing voice."

I'm reminded of a workshop I did with Natalie in New York City, where she led the entire group of one hundred students out of the building and down the street to do walking meditation in Washington Square Park. It was one of the first warm days of spring, and everyone was out—people walking dogs, people playing Frisbee and strumming guitars, bike couriers munching sandwiches on the lawn beside their steeds, old men playing checkers. As we walked step by slow step past them all, beneath trees with the first pale shoots leafing out from their tips, a silence fell across the multitudes. People stopped what they were doing to whisper amongst themselves: "What are they doing?" Then finally to call out: "Hey, what are you all demonstrating for?" Meanwhile, a man walked past, pushing a shopping cart laden with all his belongings and shouting the one thousand names of God in three languages, while no one paid him any mind at all.

"We're just walking," answered Natalie, and for the next twenty minutes we continued to do just that, until we'd become just another part of the afternoon scene in the park, and everyone returned to their lunches and games.

But now, here in the zendo, I can tell she's about to go off on one of her rolls. She's trusting her own mind, and every word, it seems, is golden:

"Our conscious mind doesn't know much. It maybe knows to go out and get some more milk when we've run out. And maybe we should just leave the conscious mind for those things. Our real life unfolds some other way. We never really know who we are. Odd, isn't it? The deeper you go the less you know—but the more awake you are.

"Our work is to move closer and closer. To abstract is to move further and further away. Until in politics you can drop bombs and you don't really know there are people there.

"Life doesn't make sense. Stand around waiting for your life to make sense and you'll spend your life waiting on the sidelines.

"The mind, if you get out of the way, already knows the rules of art—because the rules of art come from Wild Mind. I still don't know a thing about writing."

Is she talking writing or is she talking Zen? The distinction has dropped away. Meanwhile, across the street the Mississippi, artery of the nation, rolls past, and over it all broods the giant brick smokestack of the Schmidt's Brewery, which you can smell from just about anywhere in the city if the wind is blowing in the right direction. *The wisdom of the yeast,* I can't help thinking to myself.

Natalie, in fact, assigns the class to meet for the first hour next week in the parking lot below the brewery, whose architecture she's fond of. There they'll do walking meditation as a warm up before writing practice.

"But what if it snows?" someone protests.

"Bring a coat," responds Natalie, and here it comes again, that unquenchable enthusiasm: "Can you imagine walking meditation in the snow in the Schmidt's Brewery parking lot? Holy, Holy, Holy."

Freud Meets Buddha: Psychotherapy and the Dharma

One night, a psychiatrist was giving a talk at Plum Village and Thich Nhat Hanh raised his hand. With the utmost seriousness he asked, "Are the children of psychologists happier than other children?"

"I'd done a fair amount of therapy," says Hozan Alan Senauke, a dharma successor to Sojun Mel Weitsman, "and I was in the middle of that process when it came to me that there was a whole realm of questions I had that were outside the scope of psychotherapy. Questions like 'Why am I here?' and 'What's my purpose in life, and how can I function in harmony with it?' I talked to my therapist about it, and she confirmed that I needed to look elsewhere for answers to those kinds of questions. After I got involved with Zen, I ended up doing the two, psychotherapy and Zen practice, for a long time—and I never thought they were in any tension with each other."

Buddhism has always adapted to the prevailing religion of each country to which it has traveled. But what *is* the prevailing religion of our increasingly secular American culture? Christianity? Science? Capitalism? Consumerism? While any of these might arguably fill the role, may people might point to another alternative: psychology. As the reigning means the Western world has discovered for working with and freeing the mind and emotions, many people point to psychotherapy as the closest thing we have to the paths of liberation available in the East. But are "self-actualization" or "peak experience" the same thing as spiritual liberation? Do Western approaches to psychological well-being have anything to offer the East? The jury is still out, but one thing seems certain: the two are going to have to deal with each other.

"We can look at Zen practice and psychotherapy as existing on a continuum," says Zen teacher and psychotherapist Lawson Sachter, a dharma heir to Philip Kapleau. "Or we can look at them as two distinctly different ways of working. Maybe it's useful to see psychological work as focusing more on what we feel—or avoid feeling—and Zen as looking into who it is that is experiencing all this. It's an amazing experience to work with someone in therapy right after they've completed a seven day sesshin. The psyche is almost always more fluid and accessible in a way that is rarely encountered under ordinary circumstances.

"As a Zen teacher, my experience has been that not all practice-related difficulties that come up for Western students are addressed through traditional forms of training. Unconscious obstructions arising from early grief and deeply buried anger, and a whole range of related defensive structures, can be stirred up by intensive zazen. And, at least to some degree, it's our defensive structures with which we identify. I've had students say, 'Without my defenses, who am I?' That's a big question.

"Based on my experience over the years, I've become convinced that for many of us in the West, both practice and therapy are vital; that together they lead to deeper, and more lasting change. Some teachers resist this view, but I expect that in the years to come more and more effective forms of integrating these two ways of working will naturally evolve."

A contender for the reigning "religion" of the West—and certainly the major Western-developed model of working with the mind—psychology has been tangled up with Buddhist practice at least since Carl Jung, early in the last century, coined the term "transpersonal." The two have been even more deeply associated since the human potential movement of the Sixties and Seventies, where the distinction between spiritual and psychological work, if it was made at all, was often unclear. The relation between the two worlds has continued to be explored and developed by such pioneers as Ken Wilber, Mark Epstein, Daniel Goleman, and Tara Bennett Goleman.

"If we can't take the teachings to heart," says Zen teacher Cynthia Jurs, "and apply them to our own lives, the habitual patterns that keep us locked into our suffering—if we can't use the dharma to address those things directly, then there's no hope. And there's no real awakening. I feel Western culture has a great deal to offer Buddhism in the psychological realm, as far as how to address our *stuff*—our habitual, reactive patterns. Psychology gives us some tools. But what Buddhism is about is cutting *all* of those patterns of self-clinging, utterly and completely. Psychological training is helpful, because it teaches you to identify that stuff. And if you take that into your practice, look deeply, and don't avoid it, you can unravel it. But you have to be willing to face it: what is keeping me from being free and really helping others? The point of all this is, if you're really practicing dharma, you're out to let go of self-clinging. There's no such a thing as the self. You might as well forget it and start dying now! There's nothing to hold onto."

The Way to Mental Health (105)

Psychoanalyst Erich Fromm, who studied Zen and sought to integrate it into his psychoanalytic practice, was asked once whether he thought mental health could be attained through Zen.

"It's the only way to mental health," answered Fromm.

The Ordinary Mind School of Zen

"With unfailing kindness," says Charlotte Joko Beck, "your life always presents what you need to learn."

"There can be some confusion between our approach to Zen practice and traditional psychotherapy," says Zen teacher Diane Rizzetto of the Bay Zen Center in Oakland, California, speaking about the approach of Charlotte Joko Beck's "Ordinary Mind" school of American Zen. "In the beginning, our approach to practice can seem very psychotherapeutic because we include experiential inquiry into the thought, emotion, and bodily patterns that keep us from living our lives from the openness of wisdom and compassion that is our true nature. We investigate the behavioral patterns in our everyday lives, because it is within the context of the frustration on the freeway, the snide remark from our co-worker, or whatever else gets our feathers ruffled, that we can begin to see how the ego-self holds on. This differs from traditional psychotherapy because we do not approach our experience of self as something to be fixed. Rather, we view these situations as teachers that point us to our habitual modes of suffering.

"We're not trying to 'fix' our lives, or trying to make ourselves feel better in some way, although that is usually a result of practice over time. Rather we learn how to observe what we believe our life to be in a non-judgmental way. Psychotherapy's aim is really to reinforce the self, and make it feel good. But the purpose of Zen practice is to take us further.

"An image I use a lot," says Rizzetto, "is that of a house. We can think of the self as a house that has difficulties such as doors that won't open and windows that won't shut, but we manage to get by. Maybe we have trouble with relationships, and so forth, but with a little stomping and pushing we manage to keep things going. But it can be difficult to live this way over a long period of time, so at some point we may seek help from a psychotherapist. The therapist will help us understand why that door won't open and shut, maybe help us fix the door in a certain way—or, at least learn ways of getting by. This work can be very useful, and we need to respect it, because we need that kind of help sometimes.

"But the purpose of Zen practice is to take us further than the house. We may enter through the house—at times we may even teach people how to kick the stuck door open, to maintain, because they're not ready to see the house for what it *isn't*. But eventually what happens, through the practice, is we begin to see the house in a more transparent way. The more we learn about what we *think* the house is, the less able we are to solidify it. Eventually we find that there really *is* no permanent house separate from our experience in each moment."

Rizzetto illustrates the approach by telling a story of when she was a senior student, living in Oakland and coordinating a sitting group affiliated with Joko Beck's San Diego Zen Center. Rizzetto was often called upon to help weekend retreats get started on Thursday nights, in preparation for Beck's arrival on Friday, a task that involved giving basic practice instruction. One technique the Ordinary Mind school has pioneered is the practice of "eye-gazing," in which two students sit for a period of time looking into one another's eyes. One evening at the beginning of a retreat Rizzetto was giving basic instruction for this technique and, as she tells it:

"Somebody had glasses on and I said, 'If you're wearing glasses, take your glasses off.' It just seemed sensible to me. Now, I wasn't wearing glasses in those days, and so I didn't have a clue that some people need glasses just to see the person in front of them. I shouldn't have said anything.

"The next day, Joko was here. She gave her talk and the topic of eye-gazing came up, and the woman to whom I said 'take your glasses off' said, 'If I don't have my glasses on, I can't see anything. I was told that you're supposed to leave them off.'

"And Joko said, 'Whoever told you that doesn't know what they're talking about.'

"First," says Rizzetto, "I was crushed, and then all these thoughts started to come up, 'what story am I going to tell' and 'how am I going to cover myself,' and 'what are the other students all thinking?' And that was really wonderful to practice with.

"For me, the bodily sensation was just like a deflating balloon. I could feel my body sinking and getting smaller and kind of shriveling up into nothing, and I just sat with that. And then sadness came up. I started crying. If I were in therapy, perhaps at that point I'd start looking for the story, the history behind the sadness. But I didn't take that direction. I remained present observing the pure energy labeled 'sadness' and at some point it became not my sadness, but *just* sadness. So it went from 'someone did this to me,' to *my* sadness, and then just sadness. And then it opened up again and became the sadness of the entire universe.

"By the time I got into the interview room with Joko," says Rizzetto, "I just explained the process to her and tears came to her eyes. That was it. She looked at me and said: 'It is from this place that you help others.'"

"Suppose," explained Joko Beck in an interview in *Tricycle Magazine*, "someone has hurt my feelings—or so I think. What I *want* to do is to go over and over and over that drama so I can blame them and get to be right. To turn away from such thinking and just experience the painful body [that accompanies the thoughts and emotions] is to forget the self. If you really experience something without thoughts, there is no self—there's just a vibration of energy. When you practice like that 10,000 times, you will be more selfless. It doesn't mean that you're a ghost. It means that you'd much more non-reactive—in the world, but not of it."

"One of the things Joko helped me with greatly," says another of her students, "was the death of my son. If there's anything you want to talk about that was a 'breakthrough,' that was it—but it's taken six years. He was killed in an accident, and sitting with *that* was something. I did a lot of sesshins with Joko over that period.

"Joko was there with me in a very interesting way. On one level, she was emotionally involved. When I told her over the phone, she gasped, and it was like I could feel her getting *hit*. I could feel that reverberation back, and that sensitivity. And so that would always be there on the emotional level, the 'I understand what you're going through.' We'd talk about that.

"But still she was always, 'This is about facing it, we're not going to play any games with this. Know this and know this now: there is no such thing as death. There is no such thing as life. There's no past, and there's no future. Clear? That's what it is. Now let's deal with this.' She helped me on that level, and I see it more now and more clearly, what that aspect of no death and no birth that is spoken of in Zen.

"So that was my koan, you see? I'll tell you something—I'm not very moved by 'Mu.' I mean, *this* is a fucking koan—my life being ripped apart, my heart being broken apart. There's no choice here. And that was real clear. So yeah, that's Joko. She says everyday life is your teacher. Just be aware of it. Just look at it. See it and practice with it. Practice with that conditioned emotion, whatever it may be: anger, fear, remorse, regret, guilt, loss, utter and complete darkness. This is the face of the Buddha, buddy."

Students and Teachers: Succession and the Transmission of the Dharma in America

After Danan Henry's dharma transmission ceremony, which authorized him to teach Zen, his teacher Philip Kapleau told him: "Danan, you must understand that your greatest responsibility to your students is to protect them from your influence."

The torch has been passed—the transmission of the lamp, or the light, is a commonly used classical metaphor. But what exactly is it that has been transmitted? It still looks recognizably like Zen. But if so, will it remain Zen?

"A roshi," wrote Trudy Dixon in her introduction to *Zen Mind, Beginner's Mind*, "is a person who has actualized that perfect freedom which is the potentiality for all human beings. He exists freely in the fullness of his whole being. The flow of his consciousness is not the fixed repetitive patterns of our usual self-centered consciousness, but rather arises spontaneously and naturally . . . Because he is just himself, he is a mirror for his students. When we are with him, we feel our own strengths and shortcomings without any sense of praise or criticism from him. In his presence, we see our original face, and the extraordinariness we see is only our own true nature."

It is one thing to apply such a description to someone as apparently flawless as Dixon's teacher, Suzuki Roshi, but another to find American Zen teachers capable of living up to so high a standard—particularly in a permissive society so wrought with temptation, so infatuated with profit, power, and commerce, and so imbued with the certainty that the possession of material goods is the sure path to a satisfying and successful life. It has not always been an easy task.

The new American teachers have had enormous shoes to fill—and they have not always filled them successfully. Richard Baker, who resigned from the Abbot's position at the San Francisco Zen Center following a complex controversy around misuse of sexuality and power, has become the most prominent case in point, following a lengthy public scandal. Other teachers have not necessarily fared so well either—even among the original teachers who brought the practices from Asia there have emerged numerous reports of misuse of sexuality and authority. In examining these cases, it begins to come clear why the historical Buddha insisted that his monastics renounce sexuality, use of intoxicants, and the possession of money if they wished to join his order—and why the lifting of these restrictions in the last few hundred years, in Japan and now, America, has proven to be a problematic decision.

The brief history of Zen in the U.S. has conclusively proven, for better or worse, that Zen teachers are human. But does this invalidate the practice, or the experience of realization offered by it? Today's Zen communities have begun to address these issues by setting up codes of conduct, by forming organizations so that teachers will not operate in isolation and—though reinstating the system of absolute prohibition advocated by the Buddha does not seem to be on anyone's priority list—by returning to the fundamental teachings of the precepts, the moral and ethical teachings of Buddhism, which are designed to foster right conduct among both the monastic order and the laity. Other sanghas have experimented with both tightening and loosening the standards by which teachers are sanctioned.

"Without pointing a finger at anyone," says Robert Aitken Roshi, when asked about the rigorous standards he imposes in passing on the dharma transmission, "I'll just identify myself as being as conservative as possible in these matters."

"The original Buddhist order," said Bernie Glassman, in discussing his more liberal standards during a panel discussion I attended at Zen Mountain Monastery, "allowed teachers to emerge, or not emerge, naturally, based upon insight and talent. That's the approach, as far as I'm concerned, that's best suited for the American sangha."

Hozan Alan Senauke remembers a point with his teacher, Sojun Mel Weitsman, at which, "I realized that this person was not my father, and he was not my therapist, and he was not my friend. He was something else which I had no previous model for." But what, exactly, constitutes a Zen teacher in twenty-first century America? Charlotte Joko Beck wrote in *Everyday Zen: Love and Work* about the ultimate authority in spiritual life: "You may say, 'Well, I need a teacher who can free me from my suffering. I'm hurting and I don't understand it. I need someone who can tell me what to do, don't I?' No! You may need a guide, you may need it made clear how to practice with your life—what is needed is a guide who will make it clear to you that the authority in your life, your true teacher, is you—and we practice to realize this 'you.'"

Norman Fischer, former abbot of the San Francisco Zen Center, examined the issue from the perspective of his own experience after receiving the dharma transmission, during a conversation we had at a conference on Buddhism in the Twenty-first Century, organized by the Naropa Institute: "Here I was, a dharma teacher with the responsibility to continue this lineage, and I didn't really feel like I was a Zen master or anything like that. I remembered reading in a book by Thich Nhat Hanh, this traditional phrase: 'you should study Zen with a true teacher. And if you can't find a true teacher, it's better not to study at all.' And I thought, 'My God, am I a true teacher of Zen? What the hell am I doing?'

"So I wrote a letter to Thich Nhat Hanh, and asked him if I could see him the next time he came to the States. When I saw him and asked about this he said, 'In the dharma, everybody helps each other. The person who has more experience helps the person who has a little less experience. Everybody just does their best.' And I thought, that makes sense. I can help somebody with less experience than me.

"After that, I could do my best when necessary to teach. In Zen, doing the practice is what helps people. So the practice is like a mandala, and in the mandala there's a teacher. It's not that the teacher is so brilliant, telling everybody what's what, and they've got to listen to that. Rather, everybody advances in understanding because they continue to practice. But to this day, I feel if there's someone there who's more experienced than me, they should do it."

"My responsibility," says Danan Henry, "is to encourage my students to be what they are. They already *are* what they are—they just need to wake up to their own nature."

And Maurine Stuart puts it: "I can't *give* anything to anyone. Teaching is about being present. Just being there."

Still, nearly everyone agrees that it's a thorny matter to set off into the wilderness of the mind without a good guide. And in the Zen school at least, the mind-to-mind transmission has always been of pivotal importance. There exists a great danger, many teachers and practitioners concur, in liberalizing the process of succession and the sanctioning of teachers to the point where the baby gets thrown out with the bathwater. Still, some teachers, like Steve Allen, believe the dharma transmission to be a dead system that has completely outlived its usefulness. Others, like John Daido Loori of Zen Mountain Monastery, who only sanctioned three full dharma heirs in three decades of teaching, believe it is essential to maintaining the integrity of the practice. And Joshu Sasaki Roshi, who has been teaching in America for some five decades, has still, at most recent report, refused to sanction any full dharma heirs at all. Like so many elements in the development of American Zen, these issues are still working themselves out.

Perhaps the approach used by Master Sheng-yen of the Ch'an Meditation Center in Elmhurst, New York, can help shine some light upon the matter. Following retreats, Master Sheng-yen asks his students to prostrate toward their Shi-fu (their teacher—himself) in gratitude. Then he asks them, "Are you prostrating to Sheng-yen or to Shi-fu (the teacher)?"

He expects them to answer, "To Shi-fu."

"There is nothing special about Sheng-yen," he says. "It is only in his role as the teacher that he represents the dharma. When dharma, teacher, and student are harmonized, the student becomes enlightened."

As Robert Aitken Roshi puts it, "I'm heartened by the fact that I have a few genuine successors. That's enough."

In a conversation with Zen teacher Jitsudo Ancheta, former abbott of the Hidden Mountain Zen Center in Albuquerque, at my home outside Taos, Ancheta remembered his final meeting with his teacher, Maezumi Roshi, in the spring of 1995. Ancheta was resident priest at the Zen Mountain Center in Idyllwild, California and Maezumi was preparing for his last trip to Japan, where he would pass away quietly at the age of sixty-five, without seeing any of his students again. A late snowstorm was brewing, and in lieu of a promised last dokusan before he left, Maezumi suggested Ancheta meet him at a small café partway down the mountain, so that he could get started before the weather got any worse.

"I set off after Roshi did, driving the Zen Center pickup truck," Ancheta said. "I remember the snow was already coming down very hard and there were several inches of it on the road. I could see the tracks his tires had made, sliding and swerving on the curves. At one point, I came around a bend and lost traction completely and almost went over the edge. I had to keep going though, because I wanted to make sure Roshi was all right. The sky was completely overcast, it was all very dark. I got to the café to find it was closed. Roshi was parked in front, waiting for me. He got in the cab of the truck and we talked for a while. I told him about my idea of starting a Zen Center in New Mexico. He was supportive. I remember feeling a bit ill at ease, concerned whether he was going to get down the mountain all right.

"After a while, he said he'd better go before the storm got any worse. I remember him getting out of the cab of the truck and walking back through the snow toward his car. He was halfway there when he turned back and looked at me over his shoulder.

"Remember your vows,' he said to me. Then he turned back, got in the car, and drove off."

Ancheta never saw him again.

Teacher or Friend? (106)

Zen priest Stan White, of Hokoji temple in New Mexico, remembers one of his first meetings with Suzuki Roshi, which took place after a public talk in which Suzuki had said, "Sometimes I am your teacher and sometimes I am your friend."

"You said in your lecture," White asked, "that you were my friend. What did you mean by that?"

Suzuki-roshi replied: "I can tell by looking at you that you have suffered, and so have I. Therefore we are friends. Of course, I have a lot of experience with Zen, and you have very little. Therefore you are my student."

The Same Chord, in Harmony (107)

A student of Ch'an master Sheng-yen described the relationship with his teacher in this way: "A master is like a music teacher who sounds a particular musical chord which the student must attempt to perform. Without the master, a student might aimlessly search for the correct combination of notes, but just one clue from the master—'Put this finger here ...'—and student and master strike the same chord in harmony."

Nothing to Give (108)

John Daido Loori remembers once giving Maezumi Roshi a birthday present.

Maezumi thanked him, saying, "I am sorry I have nothing to give you."

"But Roshi," Loori responded. "You give me so much!"

With that Maezumi wheeled and walked away.

"Without realizing it," says Loori, "I'd insulted him. A true Zen teacher has nothing to give."

A student from another Zen center attended a week-long retreat with Kobun Chino Roshi and, having been very struck by his presence and teaching style, was feeling confused about who to study with. "I already have a teacher," she told him during an interview, "but I feel a quality of connectedness with you that I've never felt before. What should I do?"

Kobun looked at her. "When the last teacher on earth is gone," he asked, "Who will be your teacher?"

The student didn't know how to reply. "Everything," she answered finally.

"No," he said. "It will be you."

ENDNOTES

Frontispiece quote: "Shunryu Suzuki Roshi once said to Sojun Mel Weitsman, 'You have a saying...'" From personal interview with Sojun Mel Weitsman, August 2000.

Preface
"The self is, of course, a story..." Halifax, Joan. Personal interview, August 2000.

Part One
Opener: "There was a fisherman . . ." From Sokei-an, *Zen Pivots: Lectures on Buddhism and Zen*. Mary Farkas, ed., and Robert Lopez. New York & Tokyo: Weatherhill, 1998.

Bodhidharma story and quotes: passed down through oral tradition. This is the author's version, derived from a number of different translations.

"A special transmission . . ." Passed down through oral tradition. This is the author's version, derived from a number of different translations.

"It seems to me . . ." Loori, John Daido. Personal interview, spring 2000.

Chapter One: The Land of the White Barbarians
"To be awake is to be alive . . ." Henry David Thoreau. *Walden.* Boston: Houghton Mifflin, 1906.

"The land of the white barbarians is beneath the dignity of a Zen master . . ." Tworkov, Helen. *Zen in America.* San Francisco: North Point Press, 1989, p. 3.

"An idealistic universal religion . . ." Shaku, Soyen. (Provided by Joe McNeely.)

"depend on miracles or faith . . ." Fields, Rick. *How the Swans Came to the Lake.* Boulder: Shambhala, 1981, p. 128.

"I have studied Buddhism for more than forty years . . .." Nordstrom, Louis, ed. *Namu Dai Bosa: A Transmission of Zen Buddhism to America.* New York: Theatre Arts Books, 1976, p. 128.

"Just face this great . . ." Shaku, Soyen. Reported by Nyogen Senzaki in "Commemoration of Soyen Shaku, 1954," quoted in *How the Swans Came to the Lake,* p. 172.

"I have never made any demarcation of my learning . . ." Senzaki, Nyogen. *Zen Notes,* Vol. IV, No. 4 (April 1957), p. 1. First Zen Institute of America, Inc.

"(Senzaki) studied English and Western philosophy . . ." Aitken, Robert, in introduction to Senzaki, Nyogen and McCandless, Ruth Strout. *Buddhism and Zen.* San Francisco: North Point Press, 1987, p. x.

"Americans in general are lovers . . ." Senzaki, Nyogen. From *Namu Dai Bosa,* pp. 89–91.

Zen Story: "The Most Beautiful Vow." From *Wind Bell,* Vol. VIII, Nos. 1–2 (Fall 1969), p. 36.

Zen Story: "The True Meaning of Cleanliness." From *Zen Notes,* Vol. XXI, No. 5 (May 1974), p. 1. First Zen Institute of America, Inc.

"Dharma Words from Nyogen Senzaki." Senzaki, Nyogen. From *Namu Dai Bosa.*

"Very much the bohemian, with long swirling hair . . ." Watts, Alan. *In My Own Way: Autobiography 1915–1965.* New York: Pantheon Books, 1972, p. 144.

"I had a house and one chair . . ." Sasaki, Sokei-an. Reported by Mary Farkas in "Footsteps in the Invisible World," *Wind Bell,* Vol. VIII, Nos. 1–2 (Fall 1969), p. 15.

Zen Story: "Carve Me a Buddha." From First Zen Institute archives. First Zen Institute of America, Inc.

Zen Story: "Long Time Dead." From First Zen Institute archives. First Zen Institute of America, Inc.

"Utterly transported out of . . ." Sasaki, Ruth Fuller. Reported by Mary Farkas in "Footsteps in the Invisible World," *Wind Bell*, Vol. VIII, Nos. 1–2 (Fall 1969), p. 18.

"In Buddhism, purposelessness is fundamental . . ." Sasaki, Sokei-an. Reported by Alan Watts in *In My Own Way*, p. 144.

"I have always taken nature's orders . . ." Sasaki, Sokei-an. *How the Swans Came to the Lake*, p. 192.

"The first master to carry Zen to America . . ." Reported by Mary Farkas in introduction to *The Zen Eye: A collection of Zen Talks by Sokei-an.* Mary Farkas, ed. New York: Weatherhill, 1994, p. ix.

Zen story: "I Am from Missouri." From First Zen Institute archives. © First Zen Institute of America, Inc.

"When you go to Riverside Drive . . ." Sasaki, Sokei-an. From *Zen Notes*, Vol. XLV, No. 3, Summer 1998.

"One day, when I was traveling through Idaho . . ." Sasaki, Sokei-an. From *Zen Notes*, First Zen Institute of America, Inc.Vol. XXVIII, No. 11, 1981.

"The Mountain of Compassion" and "eastbound tendency of the teachings," Tworkov, Helen. *Zen in America*. San Francisco: North Point Press, 1989, p. 11.

"Even as a kid seeing him . . ." Saijo, Albert. From *Big Sky Mind: Buddhism and the Beat Generation*. Carole Tonkinson, ed. New York: Riverhead Books, 1995, pp. 244–245.

"Parting." Poem by Senzaki, Nyogen. From *Like a Dream, Like a Fantasy: The Zen Writings and Translations of Nyogen Senzaki*. Edited and with an introduction by Eido Shimano Roshi. Japan Publications, Inc, 1978, p. 45. Used by permission.

"Friends in the Dharma, be satisfied with your own head . . ." Senzaki, Nyogen. Reported by Eido Tai Shimano in *Wind Bell*, Vol. VIII, Nos. 1–2 (Fall 1969), p. 37.

"Do not erect a tombstone . . ." Senzaki, Nyogen. From *Namu Dai Bosa*.

"The Fifth Patriarch told a new monk . . ." poem by Shaku, Soyen. From *Namu Dai Bosa*.

"Bringing Zen to America," Sokei-an. Reported by Mary Farkas in introduction to *The Zen Eye*, p. ix.

Chapter Two

"What makes a man in his middle years," "painful tensions," and "need to understand the appalling sufferings," Kapleau, Philip. *Zen Dawn in the West*. Garden City, New York: Anchor Press/ Doubleday, 1980, p. 259.

"That damn 'nothing' feeling . . ." Kapleau, Philip. *The Three Pillars of Zen*. Boston: Beacon Press, 1967, p. 208.

"Because we Japanese have inflicted," and "the law of karmic retribution . . ." Kapleau, Philip. *Zen Dawn in the West*, p. 263.

"A mood of black depression" and "in bondage to the joyless pursuit," Kapleau, Philip. *Zen Dawn in the West*, p. 262.

"My vacuous life no longer had meaning . . ." Kapleau, Philip. *Zen Dawn in the West*, p. 264.

"If you really want to learn Buddhism" and "transfusion of courage," Kapleau, Philip. *The Three Pillars of Zen*, p. 209.

"Free as a fish swimming in an ocean . . ." Kapleau, Philip. *The Three Pillars of Zen*, p. 229.

"After several months of agonizing . . ." Kapleau, Philip. *Zen Dawn in the West*, p. 266.

Zen Story: "First Lesson." From personal interview with Philip Kapleau, October, 2000, with additional details from *The Three Pillars of Zen*, pp. 210–211.

Zen Story: "You Spit, I Bow." From personal interview with Philip Kapleau, October 2000, with additional details from *The Three Pillars of Zen*, pp. 211–212.

"Shivered for three days afterward . . ." Shimano, Eido T. *Endless Vow: The Zen Path of Soen Nakagawa*. Boston and London: Shambhala, 1996, p. 10.

Zen Story: "It's Not What You Say . . ." From personal interview with Philip Kapleau, October 2000.

Zen Story: "The Point of Zen." From *Namu Dai Bosa*, pp. 127–128.

"Now you are a pillar of this temple . . ." Farkas, Mary. "My Early Life." *Mary Farkas: Appreciations and Conversations.* Commemorative publication by First Zen Institute of America, 1992, p. 53.

"Upholstered in bright green velour . . ." Sasaki, Ruth Fuller. Reported by David Guy in "Dragon Wisdom: The Life of Ruth Fuller Sasaki." *Tricycle.* Winter 1994, p. 17.

"If I put them down on cushions and made them do zazen . . ." Sasaki, Sokei-an, from *Wind Bell*, Vol. VIII, Nos. 1–2 (Fall 1969), p. 18.

". . . making traditional Zen study available . . ." Sasaki, Ruth Fuller. *Zen Notes.* Vol. V, No. 7 (1958).

"A Letter from Japan." Sasaki, Ruth Fuller. *Zen Notes.* Vol. V, No. 7 (1958).

"The Forest of Zen" and all Walter Nowick quotes from personal interview, October 2000. (The poem is his remembered version of an ancient traditional verse.)

Zen Story: "Ready or Not . . ." From personal interview with Walter Nowick, October 2000.

"especially gentle and quiet man . . ." Snyder, Gary. *The Real Work.* New Directions, 1980, pp. 97–98.

Zen Story: "What Is Serious?" Snyder, Gary. *Jimmy and Lucy's House of 'K'*, No. 9 (January 1989), p. 23.

"Zen of eccentrics, loners . . ." Chandler, Ian. "Without Titles or Ranks." *Mary Farkas: Appreciations and Conversations*, p. 18.

"Many visitors would arrive expecting to be greeted . . ." Robison, Fay E. "Early Days." *Mary Farkas: Appreciations and Conversations*, p. 27.

"Don't you think we've made . . ." Farkas, Mary. *Zen Notes,* Vol. X, No. 10 (October 1963). First Zen Institute of America, Inc.

Zen Story: "What Is 'Spiritual'?" From First Zen Institute archives. © First Zen Institute of America, Inc.

Zen Story: "Worthwhile to Help, Zen Notes." From Vol. XXVIII, No. 11 (1981). ©1981 First Zen Institute of America, Inc.

"There is an initial experience . . ." Aitken, Robert. *The Practice of Perfection.* Counterpoint Press, 1994, pp. 20–21.

"The world seemed transparent . . ." Aitken, Robert. "Willy-Nilly Zen." From *Taking the Path of Zen.* San Francisco: North Point Press, 1982, p. 115.

"We climbed to the highest peak . ." Aitken, Robert. *Zen in America*, p. 28.

"All my work comes from the profound vow . . ." Aitken, Robert. *The Practice of Perfection*, p. 21.

"If we had not met I might well have spent my life . . ." Aitken, Robert. *Original Dwelling Place.* Counterpoint Press, 1996.

"It was as though all the beliefs I had . . ." Aitken, Robert. *Zen in America*, p. 35.

". . . a sign of throwing everything away . . ." Aitken, Robert. *Taking the Path of Zen,* p. 30.

"It was the only thing I could do . . ." Aitken, Robert. *Zen in America*, p. 37.

". . . a little bit of light. I knew he was referring to . . ." Aitken, Robert. "Willy-Nilly Zen." From *Taking the Path of Zen.* pp. 123–124.

Zen Story: "Just Like Riding a Bicycle." Aitken, Robert. Reported by Bonnie Myotai Treace in "The Broken Tray." *Mountain Record* Vol. XVI, No. 4 (Summer 1998), p. 15.

Zen Story: "A True Person of Zen." Tarrant, John. Reported in "The Fortunate and Ongoing Disaster of Lay Life." *Mountain Record*, Vol. XII, No. 2 (Winter 1993), p. 21.

"Skinny hawklike man" and "like teacups," *How the Swans Came to the Lake*, pp. 231–232

". . . could often be seen trotting about Tokyo . . ." Kapleau, Philip. *The Three Pillars of Zen*, p. 26.

". . . a distillation of pure energy." Aitken, Robert. "Willy-Nilly Zen." *Taking the Path of Zen,* p. 121.

"He devoted himself fully to us . . ." Aitken, Robert. Quoted in translator's introduction to Yasutani, Hakuun. *Flowers Fall: A*

Commentary on Zen Master Dogen's Genjokoan. Boston and London: Shambhala, 1996, p. xxvi.

"When you die, does everything around you die too?" Yasutani, Hakuun. From *The Three Pillars of Zen*, p. 114.

"I know what I'm supposed to do . . ." Yasutani, Hakuun. From *The Three Pillars of Zen*, p. 116.

"Dogen experienced full enlightenment . . ." Yasutani, Hakuun. *Wind Bell*, Vol. VII, Nos. 3-4 (Fall 1968), pp. 11–12.

"The fundamental delusion of humanity . . ." Yasutani, Hakuun. From Schiller, David. *The Little Zen Companion.* Workman Publishing Company, 1994.

Zen Story: "More Things in Heaven and Earth . . ." Reported in *How the Swans Came to the Lake*, p. 236.

"An electric news screen . . ." Yasutani, Hakuun. *Flowers Fall*, p. 57.

". . . not to lighten the load of a disciple . . ." *Tricycle,* Spring 1997, p. 78.

Zen story: "The Next Best Thing." Kennett, Jiyu. Reported in *The Wild White Goose*. Shasta Abbey, 1978, p. 51.

Closing anecdote: "Suppleness is very important . . ." Reported in *Zen Notes,* Vol. I, No. 9 (Sept. 1954).

Chapter Three

Chapter Opener: "1958 will be great year, year of Buddhism . . ." Kerouac, Jack. From 1957 letter to Philip Whalen, in *Jack Kerouac: Selected Letters 1957–1969.* Ann Charters, ed. New York: Viking 1999. Used by permission.

"I clearly remember when I first read . . ." Snyder, Gary. "On the Road with D.T. Suzuki." From *A Zen Life: D.T. Suzuki Remembered.* Maseo Abe, ed. New York/Tokyo: Weatherhill, 1986, pp. 207–209.

"When I am listening to Dr. Suzuki's lectures . . ." *A Zen Life: D.T. Suzuki Remembered.*

"hurried off in all directions" and "delayed his departure because," From Benz, Ernst. "In Memoriam" from *The Eastern Buddhist D.T. Suzuki Memorial Issue.* Vol. 2, No. 1, (August 1967).

"In meeting him . . ." Merton, Thomas. "D.T. Suzuki: The Man and His Work." *The Eastern Buddhist D.T. Suzuki Memorial Issue.* Vol. 2, No. 1, (August 1967).

". . . ever-present interest in everything . . ." Fromm, Erich. From "Memories of Dr. D.T. Suzuki. *The Eastern Buddhist.* Vol. II, No. 1, (August 1967).

Zen Story: "Supreme Spiritual Ideal?" Watts, Alan. From "The Mind-less Scholar." *The Eastern Buddhist.* Vol. II, No 1, (August 1967).

Zen Story: "Who's in Charge Here?" Reported by DeMartino, Richard in "On My First Coming to Meet Dr. D.T. Suzuki," from *A Zen Life: D.T. Suzuki Remembered*, p. 199.

Zen Story: "Know Your Own Mind." Ibid, p. 197.

". . . did not feel any great change occurred . . ." Okamura, Mihoko. Reported by Keiji Nishitani in *Memories of Suzuki Daisetz.* Tokyo: Shunjusha, 1975.

"Don't worry. Thank you! Thank you!" Suzuki, D.T. Quoted by Akishesa Kondo in "The Stone Bridge of Joshu," *The Eastern Buddhist.* Vol. II, No 1, (August 1967), p. 36.

Zen Story: "Change We Must." Reported by DeMartino, Richard in "On My First Coming to Meet Dr. D.T. Suzuki," from *A Zen Life: D.T. Suzuki Remembered*, pp.198–99.

"Man is a thinking reed . . ." Suzuki, D.T. (Quoted in *A Zen Life, D.T. Suzuki Remembered.*)

"It is said, perhaps with truth . . ." Watts, Alan. *In My Own Way*, p. 262.

". . . trying to find a needle in a haystack . . ." Watts, Alan. *In My Own Way*, p. 142.

"From the beginning I was never interested . . ." Watts, Alan. *In My Own Way*, p. 262.

". . . somewhat severe . . ." Watts, Alan. *In My Own Way*, p. 309.

"My only regret . . ." Watts, Alan. *In My Own Way*, p. 267.

"Whether his books are 'real Zen'. . ." Snyder, Gary. *Wind Bell*, Vol. VIII, Nos. 1–2 (Fall 1969), p. 29.

"You completely miss the point . . ." Suzuki, Shunryu. Quoted in Chadwick, David. *Crooked Cucumber: The Life and Zen Teachings of Shunryu Suzuki.* New York: Broadway Books, 1999.

Zen Story: "Beyond Words." Reported by Alan Watts. *In My Own Way,* p. 386.

". . . discovery . . . of sweet Buddha . . . I always did suspect . . ." Kerouac, Jack. From 1954 letter to Allen Ginsberg, in *Jack Kerouac: Selected Letters 1940–1956.* Ann Charters, ed. New York: Viking, 1995. Used by permission.

"I'm really humbled now" and "O what a dream or vision," Kerouac, Jack. From 1956 letter to Gary Snyder, in *Jack Kerouac: Selected Letters 1940–1956.* Ann Charters, ed. New York: Viking, 1995, p. 584. Used by permission.

"Word came out that DT Suzuki wanted to see me . . ." Kerouac, Jack. From early November 1958 letter to Philip Whalen, in *Jack Kerouac: Selected Letters 1957–1969.* Ann Charters, ed. New York: Viking, 1999. Used by permission.

"Dear Phil, A golden giant . . ." Kerouac, Jack. From November 1958 letter to Philip Whalen, in *Jack Kerouac: Selected Letters 1957–1969.* Ann Charters, ed. New York: Viking, 1999. Used by permission.

"It was a big guard station . . ." Whalen, Philip. From interview with Aram Saroyan in *Off the Wall.* Donald Allen, ed. Four Seasons Press, 1972.

"I am on a new kick 2 weeks old . . ." Ginsberg, Allen. From *As Ever: The Collected Correspondence of Allen Ginsberg and Neal Cassady.* Barry Gifford, ed. Creative Arts, 1978, pp. 139–142. Used by permission.

"'The Dharma Bums' is a surprising story of two young . . ." Kerouac, Jack. From July 1958 letter to Viking Press Editor Tom Guinzburg, in *Jack Kerouac: Selected Letters 1957–1969.* Ann Charters, ed. New York: Viking, 1999. Used by permission.

" . . . study with D.T. Suzuki, I've thought of music as . . ." Cage, John. *Zero: Contemporary Buddhist Life and Thought.* Vol. III, 1979, p. 69.

"Our poetry now . . ." Cage, John. *Silence: Lectures and Writings.* Middletown, CT: Wesleyan University Press, 1961.

"the melodies of silence" and "After a while one hears," Watts, Alan. *In My Own Way,* p. 231.

"In connection with my study of Zen . . ." Cage, John. *Zero: Contemporary Buddhist Life and Thought.* Vol. III, 1979, p. 69.

"I attempt to let sounds be themselves . . ." Cage, John. From a letter to the *New York Herald Tribune,* May 22, 1956.

Zen Story: "The Sleep of Babes." Reported in *In My Own Way,* p. 231.

Closing anecdote: "Mind your own business . . ." Miura, Isshu. From phone interview with Michael Hotz of the First Zen Institute of New York.

Part Two

"I feel Americans, especially young Americans . . ." Suzuki, Shunryu. *Zen Mind, Beginner's Mind.* Trudy Dixon, ed. New York: Weatherhill, 1970, p. 138.

"This kind of group practice . . ." Maezumi, Taizan. *Mountain Record* (July 1982).

Chapter Four

"[There are] boys that look like beatniks . . ." *How the Swans Came to the Lake,* p.227.

"He was just very present . . ." Kwong, Jakusho Bill. *Zen in America,* p.84.

"By the time I started to practice . . ." Weitsman, Sojun Mel. Personal interview, Sept. 2000.

"When I began to practice . . ." Hartman, Blanche. Personal interview, August 2000.

Zen Story: "Absolute Freedom?" Reported by David Chadwick in *Crooked Cucumber,* pp. 187–189.

Zen Story: "Not Two." Wilkie, Margot. Reported in interview with David Chadwick, from Shunryu Suzuki archive site, *www.cuke.com*

Zen Story: "Every Day Is Important." Mitchell, Elsie. *Sun Faced, Moon Faced Buddha, A Zen Quest.* New York/Tokyo: Weatherhill, 1973, Ch. 13.

Zen Story: "Follow the Yes." Thanas, Katharine. Personal Interview, Sept. 2000.

"Before you attain enlightenment, enlightenment is there . . ." Suzuki, Shunryu. *Wind Bell*, Vol. VII, Nos. 3–4 (Fall 1968), p. 27.

"To take this posture itself . . ." Suzuki, Shunryu. *Zen Mind, Beginner's Mind,* p. 25.

"What's here right now? Delusion . . ." Maezumi, Taizan. *Mountain Record* (August 1982).

Zen Story: "Better Not to Ask." Wick, Gerry Shishin. Personal interview, April 2000.

Zen Story: "What Is It Like?" Loori, John Daido. Personal interview, March 2001.

Zen Story: "Never Mind That." Anonymous, personal remembrance.

Zen Story: "We're Responsible." Wick, Gerry Shishin, Personal interview, April 2000.

Zen Story: "A Matter of Life and Death." Loori, John Daido. Personal interview, Spring 2001.

"Our practice rests on a physical base . . ." Maezumi, Taizan, with Glassman, Bernard Tetsugen. *On Zen Practice.* Los Angeles: Zen Center Publications, 1976.

"To get this chance . . ." Nakagawa, Soen. *The Soen Roku: The Sayings and Doings of Master Soen.* Eido Tai Shimano, ed. New York: The Zen Studies Society, p. 20.

"I've taken off my mask . . ." Nakagawa, Soen. Reported by John Daido Loori, personal interview, March 2001.

"Look at Buddha," "tradition," and "Without getting in a space-ship," as well as Beecher Lake invisible tea party, reported by Mick Sopko, personal interview, Sept. 2000.

Floating unsinkable on the surface of the Dead Sea. Reported in *Endless Vow: The Zen Path of Soen Nakagawa*. Presented, with an introduction by Eido T. Shimano, compiled and translated by Kazuaki Tanahashi and Roko Sherry Chayat. Boston and London: Shambhala, 1996, p. 120.

"There, now you make the water . . ." Reported by Derrick, Joan Yushin, June 2000.

Zen Story: "Does a Dog Have Buddha Nature?" Johnson, Wendy. Personal interview Sept. 2000.

Zen Story: "Nobody Home." Matthiessen, Peter. *Nine-Headed Dragon River: Zen Journals 1969-1982*. Boston: Shambhala, 1987, p. 50.

Zen Story: "Shaking Hands with Essence." Nakagawa, Soen. *The Soen Roku*, pp. 17–18.

Zen Story: "Nobody Home." Konigsberg, Harvey. Phone interview, Oct. 2001. First reported by Kathy Fusho Nolan, personal interview, June 2000.

"Most people think that we live . . ." Nakagawa, Soen. *Endless Vow,* pp. 101–102.

"There is a wonderful Buddha statue . . ." Nakagawa, Soen. *The Soen Roku*, pp. 1–2.

"Cooking, eating, sleeping, every deed . . ." Nakagawa, Soen. Reported by Peter Matthiessen in *Nine-Headed Dragon River*, p. 275.

"During the war in Vietnam . . ." Hanh, Thich Nhat. From Brown, Jerry. *Dialogues*. Berkeley: Berkeley Hills Books, 1998, p. 123.

Zen Story: "Not Taking Sides." Hanh, Thich Nhat. Reported by Wendy Johnson. Personal interview, Sept. 2000.

Zen Story: "Don't Just Do Something . . ." Hanh, Thich Nhat. *Being Peace*. Berkeley: Parallax Press, 1987, pp. 109–110.

Zen Story: "Touching the Present Moment." Reported in *How the Swans Came to the Lake*.

Zen Story: "The True Secret of Mindfulness." O'Neill, Kate. Personal interview, Spring, 2001.

"In 1976 I went to the gulf of Siam . . ." Hanh, Thich Nhat. *The Long Road Turns to Joy: A Guide to Walking Meditation.* Berkeley: Parallax Press, 1996, p. 46.

"If I had supernatural powers . . ." Ibid. p. 61.

"Just the way he opens a door . . ." Merton, Thomas. Reported in Hanh, Thich Nhat and friends. *A Joyful Path.* Berkeley: Parallax Press, 1994, p. 136.

"We may like to use the word self . . ." Hanh, Thich Nhat. *Dialogues*, p. 121.

"When you are guided by compassion . . ." Hanh, Thich Nhat. *Dialogues*, pp. 129–130.

"Wendy Johnson reports on a Peace March with Thich Nhat Hanh." From *Gardening at the Dragon's Gate: At Work in the Wild and Cultivated World*, Bantam Books, 2008.

"Moment to moment, how do you help others? " Sahn, Seung. *The Best of Primary Point.* Rhode Island: Kwan Um School of Zen, 1992, 1994, p. 50.

". . . his young hippie students . . ." Mitchell, Stephen. From foreword to Sahn, Seung. *The Whole World Is a Single Flower: 365 Kongans for Everyday Life.* Jane McLaughlin and Paul Muenzen, eds. Boston/Tokyo: The Charles E. Tuttle Company, 1992, p. viii.

"I just loved Soen-sa-nim's humor . . ." Halifax, Joan. From personal interview, August 2000.

"Soen-sa bowed to him . . ." Mitchell, Stephen. From "The Story of Seung Sanh Soen-sa," in *The Whole World Is a Single Flower*, pp. 230–231.

Zen Story: "Already a Corpse." Goodman, Trudy. Personal interview, February, 2000.

Zen Stories: "No More Reading, An Old, Old, Thing," and "But Why?" Dobisc, Jane. Personal interview, Sept. 2000.

Zen Story: "Very Good Demonstration." Multiple sources—oral tradition.

"Human beings understand too much . . ." Sahn, Seung. *Tricycle* (Winter 1996), p. 26.

"What we call 'world' is only an opinion . . ." Ibid. p. 28.

Chapter Five

"Katagiri Roshi once said . . ." Goldberg, Natalie. Personal interview, Nov. 2000.

Zen Story: "Changing the World." Schelling, Andrew. Personal interview, Oct. 2000.

Zen Story: "No Thought Required." Goodman, Trudy. Personal interview, Feb. 2000.

Zen Story: "New Tricks?" Boissevain, Angie. Personal interview, Spring, 2000.

Zen Story: "Form Is Emptiness." Boissevain, Angie. Personal interview, Spring, 2000.

"I'm not sitting only . . ." Reported by Natalie Goldberg. Personal interview, Summer 2001.

"Have kind consideration . . ." Goldberg, Natalie. *Writing Down the Bones.* Boston: Shambhala, 1986.

"The night before I'd been in the zendo . . ." Johnson, Wendy. Personal interview, Sept. 2000.

"Some of the leaders . . ." Rand, Yvonne. Personal interview, Sept. 2000.

"It's like war coming up . . ." and "infinite potential . . ." Anonymous. Personal interview, Nov. 2000.

"Katagiri wanted the challenge . . ." Reported by Clusin, Jodo Cliff. E-mail correspondence, Sept. 2001.

"If you showed up for dawn zazen . . ." Goldberg, Natalie. Personal interview, Nov. 2000.

"I was the Ino . . ." Anonymous. Personal interview, Nov. 2000.

"You could see it . . ." Courtney, Paul. Personal interview, Nov. 2000.

"I was working for an insurance company . . ." Clusin, Jodo Cliff. Personal interview, Oct. 2000.

"In Zen you rest your frontal lobe . . ." Courtney, Paul. Personal interview, Nov. 2000.

"Katagiri Roshi gave me a vision . . ." Goldberg, Natalie. Personal interview, Nov. 2000.

Zen Story: "No Matter Where You Go, There You Are." Reported by Jodo Cliff Clusin. Personal interview, Oct. 2000.

Zen Story: "Yeah, So What Good Is It?" Anonymous. Personal interview, Nov. 2000.

Zen Story: "An Unpaid Debt." Clusin, Jodo Cliff. Personal interview, Oct. 2000.

Zen Story: "Gathering No Moss." Leyshon, Jean. Personal interview, Oct. 2000.

"Buddhism, the real Buddhism . . ." Tsung Tsai. Reported by George Crane in *Bones of the Master: A Buddhist Monk's Search for the Lost Heart of China.* New York: Bantam, 2000.

"The most fascinating thing . . ." Crane, George. Personal interview, May 2000.

Zen Stories: "Who's the Boss?" and "A Little Advice." Crane, George. Personal interview, May 2000.

"Sparse Plum" by Zhou Lu Jing, "Hermit Crazy About Plum" translated by Tsung Tsai and George Crane. Used by permission.

"I became legal . . ." From interview with Tsung Tsai and George Crane by Mary Talbot. *Tricycle* (Spring 2000), p. 98.

Zen Story: "Hitting Bottom." Strand, Clark. Personal interview, 2000.

Zen Stories: "Making Firewood" and "What Next?" Reported by Michael Sierchio.

Zen Story: "Every Little Bit Counts." Reported by Steve Sanfield in "The Inner Passage," from *Zen and Hasidism.* Ed: Harold Heifetz. Wheaton, IL/Madras/London: The Theosophical Publishing House, 1978, p. 226.

Zen Story: "Close, but No Cigar." Anonymous. Personal remembrance, June 2000.

Zen Story: "Berry Pie." Reported by Hung Ju in *Three Steps, One Bow.* San Francisco: Ten Thousand Buddhas Press/The Buddhist Text Translation Society, 1977, pp. 24–25.

Zen Story: "Throwing Away the Key." Reported by Stan White. Personal interview, April 2000.

Zen Story: "The True Reason." Personal remembrance, August 2000.

"Jane Dobisc, who later became . . ." Dobisc, Jane. Personal interview, October 2000.

Chapter Six

"You yourself are time . . ." Kapleau, Philip. *Zen Dawn in the West*, p. 160.

Zen Story: "A Case of Unmistakable Identity." Reported in *American Zen: Twenty Years* (commemorative booklet). Rochester: The Zen Center, 1986, p. 24.

Zen Story: "Neither Hard Nor Easy." From *Zen Dawn in the West*, p.84.

Zen Story: "What Does Zen Say?" From *Zen Dawn in the West*.

Zen Story: "This Side Up." Glassman, Bernie. Personal interview, Sept. 2000.

Zen Story: "Now We Can Eat Together." Rand, Yvonne. Personal interview, Sept. 2000.

Zen Story: "Now the Work Begins." Kjolhede, Sunya. Telephone interview, Winter 2001.

Zen Story: "Mountain Seat." Description by Denis Lahey in *Wind Bell*, Vol. VI (1972), pp. 11–13.

Zen Story: "Flown the Coop?" Strand, Clark. Personal interview, 2000.

Zen Story: "Only Breath, Breathing." Rand, Yvonne. Personal interview, Sept. 2000.

"Dainin Katagiri visited Suzuki Roshi . . ." Goldberg, Natalie. Personal interview, Nov. 2001.

"Shortly before his death . . ." White, Stan. Personal interview, April 2000.

Zen Story: "Tea for Four." Loori, John Daido. Personal interview, Spring 2001.

"The Dharma of Thusness . . ." poem by Taizan Maezumi. *Mountain Record* (Summer 1995).

Part Three

"Zen teacher Danan Henry . . ." Henry, Danan. Personal interview, Oct. 2000.

"Walter Nowick used to tell the story . . ." Leff, Stephen. Personal interview, June 2000.

Zen Story: "Eyes That See in the Dark." Leff, Stephen. Personal interview, June 2000.

Zen Story: "Don't Hurt the Bird." Leff, Stephen. Personal interview, June 2000.

Zen Story: "Light and Shadow." Leff, Stephen. Personal interview, June 2000.

Chapter Seven

"When Zen teacher Mitra Bishop . . ." Bishop, Mitra. Personal interview, Winter 2001.

"The mercy of the West has been . . ." Snyder, Gary. "Buddhism and the Coming Revolution." From *Earth House Hold: Technical Notes and Queries to Fellow Dharma Revolutionaries.* New York: New Directions, 1969.

"The whole notion of engaged Buddhism . . ." Jurs, Cynthia. Personal interview, Sept. 2001.

"[Social action] arises from the sense that . . ." Aitken, Robert. Phone interview, Sept. 2001.

"All people, whether perpetrators . . ." Senauke, Hozan Alan. Personal interview, Sept. 2000.

"If there's a gash . . ." Glassman, Bernie. *Bearing Witness: A Zen Master's Lessons in Making Peace.* New York: Bell Tower, 1998, p. 50.

Zen Story: "True Intimacy." Kapleau, Philip. *Zen Dawn in the West,* p. 200.

Zen Story: "Taking Care of Each Other." Allen, Steve. Phone interview, Sept. 2001.

"Right action then, means sweeping . . ." Snyder, Gary. Snyder, Gary. *The Real Work,* p. 119.

"What happens in practice . . ." Halifax, Joan. Personal interview, August 2000.

Prison interview material. From personal interview with Geoffrey Shugen Arnold, June 2000.

"Your life is your practice . . . ." Stuart, Maurine. Reported in *Zen in America*, p. 165.

Zen Story: "Identity, or Responsibility?" Allen, Steve. Phone interview, Sept. 2001.

"A student visiting with . . . ." Hahn, Thich Nhat. *The Miracle of Mindfulness*. Boston: Beacon Press, 1975, p. 7.

"I learned something very interesting . . ." Kaye, Les. *Zen at Work*. New York: Crown Trade Paperbacks, 1996, p. 14.

"I remember . . . I was working at Greens . . ." Wenger, Dairyu Michael. Personal interview, Aug. 2000.

Zen Story: "Sacred Vessels." Brother David. *Wind Bell*, Vol. VII, Nos. 3–4 (Fall 1968), p. 17.

"During a retreat with Thich Nhat Hanh . . ." Vineyard, Mary. From "Psychotherapy and Meditation," in *Radical Grace*, publication of the Center for Action and Contemplation in Albuquerque. Vol. 2, No. 4.

"I'd been studying Zen maybe eight years . . ." Green, Ron Hogen. Personal interview, May 2000.

Zen Story: "Transformation." Ho, Mobi. "Animal Dharma." *Dharma Gaia: A Harvest of Essays in Buddhism and Ecology*. Allan Hunt Badiner, ed. Berkeley: Parallax Press, 1990, p. 130.

Zen Story: "Performing Magic." Loori, John Daido. Personal interview, May 2000.

Zen Story: "A Turning of the Heart." Fischer, Zoketsu Norman. Personal interview, Oct. 2000.

"A long time Zen practitioner . . ." Leff, Stephen. Personal interview, June 2000.

"A life-long Catholic . . ." Ancheta, Jitsudo. Personal interview, June 2000.

". . . presumptuous statements" etc. Kapleau, Philip. *Zen: Dawn in the West.*

Zen Story: "How Original Can You Get?" Personal experience.

Zen Story: "Making Contact." Brown, Jerry. Personal interview, August 2000.

Chapter Eight

"We all carry this very deep territory . . ." Martin, Rafe. Personal interview, Oct. 2000.

"Whatever made people think Mind isn't . . ." Snyder, Gary. *Jimmy and Lucy's House of 'K',* No. 9 (January 1989), p. 12.

"Zazen, certainly, is the most important . . ." Aitken, Robert. Phone interview, Sept. 2001.

"What does zazen do . . ." Leff, Stephen. Personal interview, Oct. 2000.

". . . to fathom all the intricate layers of who we think we are . . ." Kwong, Jakusho Bill. *Zen in America,* p. 73.

Zen Story: "Press "C"." Rhodes, Barbara. From talk at Zen Mountain Monastery.

"In Zen practice we use incense a great deal . . ." Kaye, Les. *Zen at Work,* p. 130.

"Kapleau-san, when you make prostrations . . ." reported by Philip Kapleau in *Zen Dawn in the West,* p. 191.

Zen Story: "Gesture Reciprocated." Fischer, Zoketsu Norman. Personal interview, Oct. 2000.

When his students asked Shunryu Suzuki . . ." *Zen in America,* p. 225.

"Enlightenment? You won't hear that word . . ." Aitken, Robert. Phone interview, Sept. 2001.

"I think big experiences . . ." Wenger, Dairyu Michael. Personal interview, Aug. 2000.

"The enlightened man neither opposes nor evades . . ." Kapleau, Philip. *Zen Dawn in the West,* p. 160.

"The definition of an enlightened person . . ." Baker, Richard. *Tricycle,* Fall 1996, p. 109.

"How do you establish a foundation . . ." Master Sheng-yen. *Getting the Buddha Mind.* New York: Dharma Drum Publications, 1982, p. 93.

"If a candle is brought into an absolutely dark room . . ." Suzuki, D.T., Fromm, Erich, and DeMartino, Richard. *Zen Buddhism and Psychoanalysis.* New York: Harper and Brothers, 1963, p. 138.

"The moment of awakening may be marked . . . ." Hanh, Thich Nhat. *Zen Keys: A Guide to Zen Practice.* Garden City, New York: Anchor Press/Doubleday, 1974, p. 44.

"Enlightenment is not anything a person with an inquiring mind . . ." Farkas, Mary. "My Early Life." *Mary Farkas: Appreciations and Conversations,* p. 72.

"As for realization . . ." Senzaki, Nyogen. *Zen Notes.* Vol. VI, No. 4, (1957).

Zen Story: "Expressing Enlightenment." Kaye, Les, *Zen at Work,* pp. 37–38.

Zen Story: "Hitting the 900-Year-Old Bell." Leyshon, Jean. Personal interview, Oct. 2000.

"I must confess that I don't have the faintest idea . . . ." Snyder, Gary. *Jimmy and Lucy's House of 'K',* No. 9 (January 1989), p. 22.

"The practice is so simple, really . . ." Glassman, Bernie. Personal interview, Sept. 2000.

Zen Story: "Sometimes It's Better Not to Know." Marchaj, Konrad Ryushin. Personal interview, June 2000.

Zen Story: "Nothing but the Truth." Ancheta, Jitsudo. Personal interview, June 2000.

"Zen Mind is one of those enigmatic phrases . . ." Baker, Richard. *Zen Mind, Beginner's Mind,* p.13.

"When we see into the emptiness or illusory nature . . ." Arnold, Geoffrey Shugen. *Mountain Record,* Summer 1998, p. 24.

"Given the Truth that nothing exists . . ." Master Sheng-yen. *Getting the Buddha Mind,* pp. 187–188.

Zen Story: "Full of Everything." Whalen, Philip. *Jimmy and Lucy's House of 'K',* No. 9 (January 1989), p. 21.

Zen Story: "Absolutely Not." Warner, Jisho. Personal interview, Sept. 2000.

"Some people think that . . ." Hanh, Thich Nhat. "Remarks on Buddhism and Psychotherapy." From *Reseedings: Dharma and Drama: Reseedings from the National Conference on Buddhism and Psychotherapy.* Ed: Rowan Conrad. Buddhist Peace Fellowship/Order of Interbeing, 1990, p. 7.

"Forgetting the self is a peak experience . . ." Aitken, Robert. Phone interview, Sept. 2001.

"Life and death are nothing but movement . . ." Loori, John Daido. *Mountain Record,* Summer 1998 pp. 7–8.

"The self is not to be despised . . ." Master Sheng-yen. *Getting the Buddha Mind.*

"All we have is what we notice." Baker, Richard. Reported by Joan Halifax in *Tricycle,* Spring 1996, p. 28.

"Wherever you are, you are in the zendo . . ." Glassman, Bernie. *Zen in America,* p. 116.

"One day when I was walking . . ." Halifax, Joan. *Tricycle,* Spring 1996, p. 28.

Zen Story: "Ask Not for Whom the Bell Tolls . . ." Jurs, Cynthia. Personal interview, Sept. 2001.

"No matter how far out on the sea . . ." Treace, Bonnie Myotai. *Mountain Record,* Summer 1998, p. 18.

"What the Buddha actually came for . . ." Reps, Paul. *Wind Bell,* Fall 1990, p. 6.

"If you could change one thing in your life . . ." Ford, Maureen Jisho. *Mountain Record,* Winter 1993, p. 34.

Zen Story: "Just as It Is." O'Hara, Pat Enkyo. *Tricycle,* Fall 1998, p. 76.

Zen Story: "The Wish-Fulfilling Jewel." Allen, Steve. Phone interview, Sept. 2001.

"Cancer—it stops you in your tracks . . ." Thanas, Katharine. Personal interview, Sept. 2000.

"It had rained during the night . . ." Rand, Yvonne. Personal interview, Sept. 2000.

Zen Story: "I'm O.K.—How About You?" Strassman, Rick. Personal interview, May 2001.

Zen Story: "Problem or Challenge?" Goodman, Trudy. Personal interview, February, 2000.

Zen Story: "Nowhere to Go." Allen, Steve. From Issan Dorsey memorial service, Sept. 2000.

Zen Story: "Trading Places." Allen, Steve. From Issan Dorsey memorial service, Sept. 2000.

Zen Story: "Universal Sound." Dobisc, Jane. Personal interview, Sept. 2000.

Zen Story: "How You Play the Game . . ." Personal remembrance.

Zen Story: "Die Now." Personal interview, Nov. 2000.

"People want so much . . ." Kwong, Jakusho Bill. *Zen in America*, p. 86.

Chapter Nine

"Zen is not about nonmovement . . ." Glassman, Bernie. *Zen in America*, p. 113.

"Bearing witness is an experience . . ." Gordon, Rose. Personal interview, May 2001.

Description of Glassman street retreats. Schelling, Andrew, and Waldman, Anne. Personal interviews, October 2000.

"Spring Sesshin in the Bowery (II) April 1992." Poem by Andrew Schelling. Used by permission.

Zen Story: "Living in the Now." Glassman, Bernie. Personal interview, Sept. 2000.

Natalie Goldberg material from personal interviews and experience, Nov. 2000 and July 2001.

"One night there was a psychiatrist . . ." O'Neill, Kate. Personal interview, Spring 2001.

"I'd done a fair amount of therapy . . ." Senauke, Hozan Alan. Personal interview, Aug. 2000.

"One way to look at the difference between Zen practice . . ." Sachter, Lawson. Personal interview, Oct. 2000.

"If we can't take the teachings to heart . . ." Jurs, Cynthia. Personal interview, Sept. 2001.

Zen Story: "The Way to Mental Health." Fromm, Erich. *A Zen Life: D. T. Suzuki Remembered.*

"With unfailing kindness . . ." Beck, Charlotte Joko. *Tricycle,* Summer 1998, p. 39.

"There's a confusion between our kind of work and psychotherapy . . ." Rizzetto, Diane. Personal interview, Sept. 2000.

"Suppose someone has hurt my feelings . . ." Beck, Charlotte Joko. *Tricycle,* Summer 1998, p. 39.

"One of the things Joko helped me with greatly . . ." Goodkind, Joel. Personal interview, Spring 2000.

"After Danan Henry's transmission ceremony . . ." Henry, Danan. Personal interview, Oct. 2000.

"A roshi is a person . . ." Dixon, Trudy. From introduction to *Zen Mind, Beginner's Mind,* p. 18.

"Without pointing a finger at anyone . . ." Aitken, Robert. Phone interview, Sept. 2001.

"In the original Buddhist order . . ." Glassman, Bernie. Personal experience, June 2000.

"I realized that this person was not my father . . ." Senauke, Hozan Alan. Personal interview, Aug. 2000.

"You may say, 'Well, I need a teacher' . . ." Beck, Charlotte Joko. *Everyday Zen: Love and Work.* San Francisco: Harper.

"Here I was, a dharma teacher . . ." Fischer, Zoketsu Norman. Personal interview, Oct. 2000.

"My responsibility is to encourage . . ." Henry, Danan. Personal interview, Oct. 2000.

"I can't give anything to anyone . . ." Stuart, Maurine. From *Zen in America,* p. 164.

"To Shi-fu . . . There is nothing special . . ." Master Sheng-yen. *Getting the Buddha Mind,* p. 85.

"I'm heartened by the fact that I have a few . . ." Aitken, Robert. Phone interview, Sept. 2001.

"I set off after Roshi did . . ." Ancheta, Jitsudo. Personal interview, June 2000.

Zen Story: "Teacher or Friend?" White, Stan. Personal interview, April 2000.

Zen Story: "The Same Chord, in Harmony." Master Sheng-yen. *Getting the Buddha Mind,* p. 171.

Zen Story: "Nothing to Give." Loori, John Daido. Personal interview, May 2000.

"A student from another Zen center . . ." Goodman, Trudy. Personal interview, Feb. 2000.

GLOSSARY

absolute: the fundamental nature of reality; oneness, emptiness.

Avalokitesvara (Sanskrit): the Bodhisattva of Compassion, also known as Kuan Yin in Chinese, Kannon, or Kanzeon in Japanese.

Bodhidharma: founder of the Zen school of Buddhism in China; the first Chinese ancestor.

bodhisattva (Sanskrit): the ideal of compassionate practice in all forms of Mahayana Buddhism, including Zen. One who makes the commitment not to enter complete enlightenment until all beings have been liberated from delusion.

Buddha hall: literally, a hall of Buddhas, often used in Zen practice centers for services and devotional practices.

Buddha mind seal: recognition of the Buddha mind, a sanction of realization from teacher to student, entrusting the teachings to the next generation.

Buddha nature: one's true nature; the true mind of enlightenment.

Ch'an (Chinese): Chinese word for Zen, derived from Sanskrit Dhyana, meaning Samadhi, or complete meditative absorption.

daiosho (Japanese): great teacher.

dharani (Sanskrit): a brief sutra or scripture, generally consisting of monosyllabic sounds intended for chanting out loud.

dharma brother/sister, "nephew" or "grandson," etc.: someone from the same lineage; two students having the same teacher would be dharma brothers or sisters, etc.

dharma combat: dialogue in which two or more Zen practitioners test and sharpen their understanding of the dharma.

dharma heir or dharma successor: a recipient of dharma transmission from a particular teacher, generally carrying sanction or authority to teach.

dharma transmission: the confirmation of a student's realization, signifying the unity of the student's mind with the teacher's (and therefore with the Buddha's); generally bestowed along with the authority to teach Zen.

dharma wheel: the turning of the dharma wheel is an expression signifying the teaching of the dharma by the Buddha or other esteemed teacher; in general, the spreading of the teachings of the dharma.

Dogen Zenji (Japanese 1200–1253): founder of the Japanese Soto Zen school, established Eiheiji Monastery and authored the *Shobogenzo*, a primary text of the Soto sect.

dokusan/daisan (Japanese): formal private meeting with a Zen teacher in which students present or clarify their insight into the dharma.

engaged Buddhism: current movement in Buddhism toward bringing practice into engagement with social, environmental, and political issues.

Four Great Bodhisattva Vows: also known as the Four Great Vows, or simply the Fours. Traditionally chanted at Zen monasteries, these express the commitment to postpone complete enlightenment until all beings have been liberated from delusion.

Four Noble Truths: the first public teaching of the Buddha, in which he described the condition of suffering, its cause, and the path out of suffering to liberation.

gassho (Japanese): a gesture of hands together, palm to palm, in prayer position, signifying gratitude or the bringing together of opposites.

gatha (Sanskrit): a brief scriptural verse, often intended for chanting.

Gautama: a family name of the historical Buddha, Siddhartha Gautama, also known as Shakyamuni.

Genjo koan (Japanese): title of the first and most widely known fascicle of Dogen Zenji's Shobogenzo; often translated as, and used to signify, the way of everyday life.

Haiku (Japanese): a classical seventeen-syllable poem form, traditionally embracing nature and the change of seasons, often associated with Zen practice.

Hakuin Ekaku Zenji (1685–1768): primary Japanese ancestor and revitalizer of Rinzai sect in Japan, through whom all current Japanese Rinzai lineages are traced; systematized koan study into its current form.

Heart Sutra: primary text of Mahayana Buddhism, chanted daily in Zen monasteries; contains the famous line "form is emptiness, emptiness is form."

Indra's Net: an image from the Avatamsaka Sutra, envisioning the universe as a vast interlinked network of jewels, each one perfectly reflecting and containing all others.

inka (Japanese): authentication of a practitioner's awakening, bestowing full sanction as a Zen teacher.

jukai (Japanese): the taking of the Buddhist precepts; a public ceremony of commitment to practice the moral and ethical teachings of Buddhism.

kalpa (Japanese): an enormously long period of time; a full world cycle.

Kannon (Japanese): see Avalokitesvara.

Kanzeon (Japanese): see Avalokitesvara.

karma (Sanskrit): the law of causation; the inescapable fruit of action and intention.

kensho (Japanese): an experience, often the first experience, of seeing into one's true nature; enlightenment or realization.

koan (Japanese): apparently paradoxical question or statement, used as an object of meditation during zazen practice; at more advanced stages, a dialogue between practitioners, demonstrating one or more points of the dharma, used as a "case" to be examined deeply during the practice of zazen.

koi (Japanese): large ornamental carp, similar to goldfish, typical of Zen temple ponds.

kokushi (Japanese): title of national Zen teacher, generally bestowed by Emperor.

Kuan Yin (Chinese): see Avalokitesvara.

Mahakashyapa (Sanskrit): the Buddha's first dharma heir.

Mahayana (Sanskrit): the Northern School of Indian Buddhism, which traveled to Tibet, China, Korea, and Japan, in which the bodhisattva path is held forth as the ideal of practice.

mandala: esoteric symbol used in Tantric Buddhism. A symbol of wholeness and integration, often used as an object of meditation.

Manjushri (Sanskrit): the Bodhisattva of Wisdom, a common Zen altar figure, often depicted as holding the sword that cuts through delusion.

mindfulness: traditional Buddhist awareness practice, the application of close moment-to-moment attention to one's activity in the present.

monastic: non-gender-based term for a monk or nun.

nirvana (Sanskrit): union with the absolute basis of reality.

patriarch: early ancestor of Buddhism in China; Bodhidharma was the First Patriarch of Zen in China.

precepts: the ethical and moral teachings of Buddhism; generally taken on as part of the Jukai ceremony of formally joining the Buddhist order.

Pure Land: in Mahayana Buddhist mythology, a heavenly realm into which some believe it is possible to be reborn through the performance of good works, or through faith in Amitabha Buddha.

realization: awakening; seeing into one's true nature. The experience of enlightenment.

Rinzai (Japanese): one of the two primary schools of Zen (the other being Soto), generally known for its emphasis on koan study and direct experience of realization.

Rohatsu sesshin (Japanese): particularly intensive Zen training retreat, generally held in December, the anniversary of the Buddha's enlightenment.

roshi (Japanese): honorific title used for a Zen teacher. In the west this tends to refer to a particularly venerated or accomplished master.

samadhi (Sanskrit): a state of deep, concentrated absorption, experienced through the practice of zazen.

samsara (Sanskrit): the condition of suffering experienced in worldly existence prior to the experience of realization.

sangha (Sanskrit): the community of practitioners. In the broadest sense, the community of all beings.

sanzen (Japanese, Rinzai sect): private meeting with a Zen teacher in which students present or clarify their understanding of a koan.

satori (Japanese): the experience of enlightenment. Awakening to one's true nature; experiencing deep realization.

sensei (Japanese): a Zen teacher; in Japan, may refer to an esteemed teacher.

sentient beings: literally, a "knowing" or conscious being; any living being.

sesshin (Japanese): literally, "to unify the mind." An intensive Zen training retreat.

shakuhachi (Japanese): traditional wooden flute of Japan, closely associated with Zen practice.

shakyamuni (Sanskrit): literally, "sage of the Shakya clan." One of the names of the historical Buddha.

shikantaza (Japanese): "Just sitting": a form of zazen practice in which no particular object is used as a point of focus; the practice of pure awareness.

shosan (Japanese): public formal question-and-answer session with a Zen teacher.

shunyata (Sanskrit): Emptiness; the fundamental nature of reality.

Siddhartha: the birth name of the historical Buddha.

Soto (Japanese): one of the two primary schools of Zen (the other being Rinzai), characterized by emphasis on shikantaza practice.

suchness: the absolute state of phenomena, beyond all conceptual distinctions.

sutra (Sanskrit): Buddhist scripture

tan (Japanese): woven mat of rice stalks, often used for a surface for sitting.

Tathagatha (Sanskrit): one of the traditional names of the Buddha, signifying the state of perfect enlightenment.

teisho (Japanese): formal talk on some aspect of the dharma; non-intellectual and sometimes even paradoxical in nature, such a talk is intended to be a direct demonstration of the teacher's understanding, rather than a discussion of philosophy or doctrine.

transmission: see dharma transmission.

true dharma eye: the eye of realization, of awakening, which sees the absolute nature of reality.

zabuton (Japanese): flat cushion used to support a zafu, against which one's knees rest when seated in zazen position.

zafu (Japanese): the round cushion on which a practitioner sits during the practice of zazen.

zazen (Japanese): Zen meditation, leading to unity of mind, body, and breath; the Zen practice of realization.

zendo (Japanese): hall where zazen is practiced.

SUGGESTED READING

Contemporary Zen Teachers in America:
Aitken, Robert, *Taking the Path of Zen*.
Beck, Charlotte Joko, *Everyday Zen*.
Friedman, Lenore, *Meetings with Remarkable Women*.
Glassman, Bernard, *Bearing Witness*.
Hanh, Thich Nhat, *The Miracle of Mindfulness* and *Zen Keys*.
Kapleau, Philip, *The Three Pillars of Zen*.
Katagiri, Dainin, *Returning to Silence*.
Loori, John Daido, *The Eight Gates of Zen*.
Sahn, Seung, *Dropping Ashes on the Buddha*.
Suzuki, Shunryu, *Zen Mind, Beginner's Mind*.
Wick, Gerry Shishin and Perez, Ilia Shinko, *The Great Heart Way*.

On Koan Practice:
Loori, John Daido, *Two Arrows Meeting in Mid-Air*.
Sahn Seung, *The Whole World Is a Single Flower*.

Contemporary Personal Accounts of Zen Training:
Goldberg, Natalie, *Long Quiet Highway*.
Matthiessen, Peter, *Nine-Headed Dragon River*.
Shainberg, Lawrence, *Ambivalent Zen*.
Strand, Clark, *The Wooden Bowl*.

On Zen in America:
Chadwich, David, *Crooked Cucumber*. [Biography of Suzuki Roshi.]
Fields, Rick, *How the Swans Came to the Lake*. [Comprehensive history of American Buddhism.]

Shimano, Eido T., *Endless Vow: The Zen Path of Soen Nakgawa*.

On Ancient Masters and History of Zen in the East:

Foster, Nelson and Shoemaker, Jack, *The Roaring Stream: A New Zen Reader*.

General Zen Readers/Anthologies:

Tonkinson, Carole, *Big Sky Mind: Buddhism and the Beat Generation*.
Reps, Paul and Senzaki, Nyogen, *Zen Flesh, Zen Bones*. [101 traditional Zen stories, and more.]
Smith, Jean, *365 Zen*.
Tanahashi, Kazuaki, and Schneider, Tensho David, *Essential Zen* [Stories from Eastern and Western sources.]

Zen, Travel, and Adventure:

Chadwick, David, *Thank You and OK! An American Zen Failure in Japan*.
Crane, George, *The Bones of the Master*.
Matthiessen, Peter, *The Snow Leopard*.

Zen, Creativity, and the Arts:

Goldberg, Natalie, *Writing Down the Bones*, *Wild Mind*, and *Thunder and Lightning*.
Loori, John Daido, *The Zen of Creativity*.
Strand, Clark, *Seeds from a Birch Tree: Writing Haiku and the Spiritual Journey*.

INDEX

A

Absolute/Absoluteness, 8, 11, 165, 177–78
Aitken, Robert, 9, 16–17, 24, 33–36, 75, 127, 168
    on dharma transmission, 211, 214
    on enlightenment, 170
    on responsibility, 158
    on self & no-self, 178
    social activism and, 152–53
Akiyama, Rev. Tozen, 178
Allen, Steve, 61, 158, 182, 213
Ancheta, Jitsudo, 176, 214–15
Anderson, Tenshin Reb, 166
Arnold, Geoffrey Shugen, 155–57, 177
Asahina, Sogen, 33–34, 39
Auschwitz-Birkenau, Zen at, 192–94
Avalokitesvara (Bodhisattva of Compassion), 102, 153

B

Baker, Richard, 130–33, 172, 177, 185, 211
Bearing Witness (Glassman), 153
Beat movement, 16, 30, 42, 47–54, 59–60, 65, 110
Beck, Charlotte Joko, 206–210, 212
Bennett Goleman, Tara, 205
Berkeley Zen Center, 65, 170
Big Sky Mind (anthology), 50
Blyth, R.H., 33
Bodhidharma, 3–4, 126, 151
bodhisattvas, 79–80, 102, 122, 130, 142, 153, 170, 197
Boissevain, Angie, 98–99
Bones of the Master (Crane), 106–7
Brown, Jerry, 81, 165

on enlightenment, 172
interview with, 119–125
"Mu" koan and, 126–27
on religion, 164
Katagiri, Dainin, 63, 91, 94, 99–106, 120, 122, 130, 134, 199–202
Kaye, Les, 159, 169, 173
Kennedy, Father Robert Jinsen, 165
kensho, 14, 42, 120, 170–71
Kerouac, Jack, 41, 42, 47–51, 53–54, 59
Kjolhede, Sunya, 129
Kjolhede, Bodhin, 161
koans, 8, 12, 21, 27, 30, 31, 35, 46, 47, 50, 74, 76, 77, 95, 113, 125, 129, 132, 136,
    see also "Mu" koan
Kobun Chino Roshi, 94–102, 125, 225
Koryu, Osaka, 74
Kuan Yin (Bodhisattva of Compassion), 125, 153
Kuroda Roshi, 74
Kwan Um School of Zen, 86
Kwong, Jakusho Bill, 65, 66, 131, 168, 187

L
Lahey, Dennis, 130
Lassalle, Father, 165–66
Leyshon, Jean, 104–05, 173–74
Long Quiet Highway (Goldberg), 100, 202
Loori, Abbot John Daido, 5, 72, 120, 134–36, 154, 163, 176, 215
    dharma transmission and, 213
    on self, 178

M
Maezumi, Hakuyu Taizan, 36, 59–60, 68–75, 101, 127–28, 182, 189, 192, 214–15
    death of, 136
    dharma words from, 68

Providence Zen Center, 86–87
psychotherapy, 204–07

R

S

ABOUT THE AUTHOR

 Sean Murphy has been a Zen practitioner for 25 years. A graduate of the Naropa Institute MFA Writing program, he is also the author of three novels, including *The Hope Valley Hubcap King*, which won the Hemingway Award for a First Novel. His most recent novel is *The Time of New Weather*. He teaches meditation and creative writing at the University of New Mexico in Taos, as well as at conferences, workshops, and retreats nationally. He is the founder of the non-profit Sage Institute for Creativity, Consciousness, and the Environment, which sponsors a variety of trainings in meditation, mindfulness, and creativity, including an innovative meditation teacher training program.

www.murphyzen.com

Hampton Roads Publishing Company
. . . for the evolving human spirit

Hampton Roads Publishing Company publishes books on
a variety of subjects, including spirituality, health, and other
related topics.

For a copy of our latest trade catalog, call (978) 465-0504 or
visit our distributor's website at *www.redwheelweiser.com.* You can
also sign up for our newsletter and special offers by going to
www.redwheelweiser.com/newsletter.